A GREEN ECONOMY

India's Sustainable Development

N. R. Krishnan

INDIA • SINGAPORE • MALAYSIA

ISBN 979-8-88833-379-2

To

My Parents

Contents

Foreword

Dr. Nitin Desai

Our species, Homo sapiens, evolved from its hominid ancestors 200000 to 300000 years ago. For at least 95 percent of this time we humans lived as part of nature, relying, like other species, on hunting and gathering for sustenance. There was one incipient difference from other species even then. Because of the manipulability of our limbs, our larger brain size that allowed a higher rate of understanding of nature, the capacity to control fire and the emergence of language to connect with other humans we developed a capacity to form social groups that could modify nature in a modest way mainly for residential space. The capacity to adjust living and working conditions to the local environment led also to the great migration of the species into regions that had very different environmental conditions.

Around 12000 years ago the ice age ended, and climatic conditions allowed the possibility of cultivation. In the Fertile Crescent in the Middle East humans learned the art of agriculture and started moving from being hunter-gatherers to growers of food and other natural products and domesticating some species. This development of settled agriculture grew later also in other areas in Asia, notably in some river valleys in India and China. Incidentally, the evidence suggests that the lifestyle of the agriculturists was distinctly worse than that of the hunter-gatherers, in terms of the time devoted to securing food and health status.

Settled agriculture and the surpluses it produced needed built-up settlements for storage. This need marked the beginning of the transition in the relationship between humans to nature. Our history since then has seen a growing manipulation of nature by humans, a trend that accelerated hugely after the industrial revolution which was launched some 250 years ago.

Our challenge today is that this power to manipulate nature does not change the dependence of the human species on the fundamental features of the third rock from the sun where we live, namely, the incidence of solar radiation – the only source of energy for the earth, the composition of the atmosphere, the water cycle and the cycles of other natural resources. However, the scale of our transition measured by transformations of land use, the use of biotic resources, energy emissions, and intrusion of strange waste into nature is fast approaching a level that threatens the balance between humans and nature to a point at which survival could be at risk. Hence the need to rethink the manipulative relationship between humans and nature that has driven the development of our economies and societies for over 10000 years.

This concern is not new. As Mr. Krishnan presents at the very start of his book, some 2500 years ago, when the great religions of the world were born, the need for respecting nature became an integral part of religious belief and even practice. It survived for centuries during which living conditions were more or less stable and population growth at a local level was limited, though in the aggregate the numbers of the human species grew as new areas of the earth became accessible for it. As this book points out the weakening of the religious emphasis on the balance between humans and nature started with the Enlightenment and later the Industrial Revolution in Europe and spread soon to other parts of the world, initially through colonisation by Europeans.

Since the industrial revolution began around 1750, the scale and depth of human intervention in nature have escalated enormously. The proportion of water in the natural hydrological cycle diverted through man-made dams, canals, and wells, and of land converted from its natural state to man-made forests, croplands and habitations has increased sharply. But even more than scale, the depth of intervention is increasing as new chemicals and substances are brought into use, exotic plant and animal varieties are developed and even the genes are modified.

Natural resource pressures arising from economic growth are sometimes misleadingly portrayed as a conflict between environmental protection and development. The reality is that environmental deterioration affects development, and the absence of development makes environmental conservation more difficult. When the topsoil is washed away, forests denuded, and waters polluted, it is not just the environment that suffers. The prospects for development are also eroded. Equally, when incomes stagnate or decline, resources flow out and terms of trade deteriorate, the options available for environmental action are reduced. What we have to do is to combine our concern for resource management with our concern for the growth of the economy and the eradication of poverty, hunger, and marginalisation.

Our aim must be sustainable livelihoods for poor people and responsible consumption by those who are rich.

The big change we need to secure this is the driving force of what is recognised as progress. In the 19th century, progress was understood as quantum increases in production driven by revolutionary changes in technology based on new energy sources, and a substantial increase in the exploitation of renewable and non-renewable resources. In the 20ᵗʰ century the idea of progress, pioneered in the United States, was to spread the growth of consumption that was made possible by technology. In the 21ˢᵗ century, the idea of progress will have to change. As humanity comes closer to ecological limits, the idea of progress has to shift to ways of production and consumption that conserve the environment and natural resources. The measure of progress will shift from production growth and consumption growth to efficiency growth and to improvements in equity in the sharing of growth between and within countries.

Sustainable development is a concept that seeks to capture this change and looks for a balance between economic progress, environmental conservation and protection, and social equity. It figured in the debates of environmentalists and one can see a reference to that in the Founex Report prepared for the Stockholm Environment Conference of 1971 and in the World Conservation Strategy of IUCN prepared in 1980. But as a concept, it had not entered the mainstream of discussions at the political level on development.

The term 'sustainable development' entered the high-level political discourse when the Brundtland Commission adopted it as the basis for their report. It entered their discussion with a paper drafted by me that contained the now famous definition of sustainable development as one that meets the needs of the present without compromising the ability of future generations to meet their own needs. My intention in presenting this was to build a bridge between the commission members, mainly from developing countries, who wanted to give priority to poverty removal and growth, and members, mainly from developed countries, who wanted to give priority to environmental protection over growth.

The goal was achieved and soon the members accepted that poverty cannot be removed without protecting the resources on which production and incomes depend and, equally, that resources cannot be protected if one ignores the impact of conservation on the livelihoods of the people who depend on that resource. This outlook guided the outcome of the Rio Conference on Environment and Development held in 1992 with the direct participation of over 100 heads of state or government which elevated the issue to the highest political level.

Over the next three decades, there were many attempts, both at the global and the national level to move forward with the action programme of the Rio Conference, labeled Agenda 21, through the Commission on Sustainable Development (CSD), the Johannesburg Summit on Sustainable Development in 2002 and the twenty-year review held at Rio in 2012. As one who had a ringside seat at Rio, CSD, and Johannesburg I would say the main plus points of this UN process were a steady increase in awareness at the political and public level, the emergence of many influential NGO networks whose advocacy played a major role at the global and national level, a growing engagement of corporations in the deliberations and the active engagement of sectoral global agencies like FAO, WHO, UNESCO and of course UNEP.

However, the translation of sustainable development into standard procedures for designing and evaluating development policies has not yet happened. What we do have now is a global agreement on sustainable development goals reached at the Rio+20 meeting that covers virtually the full range of development activities. But perhaps the only area where the underlying idea of sustainable development has become a significant feature is in the energy sector because of its centrality in the climate change problem

Soon after the Brundtland Report was released in 1987 the global community had to face the growing evidence of anthropogenic climate change caused mainly by the large increase in carbon dioxide emissions from rapidly growing fossil fuel use. This is not a problem that can be tackled at a local level by unilateral redesign of development policy. Its impact cuts across national boundaries and the responsibility for its origins is spread very unequally among countries. Moreover, it is a long-term impact issue and requires action to be taken as a precaution before the full effects would be seen. The action to be taken requires a deep reconsideration of virtually all areas of development policy including particularly energy, carbon-intensive sectors like transport, steel and cement, urban and building design, and, what is even more important the adaptation requirements for sectors like agriculture, forests, fisheries, cities, coastal areas, health and many others that will be adversely affected by the temperature rise that is unavoidable even if mitigation actions are initiated now. But more than anything else it requires serious global cooperation in order to have a fair sharing of costs and risks. As of now, there is a process of global negotiation on climate change and an agreement on keeping the temperature increase below $1.5\text{-}2^0C$. But there is no agreement on how the burden of adjustment should be shared, and no agreed principle of climate justice.

In many ways, the climate negotiation process brings out the challenge of shifting our idea of progress in the direction of sustainable development. A key issue is that of intergenerational equity and that requires a consensus on the long-term consequences of current actions. This was done with some success in the case of climate change through the work of the Intergovernmental Panel on Climate Change (IPCC). But a similar exercise in consensus building across decision-making entities on future impacts is absent elsewhere. A shift to sustainable development will involve variations in costs and benefits born by different decision-makers and the absence of any ethical basis for burden sharing will lead to tardiness in the actions required as we see in the commitments on climate change.

The difficulty is that sustainable development is a bridge concept meant to develop a common language of discourse between economists, ecologists, engineers, and ethical philosophers. But the culture of these disciplines is very different and, like many bridges, those who live on either shore feel no sense of ownership unless they need to cross over. The challenge is to make people want to cross over.

Consider how each one of these disciplines evaluates the processes of production and consumption of material goods. The economist will look at it in terms of the efficiency of markets and the costs and benefits of alternative policies. The engineer, taught to manipulate nature for meeting human ends, will look at ways of improving the manipulation of natural forces. The ecologist will see it within the framework of ecological systems and material flows through it and their impact on the integrity of the system. The ethical philosopher will be concerned with who bears the cost and who reaps the benefit. Sustainable development requires us to do all of these things simultaneously and, quite frankly, we have not developed the analytical language or the decision-making procedures required for this.

The most immediate challenge is to redesign the procedures for formulating development policies to address the looming threats of climate change. If we do not do this the other dimensions of sustainability will become impossible to achieve. Sustainability in the face of climate risks requires us to take an integrated view of mitigation for reducing greenhouse gas emissions and adaptation to cope with the temperature rise and related climate changes – which are unavoidable even if the world stays within the agreed 1.5-2^{0}C goal – and resilience to handle the growth in weather uncertainties that are likely because of climate change.

Nowhere is the need for this balance between resilience, adaptation, and mitigation more obvious than in agriculture. We cannot design a crop research strategy only to reduce carbon emissions. It must also address the higher temperatures and water impact of temperature increase and the need for crop resilience in the face of unpredictable temperature and water uncertainties. To take another example the standards for urban design and buildings cannot be oriented only towards carbon mitigation by reducing transport requirements and energy needs for cooling and heating. It must also include standards like more urban greenery for coping with higher temperatures and safety standards to cope with more storms and sea level intrusions in coastal cities.

Sustainability from the perspective of climate change should not distort other environmental goals. For instance, reforestation should not be planned simply to maximise carbon sequestration. That could lead to a type of monoculture that could endanger the broader role of forests in the ecosystem which includes biodiversity protection and better soil and water management in adjoining areas.

In India, over the past 50 years, we have seen growing awareness of sustainability issues, particularly in rural areas where movements like the 'Chipko Andolan' have led to necessary changes in forest policy. Environmental regulation and management have been stepped up significantly, though the actual outcome in areas like air and water quality is still well short of what we need. India has been an active participant in the global processes mentioned earlier. At the Stockholm Environment Conference held in 1971, Indira Gandhi was the only head of government – other than the host country's Prime Minister Olaf Palme – to attend and participate in the Conference. Indian diplomats played an active role at Rio and Johannesburg and in the climate negotiations. India has launched an ambitious programme of renewable energy development which will contribute significantly to carbon mitigation. Environmental awareness and action have grown. What is still missing from a sustainability perspective is the integration of development and environmental policies into a coherent package.

This book traces both the global and national process of gradual change in the integration of development and environment and, in a deeper sense the ethics of the relationship between humans and nature. One may say that the basic message one derives from this book is that "प्रकृति रक्शति रक्शिता:" or "Nature Protects if Protected".

07 August 2022   Nitin Desai
New Delhi

Dr. Nitin Desai was a Government of India civil servant who worked on deputation in the Brundtland Commission on the drafting of its Report and joined the UN in 1990 as Deputy-Secretary-General of the UN Conference on Environment and Development (Rio, 1992), and as the Under-Secretary-General in charge of the Commission on Sustainable Development (1993-2003) and as the Secretary-General of the World Summit on Sustainable Development (Johannesburg, 2002)

Acknowledgements

N.R Krishnan

Writing a book on a subject like Sustainable Development which enjoys as many as seventy definitions is a task to be approached with some trepidation. Despite such reservations, one felt the need to intervene in this babel as the expression was fast trending to become a cliché. For one with a fairly close association with the developments that marked the evolution of the concept, the urge to counter this trend has been more than mild. This volume is the outcome of that urge.

A boon of this electronic age is easy access to literature on any subject over the Internet. A large number of references, often in their originals, became available through this source. Of course, the traditional and reliable source of knowledge, the well-stocked Library was ever there in the form of the facilities attached to the C.P. Ramaswamy Aiyar Environmental Education and Research Centre, and the Madras School of Economics, both located in Chennai. I am deeply indebted to these two institutions for permitting me to use their library facilities freely.

To shoulder the burden of going through the Chapters critically as they were being drafted, I could choose none better and more willing than my former colleague in the Indian Administrative Service, Ramamurthy Swaminathan who had retired after a long tenure as Secretary to the

Asian Development Bank, Manila. Swami obliged me splendidly and with patience. For comments on Chapter VI "Conceptual Foundations of Sustainability", I availed of the suggestions of Prof. K.S. KaviKumar of Madras School of Economics who drew my attention to the seminal work of Prof. Sir Partha Dasgupta on the valuation of natural ecosystem services.

As the book took a passable shape, I made bold to request Dr. Nitin Desai, former Under-Secretary-General to the UN Commission on Sustainable Development (1993-2003) to favour me with a Foreword. He responded readily. I am greatly indebted to Dr. Desai for according me this privilege.

Finally, I thank my wife, my children, and my grandchildren for cheering me up as I laboured along working on the book. Their anxiety to see me stay the course was a morale booster.

30 November 2022   N. R. Krishnan
Chennai, India

Introduction

Indian history and culture have always preached the sacred truth of the oneness of all life on earth and the symbiotic relationship of man with nature, a relationship that nurtures both the giver and the taker. This is the golden thread running through the entire fabric of ancient oriental religions like Hinduism, Buddhism, and Jainism and the philosophies they inspired. The Western industrialized world, however, long used to the theology that preached mastery of man over nature, came to discover the eastern truth only in the 20th Century, and that too after a series of human-induced mishaps. The consequence of this belated discovery was a sudden awakening of concern in the western world for nature and the environment in the latter part of the 20th Century.

The UN Conference on the Human Environment (UNCHE) held in Stockholm in June 1972 rallied international cooperation to promote, strengthen and institutionalize this awakening. The message of the Conference that environment and development should go hand in hand became an article of faith with the world community compelling it to rethink the economic growth models pursued so far. Growth was no longer viewed as an inexorable, uni-dimensional process whose sole aim was to raise national incomes. Instead, growth came to be redefined taking into account its environmental costs. The realization that the capacity of the natural environment to sustain growing human wants bordering on greed and to absorb wastes generated in the process was not unlimited, gave birth to the principle of "intergenerational equity" and the concept of "sustainable development".

Over the years, the UN and its agencies have striven to propagate and translate into practice the Stockholm principles through conferences, conventions, and protocols. The issues the global discourse has addressed relate to two broad areas, protection of the global and local "commons" from overexploitation and degradation, and evaluating economic growth in the light of its environmental sustainability. Funds to protect the environment from further degradation and to support its remediation, though far from adequate, have been forthcoming from multilateral financial institutions, bilateral cooperation, and national exchequers.

The prospect of the finiteness of resources set in motion a global discourse on how fast economies can grow and how and how far natural resources can be harnessed for this purpose. The discourse has not been smooth always, nor has its outcome been a fair one. The rich fear finiteness as that would impair their affluent lifestyles greatly. The poor, on the other hand, perceive the argument as a serious impediment to their overdue development. This perception is particularly acute with the large group of nations that after a long period of foreign rule had become independent in the aftermath of World War II and had stepped forward to catch up with the developed world. In addition, scattered over distant corners of the globe, there are small, hapless nations whose continued existence on the global map is in jeopardy due to global warming set in motion by the energy-intensive growth of the developed countries ever since the Industrial Revolution.

India is in an unenviable position. Its population of 300 million at the time of its Independence in 1947 has swelled to 1412 million today (2022) and is headed to become the largest in the world within the current decade, overtaking China's. It is feared that this may well happen as early as 2023. To raise the living standards of its populace, India set itself on a course of planned economic development in the

1950s. It has made significant progress since then with, of course, the crests, troughs, and plateaus that mark the course of any such long and arduous venture. With the economic reforms of 1991, India's growth curve became an upwardly mobile one, the result of encouraging its dynamic private enterprise to play its due role in the nation's economic development. India is now recognized as an emerging major industrial economy with its GDP a little short of USD 3 trillion. It is but natural that this development along with population growth has been accompanied by increasing consumption of natural resources, particularly fossil fuels, and change in land use through the diversion of land under agriculture, forests, and pastures for industrial and commercial purposes and urban expansion. The pressures exerted by these forces on eco-sensitive habitats have led to criticism of India's development policies by environmentalists. However, the point that is missed in such criticism is that leaving nature totally to remain in its pristine state would neither contribute to society's current welfare nor to the welfare of future generations nor would be in the best interests of nature itself. What is needed is not a hands-off approach to nature but harnessing it sensibly and conserving it wisely.

Local criticism apart, at the global level, an uninformed adverse notice has been taken off India's substantial emissions of global warming Greenhouse Gases (GHGs) accounted for by its predominantly coal-based power generation infrastructure, use of oil to power its vast road and rail communication network, and methane emitting agriculture and cattle wealth. The world would like India to bring down its emissions noticeably by reducing its dependence on fossil fuels through the use of climate-friendly renewable sources like solar energy or wind power. How far and how soon this energy transformation would happen is uncertain. Equally uncertain is the cost of transformation. Given these challenges, it would be unfair to expect India with its huge population and low per capita income to be as nimble as some of the developed countries in embracing renewable energy in full measure. Despite these challenges, India has emerged as one of the frontrunners in this transformation.

The purpose of this work is threefold; the first is to highlight the teachings of Hinduism, Buddhism, Jainism, and Islam on the man-nature relationship and how Judaism and early Christianity differed from these; in addition, to trace the global events that marked the evolution of the concept of "Sustainable Development" and examine the relevance of the concept to India. Since sustainable development is not growth per se but growth in harmony with nature, its acceptance in an ancient and spiritually rich land like India would hinge largely on its mirroring the country's spiritual and cultural ethos. This volume would attempt to show that the Indian model of planned development practiced till 2017 and now in a modified form has been in conformity with the principles of Sustainable Development.

The second purpose is to highlight how skewed and adversarial international exchanges can be to the developmental priorities of a populous and aspirational country like India. The exchanges on global warming and climate change and the responsibilities of different nations in countering the warming and adapting to the changed conditions would illustrate this point.

The third objective is to make a plea to the society at large to adopt a collegiate and not confrontational approach to the execution of development projects.

In Chapter I, we begin with the place of nature in Indian culture and civilization as portrayed in the holy scriptures of India's great religions, whether they be of Indian origin or implants that found an abiding home in India and enriched its culture and heritage. Chapter II analyses the western view of nature and how this view shaped the western political economy. In this context, the adverse impact of colonialism on the colonized people and their natural environment is explored to highlight how and how much the latter's environmental problems of today are a legacy of the rapacity and neglect on the part of the colonial masters. We then move on to the rise of environmental awareness in the West following the beginning of the Industrial Revolution as that has full relevance to our own situation today (Chapter III). Chapters IV and V trace the growth of environmentalism in the West and the global efforts made to meet the emerging challenges of the 20th Century bringing out in the process the divergence between the developed and developing countries' perceptions of each other's share of responsibility in the efforts.

Chapter VI is a digression into the conceptual foundations of sustainability, a knowledge of which is useful to visualize an appropriate environment-friendly development process for a country like India. This is followed by an introduction to the coming into being of the Millennium Development Goals (MDGs) and Sustainable Development Goals (SDGs) and an evaluation of the progress made by India in meeting the targets under these goals (Chapter VII). Further, we seek to highlight an oft-ignored truth that ever since its Independence, India has been following a socioeconomic development strategy no different in substance and intent from what is spelled out as Sustainable Development or Green Growth today (Chapters VIII, IX, and X).

The role of the corporate sector in making sustainable development its motto is highlighted in Chapter XI. In Chapter XII, we examine the nature of the environment versus development debate in India and conclude with a plea to the institutions that manage the nation's affairs and the lives of the people, the civil society, and the public at large to work in unison and understanding to make India's sustainable development efforts a success. We need to honour the Stockholm pledge.

Chapter I

The Eastern View of Nature

"No study has so potent an influence in forming a nation's mind and a nation's character as a critical and careful study of its past history."

– R.C. Dutt, "Early Hindu Civilization"

Nature and Man

The study of nature and its constituents, both animate and inanimate, has a long history. Since earth's non-human constituents came into existence far, far ahead of man and in myriad forms ranging from the minute to the gigantic, from the living to the non-living, against the backdrop of changing seasons and events like thunder, lightning, and rain happening often on a grand scale. Non-human nature looked awesome and it was but natural for early man to look upon his surroundings with fear, wonder, veneration, and total supplication. Nature was benign and generous most of the time but daunting and unforgiving not infrequently. Plants, animals, and even insects seemed to understand nature's moods and ways a lot better than man did and adapted themselves to them as if they were an integral part of nature. Their understanding of nature and adaptation to its ways contributed to their very survival. But, to man afflicted with fear and caution, nature remained a puzzle, if not a mystery.

But fear could not govern man's relationship with nature for very long. Things he feared most like thunder, lightning, fire, and wild animals were also to prove his support. Thunder and lightning brought welcome rain. The flesh of animals formed his staple consumption. Fire added succulence to the raw meat he consumed and gave him security from wild animals at night when he rested. . Metals the earth yielded were to provide him with his hunting and cutting tools. Later, as he entered the pastoral age, he learned to domesticate the cow, the bullock, and the horse and put them to useful work. His passage to the next stage of his history, the age of agriculture, brought him closer to nature as he could reap rich harvests of grain to feed himself, his kin, and his domestic animals. Times of plenty were interspersed with periods of drought and crop attacks by insects. But, barring the climatic changes that marked the arrival of different seasons, the rest of nature's behaviour was shrouded in secrecy.

The changing seasons and the varying hues on the landscape they brought about and the medley of good fortune and misery that marked the years of his life were to arouse man's curiosity over how Mother Nature went about her way 'her wonders to perform'. Though some of nature's ways became predictable, others, ever inscrutable, remained in the domain of speculation. Understanding nature was man's first intellectual inquiry and has remained to this day his most challenging one. This inquiry took two different paths, the awestruck, deeply philosophical, oriental one and the earthy, fully reason-driven occidental one.

In sharp contrast to the combative, domineering western view of man's relationship with nature, the eastern view has always been one of deep veneration and supplication shaped by its great religions and culture. It was untainted by any desire to either exploit nature for man's greed or interfere with nature's orderly ways of playing its role in man's life. Ancient East, particularly India, had great strengths of knowledge and resources that could have been deployed to such interference but it desisted from doing so out of sheer reverence to nature. Indian philosophy and culture preached moderation, not excess. A study of the teachings of India's religions will bear testimony to this claim.

The reason for undertaking an exercise to bring home the above assertion is that ever since the modern environmental movement began in the 1970s, material growth has been identified by some with greed and ecology with righteousness. This school of thought which is claiming adherents among the intelligentsia and the young implies that growth in any form impacts nature adversely and hence growth is unrighteous to the point of being irreligious. The logical extension of this line of thinking is that nature is best left to remain in its pristine state. This "Deep ecology" view is an article of faith with many and to differ with it is deemed sacrilegious. This modern-day bigotry could have been dismissed as harmless but for the fact that it has come to exert a wholly negative influence on popular thinking on economic growth in developing societies like India.

Since a good section of the current environmental movement in India draws its sustenance from a pristine view of nature, it would be useful to look into the validity of this hands-off view in the light of the teachings of India's great religions. No doubt, other factors are in play too in inspiring the nature – first, development – next movement. There is a prevalent notion that economic development as practiced in India is essentially anti-environment. Such views shall be dealt with in later chapters of this book. First, let's cast a detailed look into what India's great religions say about man-nature relationship.

Hinduism

Vedas, Upanishads and the Puranas

The Vedas, the Upanishads and the Puranas form the bedrock of Hinduism. Hinduism views man and nature as manifestations of an all-pervading unique, supreme self, referred to as "brahman".

The Brahadaranyaka Upanishad conveys the following emphatic message to man:

"The gods ignore the man who thinks of them [nature's creations] as anything apart from the self.

The creatures ignore the man who thinks of them as anything apart from the self.

Everything ignores the man who thinks of them as anything apart from the self." (Book IV)

If one were to go by the above teaching, the conclusion is inescapable that humans, animals, plant life, and inanimate matter are but the varied manifestations of a single principle, the "brahman", with man not being assigned any position superior to that of the others.

What then is the relationship of man with nature? The Rig and Atharva Vedas, provide the answer. As expressed in the words "Vasudaiva Kutumbakam", "man and nature are merely different members of the same family", that is, the whole universe is one single family. The relationship and conduct of the members with one another should be marked by harmony and not contest. The Rig Veda spells out this relationship in picturesque words thus: "Nature is to be understood as a friend, revered as mother, obeyed as father and nurtured as a beloved child." The voluminous text of the Rig Veda is replete with assertions of the need for the harmonious existence of man with nature.

Consider more Hymns from the Rig Veda:

> "May father Heaven, may mother Earth, who are all-knowing, and doers of good deeds, grant us sustenance: may Heaven and Earth, mutually cooperating and promoting the happiness of all, bestow upon us prosperity, food and riches" (Rig Veda Samhita, Mandala 6, Sukta 70).

"The divine and benevolent Savita puts forth his golden arms for (making) donations: the adorable, youthful, sagacious (deity), stretches out his hands, filled with water, in the various service [s]of the world" (Rig Veda Samhita, Mandala 6, Sukta 71, Hymn 5097).

The Atharva Veda is even more evocative in its veneration of the five elements that sustain life on this planet, air, fire, earth, water, and the sky. The earth which embraces all the other elements is singled out for lavish praise: "Tranquil, fragrant, pleasant, with sweet drink in her udder, rich in milk, let earth (bhumi) bless me, earth together with milk."(Atharva Veda Samhita, Kanda 12, Sukta 1, hymn 3348). Again, "O mother earth (bhumi) do you kindly set me down well established; in concord with the heaven, O sage (kavi), do you set me in fortune, in prosperity (bhuti)" (Atharva Veda, Kanda 12, Sukta 1, hymn 3362).

In the Atharva Veda, earth occupies a pivotal position in the Supreme Self's scheme of things. Earth's primacy as the life-giver is extolled in the following hymns in Kanda XII of the Atharva Veda:

"Great (brhant) truth, formidable right, consecration, penance, brahman, sacrifice sustain the earth; let her for us, mistress of what is and what is to be – let the earth make for us wide room (loka)."(Hymn 1) "Whose, the earth's, [are] four quarters; on whom food, plowings, came into being; who bears manifoldly what breathes, what stirs – let that earth (bhumi) set us among kine, also in inexhaustibleness (?anya)" (Hymn 4)

"She the earth (bhumi prithivi) whom the gods, sleepless, defend all the time without failure – let her yield (duh) to us honey, what is dear; then let her sprinkle us with splendor" (Hymn 7).

"On whom the circulating waters flow the same, night and day, without failure – let that earth (bhumi), of many streams (-dhara) yield (duh) us milk; then let her sprinkle [us] with splendor."(Hymn 9). "What is thy middle, O earth, and what is thy navel, what refreshments (urj) arose out of thy body – in them do thou set us; be purifying (pu) toward us; earth (bhumi) is mother, I am earth's son; parjanya is father – let him save us" (Hymn 12)

That man is mortal and earth alone can prolong his life span is put succinctly in Hymn 22 of Atharva Veda:-

"On the earth (bhumi) they give to the gods the sacrifice, the oblation, duly prepared; on the earth (bhumi) mortal men (manusya) live by svadha, by food; let that earth (bhumi) assign us breath, life-time; let earth make me one who attains old age."

Food and longevity were not the only boons that man sought from the earth. A fuller and more liveable life demanded material forms of wealth too. In Hymn 44 of the Atharva Veda, man prays for gold and jewels thus: "Bearing treasure [and] good in many places hiddenly, let the earth give me jewel (mani), gold; ...." Faith in nature as a giver of unlimited blessings even encouraged man to give expression to his avarice in an earlier hymn (Hymn 40) where he prays "Let that earth (bhumi) appoint unto us what riches we desire." The Vedas did not look down upon man's overvaulting greed but tolerated it as his inherent failing and discouraged it.

The foregoing passages from the Rig and Atharva Vedas make one thing clear. Man held nature in awe and approached her with supplication but felt equally at liberty to beseech her with requests to bestow on him food, wealth, well-being, and long life. It was not just the awe and fear of nature that ruled men's hearts and lives but also an unshakable belief that their wishes would be granted by Mother Nature. In return, as the following Hymn from Atharva Veda puts it beautifully, man was to promise to nature that he would pay her back whatever he received from her and would never do anything that caused her permanent injury nor would he ever fail to be thankful to her for her gifts:-

> "What of thee, O earth (bhumi), I dig out. Let that quickly grow over; let me not hit (arpay) thy vitals nor thy heart, O cleansing one. (Hymn 35, Kanda XII, Atharva Veda)"

Finally, man concludes his worship of nature with the following words:

"Earth my mother, set me securely with bliss

In full accord with heaven,

O Wise one,

Uphold me in grace and splendor."

While the Vedas stress the need for man to be reverential to nature and to the gods, texts like the Upanishads bring gods, nature, and humans close together by intertwining their lives and feelings. According to the Upanishads, every stage in the evolution of life on this planet from fish, amphibians, and animals to man is symbolized by a series of divine incarnations called Avataras. According to the Vaishnavism School of Hindu philosophy "man did not spring fully formed to dominate the lesser life forms, but rather evolved out of these forms itself, and is therefore integrally linked to the whole of creation."(O.P. Dwivedy) The Avataras, nine in number, follow a succession in keeping with the stages of human evolution. Thus, the first Avatar is Matsya (the fish), followed by Kurma (the turtle), Varaha (the wild boar), the small-statured human (Vamana) succeeded by other human forms like Parasurama, Rama, Balarama, Krishna, and the part-man –part horse Kalki at the end.

The Brhadaranyaka and Chandogya Upanishads compare the physiognomy of man with that of a tree: "Truly man is just like a tree. His hairs are the leaves and his skin resembles the natural bark. His blood streams forth out of his skin like the sap of a tree when he is cut.....The flesh is comparable to wood, the sinews are like the inner bark, the bones are the inner core of the wood and the marrow resembles the pith of a tree." Such expressive comparisons, by no means fanciful, reinforce Hinduism's claim that the different forms of matter are but the different manifestations of the same, single "Brahman".

The celebrated cosmic dance of Lord Shiva is an illustration of a higher order of universal harmony. In his essay "The Dance of Shiva" Ananda K. Coomaraswamy describes the dance as depicting the five activities (Pancha kritya) of Shiva in his forms of Rudra, Maheshwara, Sadashiva, Vishnu and Brahma. The activities are "Shrishti (overlooking, creation, evolution), Stithi (Preservation, support), Samhara (destruction), Tirobhava (veiling, embodiment, illusion, and also, giving rest), [and] Anugraha (release, salvation, grace)." Coomaraswamy elaborates on the cosmic dance further thus: "creation arises from the drum: protection from the hand of hope: from fire proceeds destruction: the foot held aloft gives release." The fourth hand that points to this lifted foot is the refuge of the soul. Commenting on the Dance of Shiva, Romain Rolland observed sagely that, in this universe, "everything has its place, everything has its function, and all take part in the divine concert, their different voices and their very dissonances, creating ... a most beautiful harmony." Harmony between man and nature is what Hinduism is all about.

But does harmony mean splendid isolation of each element in this universe and non-interference with the lives of others? As seen earlier, Hinduism envisages harmony with nature as a two-way process, a process of give and take with neither of the players being the loser. How can man take advantage of this harmony for his sustenance and what are the limits to such acts of man? The Atharva Veda provides a ready and telling answer in the form of a fable. It recounts the story of both angels and demons deciding to churn the ocean (Amrut Manthan) to bring out the elixir of life that the oceans were rumoured to contain. Out of their common desire to gain access to the elixir, the two warring groups go about the task working in tandem using a mountain as the churner, a huge snake (Vasuki) as the churning rope, and above all using Lord Vishnu in his incarnation as a giant turtle as the seat of the churning pot. Their labours bring out not only gems and riches and the sought after elixir from the innards of the ocean but also a deadly poison. Fearing danger to all life on earth from this unexpected side effect, Lord Shiva steps in and gulps the poison. This daring but dangerous act draws out the protective and possessive instincts in his consort Parvathi who presses his neck to prevent the poison from going down his throat. The stagnant poison casts a dull blue hue on Shiva's neck, a feature that marks his picturisation in Hindu iconography as one with a blue neck and earns him the sobriquet of Neelakanta (the one with a blue neck).

From an ecological point of view, the moral of this amusing tale of churning the ocean to bring out the elixir is simple. Nature can provide all that man desires up to a point. But if pushed further, it can bring about his destruction. Nature does not bar her being harnessed by man for his welfare and material growth but surely dictates the limits to such harnessing. Just compare this teaching with what James Lovelock cautions us today. In his "Revenge of Gaia", Gaia, the goddess representing earth with its resources, waste assimilation capacities, and ecological balance would tolerate perturbations to her equilibrium to a point – the 'tipping point' as modern science would put it-but beyond that may strike back with vengeance.

To promote the feeling of oneness with nature in man, Hindu mythology bestowed God's and nature's bounties and forces with human and animal forms and qualities. Thus, rivers were bestowed with feminine form and charm, and the Lord with amoral masculine traits in his relationship with them. River Ganga (Ganges) is portrayed as priding herself as being closest to Lord Shiva by arriving from the heavens and getting herself ensconced in his profusely matted locks, obviously to raise the ire of the other two suitors for his affections, Yamuna and Saraswati. Fighting back, Yamuna raises the passions of Shiva so much that his blazing heart sets Ganga afire with the unintended consequence of darkening her complexion. With a feeling of deep remorse, the cosmic lover consoles his distraught love with the blessing that henceforth she would become known as Harathirtha, the carrier of water sacred to Hara that is Shiva. Yamuna gets doubly rewarded when she becomes dear to both Hara and Hari (Vishnu) and acquires yet another honourific, Harithirtha. And what about Saraswati? She too gets her desserts by becoming the carrier of Shiva's famed Third Eye to the ocean. What a poetic way of bringing together gods and inanimate nature and conveying the message of universal harmony to the lay follower!

Interference by man with nature for satisfying his wants came after a long period of observation and trial during which he learnt the ways of nature and how he could turn the knowledge to his benefit in a spirit of understanding and gentleness. As Martha Vanucci observes that man learned that there were also natural phenomena with which he could interfere and with which he could collaborate after having understood how the system worked. She draws attention to the wise words of the Rig Veda "The seeker of nature's laws is rewarded; the fathers found the light (knowledge) that lay in darkness (ignorance) and with effectual words begat the morning (teaching of knowledge, or accepted science) (RV, V II 76, 4)". Vanucci concludes that "In fact, we would not be here if our forefathers had not been wise and ingenious." This wisdom and ingenuity of a pastoral society came to its help when it began its transformation into a settled community in Rig Vedic times. Its food needs were satisfied through 'rational agriculture', improvement of the wheel to draw water, and harnessing the motive power of the horse and the bullock. Thus, the scientific observation that barley grew well in the highlands made it the staple food of the pastoralists, and later when they moved into the plains in pursuit of settled life, wheat came into prominence in their diet. Similarly, knowledge of winning metals from ores ushered in the iron – age and the copper age. Steel metallurgy reportedly dates back to 400 BC and by 200 BC good quality steel was being produced employing crucible technology.

Hinduism's philosophical and practical underpinning of man's position in the universe, in one breath, stands in full agreement with the modern, scientific, ecological principle of "Man without his environment [both living and non-living] is an abstraction; in reality no such being could exist." (Dasmann). An adversarial relationship between man and nature was never contemplated in Indian religious texts nor was such a relationship ever practised in the long history of India. Hinduism neither preached a hands-off approach on the lines championed by green activists of today nor did it ever countenance harnessing nature to the point of exhaustion as a protagonist of growth *per se* would like to believe.

Buddhism

Buddhism, though negating Hinduism's basic tenet of an all-pervading 'brahman' and the presence of an indestructible 'atman' in every being, resonates with compassion for all sentient beings and spreads the message of universal love and interdependence. Interdependence of beings and not independence is at the core of Buddhism. The Hindu concept of 'self' is unacceptable to Buddhism as that "promotes a feeling of independence than interdependence." As developed by later Chinese Buddhist philosophers, this doctrine of "unimpeded interpenetration of all phenomena" propounds that "everything in the universe is literally dependent upon everything else, nothing stands alone, everything is linked together through time and space." This interlinking can be understood or interpreted in many ways. One could be to urge man to adopt a hands-off approach to nature on the argument that nature has as much right to exist as undefiled as man is. Another could be to permit limited interference, enough to satisfy man's wants, though not his greed. Buddhism tends to agree with, nay advocates, the latter view. In doing so, it propounds a middle way, that of a "moderate lifestyle" eschewing the "extremes of self-deprivation and self-indulgence."

Buddhism preaches neither extreme asceticism nor the unbridled pursuit of worldly wants. It prescribes a way of life at once practical and unworldly as one would wish it to be. In the words of Martine Batchelor, for a Buddhist, "Enlightenment is not some mystical state where visions of unearthly bliss unfold but a series of responses to the question; how am I to live in this world?"

The Buddhist doctrine of 'no self' (Anatta) does not set man apart from his environment. Instead of making him a mystic, it advocates that he follow a worldly unworldliness. It calls upon him to be aware and alive to all that surrounds him, whether they are of any significance or not. An early Buddhist text says: "Know you the grasses and the trees... Then ye the worms, and the moths, and the different sorts of ants.... Know ye also the four-footed animals small and great, the serpents, the fish... the birds...Know ye the marks that constitute species are theirs, and their species are manifold."(David Gosling) This deep reverence for creatures, big and small, is portrayed in the choice of the central characters of many a Jataka tale. Enumerating such references, Christopher Chapple finds that "half of the 550 stories have animals as their central characters; seventy types of animals appear with varying frequency; monkeys are present in 27 tales, lions appear in 19, and the humble mouse just once."

Though negating the Hindu concept of the 'self', Buddhism shares with the former the belief in the existence of disembodied spirits and their taking residence in natural objects. This leads to the Buddhist teaching of man's need to show consideration and compassion towards all objects lest the spirits residing in them throw a curse at him. The Buddhist text, Ariguttara Nikaya, recounts the story of the spirit residing in a fruit-bearing tree casting a curse on the man who partakes of its offerings but breaks a branch before leaving. The spirit thinks to itself "how astonishing it is, that a man should be so evil as to break a branch off the tree after eating his fill. Suppose the tree were to bear no more fruit." The tree becomes barren after the incident. This illustrates the revenge nature can unleash upon inconsiderate humanity.

Buddhism sets much store by the physical well-being of man. Poverty and hunger are taboo unless embraced for a worthy cause; otherwise, they are liable to lead man to sin and hence to an unhappy rebirth. This teaching of Buddhism is well brought out in the Tamil classic, Manimeghalai (circa the sixth century BCE) which speaks of the horrors of hunger and the blessedness of those who have the means to relieve the hunger of others. Buddhism sees little virtue in those who would rather suffer the pangs of hunger than partake in the bounties of nature to satisfy it. Like Hinduism, it advocates a pragmatic approach to nature.

The Buddhist scripture Sigalovada Sutta counsels man to act with nature the way a bee collects nectar from a flower. The bee harms neither the beauty nor the fragrance of the flower but only gathers nectar to be muted into honey. Likewise, striking a fine balance in the harnessing of nature enables man to fulfill his material wants and leave nature's recuperative strengths unharmed in the process. Since all worldly goods, in some way or the other, originate from nature, their overconsumption and waste are termed "criminal" by Buddhism. The man who pays little heed to this teaching is derided as a "wood apple eater", meaning one who shakes the wood apple tree to bring down all the fruits but picks up only a few and leaves the rest to waste.

The Buddhist teaching of detachment means "detachment from inappropriate human intervention" to fulfill one's desires. Non-aggressive intervention suffers from no bar. In the vivid prose of the Taoist philosopher, Chuang Tzu (369-286 BCE), "A good cook changes his knife once a year because he cuts. A mediocre cook changes his knife once a month – because he hacks." Nature is not to be savaged to part with her riches; she has to be coaxed into gifting them.

Jainism

Austerity and non-violence are the basic tenets of Jain philosophy and the way of life it preaches. Its message of "paraspararopa Jivanam" highlights the interconnectivity of all life forms and means mutual support to all living beings." Jainism does not abhor interference with nature to fulfill human needs but advocates moderation and gentleness in doing so. Jain texts refer to restraint from attachment to worldly possessions as "Aparigraha" and infatuate attachment as "Parigraha". Avarice (parigraha) is looked down upon as it is insatiable. As the Utta Sutra(8-16) puts it "Even if this whole world full of wealth is given to a man, he will not be contented, for it is very difficult to satisfy the desires of an avaricious man."

The virtue of abhorrence of avarice assumes lofty proportions in Jainism. It extends to total abnegation of anything that is not one's due, not even something lost and unclaimed by others. It puts limits even on profit that one can earn rightfully. Jain scriptures caution man thus: "A noble householder is one who does not buy valuable goods much below their cost price, does not take possession of lost properties, and remains satisfied by earning reasonable profits." Profit per se is not looked down upon but profiteering is.

What it preaches in relation to transactions in man's daily life, Jainism extends them to his interactions with nature too. This is done through fine parables like the one which tells the story of six hungry men who lose their way in a forest. To satisfy their hunger, they embark on the exercise of collecting fruits from a tree. Each comes up with his suggestion on how to collect the fruits and the measures vary from cutting down the whole tree to plucking the low-hanging ones. Finally, good sense prevails upon them to pick up only the fruits fallen on the ground as they would be enough to satisfy their hunger. So conscious of the need for restraint in approaching nature, Jainism has a special term, 'Atibharopana' for applying undue stress on natural ecosystems. Atibharopana has to be avoided at all costs through the exercise of self-restraint.

Decrying avarice, Jainism goes on to identify avarice and violence as the root causes of all conflicts in this world. Jainism believes that one who deprives another of his rightful share of resources or his basic needs is committing the sin of 'Aharavarana'. Aharavarana is causing starvation of another human being through negligence, indifference, deliberation, or bad governance. Hence, the Twenty-fourth Tirthankara, Lord Mahavira, advanced austerity, non-possession, and eschewing violence to ward off class conflicts and bring about an equitable distribution of the world's resources and sustainable development.

Islam

As with the other great religions that we have looked at, Islam preaches total harmony between man and nature. "The world is green and beautiful, and the Allah has appointed you his guardian over it," said The Prophet. Though a religious faith that sprouted and grew on desert sands and in an inhospitable climate, Islam abounds in passages extolling greenery and exhorting believers to be guardians of the Lord's creations. Such is Islam's love for nature that the Prophet advises his flock thus: "When doomsday comes, if someone has a palm shoot in his hand he should plant it." For a follower of Islam, greening the earth is an act of faith. For the true believer, living in harmony with nature is not a hands-off approach but one of symbiotic existence. For him, nature is the source of his sustenance as put beautifully in the following words:

"[Allah] Made for you the Earth a Resting Place,

And the Heaven an edifice for protection,

And caused water to pour down from The clouds. He brought you forth

Therewith a great variety of fruit for your sustenance." (Holy Qur'an Al-Baquarah 3:22)

Islam preaches total equality of man and other beings on this earth. Surah 6:38 proclaims "There is not an animal in the earth, nor a flying creature flying on two wings, but they are peoples like unto you". This means that creatures other than man have as much right to live in this world as man has. Man does not have the status of a master over nature and hence cannot proclaim his dominion over it. Further, "Environment is the gift of God to all ages, past and present and future." Man is but a resting traveller who can enjoy the offerings of nature to the extent of satisfying his immediate needs only, conscious all the time of the fact that the path of life on earth would be trodden by future generations too who would have an equal need of nature's gifts. Wise stewardship and intergenerational equity are built-in features of Islam.

Quran institutionalizes man's relationship with nature in a threefold manner, as a Trustee (**Khalifa),** as a promoter of the message of **Tawhid (**Allah's unity), and as one bound by **Akhirah** (accountability). To the sceptical angels concerned over the evil that man can do on earth, Allah replies "I know that which ye know not" thus reposing faith in humanity to nurture nature. The Qur'an speaks of humans as vice-regents of the Lord on earth. It exhorts the vice-regents never to forget the eternal truth of Allah's unity "reflected in the unity of mankind and the unity of man and nature." Hence, his appointed trustees are "responsible for maintaining the unity of his creations, the integrity of the Earth, its flora and fauna, its wildlife and natural environment." This "Unity cannot be had by discord, by setting one need against another; it is maintained by balance and harmony." Islam thus takes the middle path, neither preaching total abstinence from harnessing nature to man's good nor reckless exploitation of nature to serve man's greed.

Islam is fully alive to the fact of man's proclivity to ignore Lord's teachings and forget his dependence on the Lord for everything he needs on earth. Islam administers a stern warning to those who entertain thoughts of such errant behaviour:

"Nay, but verily man is rebellious

That he deemeth himself independent "Verily unto thy Lord is the return."

Islam believes in the Day of Reckoning when all beings will have to render an account to the Lord of what all they did on earth. This belief **(Akhirah)** is the third tenet of Islam that along with **Khalifa** and **Tawhid** governs man's conduct on earth. These three beliefs form the three pillars of Islamic environmental ethics. The point of man's total dependence on the Lord is thus driven home forcefully. In a series of lectures titled "The cultural side of Islam", delivered in Chennai in 1927, the British Islamic scholar, M.M. Pickthall put this point succinctly: "His [man's] absolute dependence on the natural laws which govern all existence; his inability to breathe or raise an arm without obeying laws he never made; the spectacle of day and night; the laws of growth and decay and new growth, of birth and death; the laws of consequences which attend on all his acts – all these should be a perpetual reminder to man that his sovereignty or province of free will is strictly bounded, and always at the mercy of an infinitely greater power." Clearly, in Islam, there is little place for either anthropocentrism or abnegation in man's relationship with nature. What Islam preaches is healthy harmony between man and nature.

The convergence of thought on the man-nature relationship among the religions of India is its greatest cultural strength so very essential for sustainable socio-economic progress.

Select References

"Rig Veda Samhita, Vol. III (Mandalas 6, 7, 8)"; translation of Wilson and Bhasya of Sayanacharya; revised by Ravi Prakash Arya, K.L. Joshi, Parimal Publications, Delhi.

Atharva Veda Samhita, Vol. II; based on the translation of W. D. Whitney and Bhasya of Sayanacharya; edited and revised by K.L. Joshi; Parimal Publications Delhi.

Atharva Veda Samhita, Vol.II; based on the translation of W. D. Whitney; Motilal Banarsi Das, Varanasi.

"The Dance of Siva: Essays on Indian Art & Culture" Ananda K. Coomaraswamy, Dover Publications, INC, Mineola, New York.

"Human Ecology In The Vedas", Martha Vanucci, Restructuring Indian History and Culture, No.19, D.K. Printworld (P) Ltd. New Delhi.

"Buddhism and Ecology", Martin Batchelor and Kerry Brown; Motilal Banarsi Das. Delhi.

"Sigalovada Sutta: The Buddha's Advice to Sigalaka" Dhammapada Verse 49 (DN 31) Translated from the Pali into English by John Kelly, Sue Sawyer and Victoria Yareham, 2005; Alternate translation by Narada Thera (1996).

"Environmental Awareness in Jainism", Geetha Ramanujam, Department of Jainology, University of Madras.

"Deep Ecology and Jainism: A critical Assessment of Theory and Practice", Blair Trelinski, Queens University, Kingston, Ontario, Canada (2010).

"The Cultural Side of Islam", M.M. Pickthall, Kitab Bhavan, India (first published by The Committee of Madras Lectures on Islam, 1927).

"Environmental Conservation", Raymond F. Dasmann, Wiley 1968

Chapter II

The Western View of Nature

Judaic and Early Christian View

The Oriental approach to nature, as we saw in Chapter I, was entirely one of veneration of nature devoid of inquisitive interest in its ways. In contrast, the Occidental approach, inspired by Judaic thought, was to regard man as a creation of God in his own image vested with lordship over nature and all its constituents. Genesis (1:27) affirms "So God created man in His own image, in the image of God created He in him; male and female created like He them." The Book of Moses says that on the sixth day of Creation, God said "Let us make man in our own image, according to our likeness; let them have dominion over the fish of the sea, over the birds of the air, over all the earth and over every creeping thing that creeps on the earth." God commended to man to "Be fruitful and multiply; fill the earth and subdue it; have dominion over the fish of the sea, over the birds of the air and over everything that moves on the earth." God supplemented this grant of largesse with the words "See, I have given you every herb that yields seed which is on the face of all the earth, and every tree whose fruit yield seed; to you it shall be for food."

What was God's purpose in creating earth? Isaiah (45:18) provides the answer thus "For thus saith the Lord that created the heavens; God Himself that formed the earth and made it; He hath established it, He created it not in vain, He formed it to be inhabited". The thoughtful Lord bestowed more on man, his supposedly favourite creation. He created a garden for man's habitation as said in Genesis (2:8-15) "And the Lord God planted a garden eastward in Eden; and there He put the man whom he had formed. And out of the ground made the Lord God to grow every tree that is pleasant to the sight, and good for food..... And the Lord God took the man, and put him into the garden to dress it and keep it."

An uncritical reading of Judaic and Christian texts would suggest that they postulated a dualistic view that nature and man were two sharply defined discontinuous entities and asserted man's superiority over nature. This postulate known as "anthropocentrism" or "homocentrism" was presented in two forms, normative and teleological. In its normative form, the postulate limited its application of moral standards and morality to human beings and their inter-relationships and not to man's relationship with God's other creations. Teleology was anchored on the premise of a grand design and purpose in nature that considered things other than man as existing for the benefit of man only. This conferment of superior status on man inspired the 12th. Century theologist, St. Thomas Aquinas to develop an 'instrumentalist' approach to guide man's attitude towards animals, a doctrine that preached that animals had their value because they served some essential purpose of man. That is, animals had their value in God's scheme of life on this planet because they were useful to man, the overlord, in some way or the other but had no intrinsic value. This view was to exert a powerful influence on the thinking of western political economists in the 18th. Century and to inspire modern man's less than considerate treatment of nature in his march towards economic development. Rene Dubos goes as far as to say that anthropocentrism provided an excuse for policies of overexploitation of natural resources.

Renaissance and the Age of Exploration

The contrary view that the biblical texts should be understood to convey man's stewardship of nature and not overlordship was lost on the western world in mediaeval times. Forgotten was God's warning to man that the land in Eden "must not be sold permanently, because the land is mine and you are aliens and my clients" (Leviticus 25.23) and that "The land shall not be sold for ever; for the land is mine; for ye are strangers and sojourners with me" (King James Bible). But the West chose to ignore this stern message for worldly reasons engendered and nourished by a profound cultural transformation called Renaissance that began to sweep it from the fourteenth century onwards.

The wave of Renaissance that swept Europe from 1300 CE to 1600 CE with its encouragement of the spirit of inquiry and reason nourished the religion-inspired egoistic notion of human superiority over the Lord's other creations. A logical development of this movement was to find ways and means to harness nature for man's personal greed without moral guilt and fear of supernatural retribution.

Renaissance was also set to overlap another milestone in world history. The spirit of inquiry that prevailed in the Age of Renaissance led adventurers turned explorers to navigate the oceans to map the geographical limits of the earth. This marked the beginning of the Age of Exploration (1420 AD – 1620 AD). To the royal courts and nobility of Europe, this was a welcome development as indigenous sources to generate wealth to support their lavish lifestyles and military spending began to dwindle. Royal patronage and explorers' adventurism synergized each other proving profitable to both and more importantly, buttressed the western portrayal of nature as a vast treasure house that could be sacked at will.

There was a third force that acted in unison with Europe's royals and explorers, namely, the merchant class, that was eager to broaden its activities from the confines of local markets to theatres afar. As the spirit of 'Exploration' opened up access to new lands and newer and newer resources, it was natural for the merchant classes to extend their areas of trade and commerce, an initiative much to the liking of the rulers as it brought immense wealth to their nations and to them personally. The monarchs were greatly taken in by the potential of foreign trade in ensuring a steady stream of revenue, a gain that made them less dependent on land revenue and tributes exacted from grudging landlords and vassals. Foreign trade led to the imposition of border taxes, a steady and strong source of revenue for the governments. With the rise of the merchant class, a great movement called 'Mercantilism' was born in Europe.

Era of Colonization and Industrial Revolution

The Age of Exploration fortified by the spirit of inquiry also spawned a new era in world history, the Age of Colonization. As the militaristic, seafaring European nations were discovering new lands on the planet, their economies began to undergo profound structural changes, thanks to the availability of cheap raw materials from the newly discovered lands and the onset of the Industrial Revolution at home. The emergence of machines with high productivity in the last quarter of the 18th. Century opened up possibilities for the conversion of natural resources into finished goods on scales never attained before. For instance, in Britain, the newly invented Spinning Jenny and the Steam Engine enabled imported cotton and wool to be spun into yarn and woven into fabric for marketing at home and abroad in large quantities. Gold, silver, and other metals of value were extracted from the mines of the discovered lands to be stored in the royal vaults in Europe, to decorate the households of the nobility, and to produce Iron, Steel, Copper, Aluminium, and

Tin in quantities the western world needed them. Tropical timber provided the sinews of the mercantile and naval fleets of Europe.

Mechanization of industry leading to high productivity and lower costs of production, a development of surpassing significance in world history originating in Britain in 1775 and spreading to the Continent, necessitated the discovery of ever new sources of raw materials and development of markets outside the traditional and the domestic. For both purposes, the new lands on the seafarer's map and their native inhabitants were the inevitable choices to be targeted by the mercantile bodies of the Continent. Britain, Netherlands, Spain, and Portugal were the leaders in these efforts, setting up trading companies and outposts abroad that gave them permanent seats of commercial establishment. The companies were soon to look upon the hinterlands of the newly discovered shores as their estates and the natives their captive source of labour. This development was to mark the beginning of what historians call "exploitation colonization".

To consolidate their control over the riches and people of the discovered lands and ensure a steady flow of raw materials to the industry back home, European nations needed to deal with the colonies at a level more proximate and effective than one of distant and itinerant trading. They needed to occupy the lands on a permanent basis and keep the natives in awe and fear of European might. This took two forms, one of establishing an elaborate administrative and governing apparatus with local participation secured more by force than by consent and the other of encouraging citizens from the home countries to settle in the new lands and make them their new home. The first strategy was adopted where the stakes and local resistance were high as in India and East Asia and the second where fear of another competing colonial power filling the vacuum loomed large as in North Africa. Both "exploitation colonization" and "settler colonization" were aided by the deployment of well-trained armies fortified with firepower, assets that native rulers and chieftains lacked. These synergistic developments, though ending in the early nineteenth century in Latin America, were to dominate much of Africa and Asia till the middle of the twentieth century.

Western Political Thought and the Natural Environment

As the Industrial Revolution progressed, it was natural for a body of academic inquiry to grow that examined the role of different elements that contributed to the production process in the industrial age and how a nation's wealth and the economy would be influenced by the Revolution. This marked the beginning of a systematic study into the role of the so-called factors of production and the role that external factors like the market played in orienting the production effort to result in maximum monetary gain to the entrepreneur and ultimately to a nation's wealth. The result was the development of the discipline of Political Economy or in its short form, Economics.

Simply put, economics as it emerged, rested on the thesis that production was a function of four internal factors and an external factor, namely, the market. The four internal factors were land, labour, capital, and organization and an efficient mix of the four supported by a favourable market resulted in the maximization of profits. The market provided the interface where demand for goods was met by supply at a price considered acceptable to the trading parties.

From an inquiry into the optimum mix of inputs that would ensure maximum returns on investment to the producer, it was a natural step forward to explore how profit maximization in industry and accumulation of surplus wealth by a nation could be sustained over the long run or even indefinitely. Since the beginning of the Industrial Revolution in 1775 "indefinite accumulation of capital and generation of surplus became the driving force behind the growth of economic activities ... With the "institution of [the] market providing the mechanics of attainment of social well-being" (Sengupta). Under this politico-economic movement that came to be known as 'Capitalism', the process of accumulation of wealth got transformed from a means of achieving the goal of material well-being into the goal itself. As Sengupta observes forcefully, "The accumulation of wealth became the purpose of wealth itself. This tautological proposition regarding the purpose of wealth took it beyond the scope of rationality. These developments in the system of values contributed to the indefinite growth of demand for natural resources and environmental services to support such a process of development."

But how could the creation and accumulation of wealth through industry be sustained in the long run? According to Adam Smith (1723-1790), the Father of the science of Political Economy, the answer lay in the size of the market. Existing markets could be enlarged and new markets could be discovered and developed to absorb the output of rising productivity. Implicit in this answer was the assumption that nature, that storehouse of material resources, was inexhaustible and hence was not a limiting factor in production. That is, in the process of wealth accumulation, nature had more of a supporting role than a determining one. Thus ran the logic of western political economy, a logic that prevailed till the last quarter of the 20th. Century.

Before proceeding further, a reference to the cautionary words of an English cleric, Reverend T.R. Malthus (1766 – 1834) would be in order. Malthus put forth the thesis that the availability of arable land was limited and not infinite. Agricultural land had a certain carrying capacity or limitation in terms of its capacity to grow food to meet the needs of the growing population. The population grew not only naturally but also due to the well-being brought about by freedom from hunger. Further, according to Malthus, since arable land was limited, agricultural production increased only in a linear manner whereas the population had a tendency to grow exponentially. This "Malthusian Trap", while highlighting the consequences of overpopulation, sowed the seeds of the concept of the finiteness of natural resources, a concept that was to find wide acceptance a century later.

To supplement Malthus's thesis of a population–food mismatch, his compatriot, the political economist David Ricardo (1772-1823), came out with the observation that fertile lands would be cultivated first to grow food and as they became less productive over the years, newer areas would need to be brought under cultivation to feed the demands of a population that grew exponentially. Both Malthus and Ricardo thus sowed the seeds of the concept of the finiteness of natural resources, a concept that was to find support in the mid-twentieth century in the form of two seminal studies, namely the "Limits to Growth" by Meadows et.al (1972) and the United Nations Report "Only One Earth"(1986).

In addition to the monumental contributions of Adam Smith, the 17th and 18th. Centuries saw the emergence of other major milestones in the history of western political thought. From an environmental point of view, the most significant was the emergence of a school of political philosophy called **Utilitarianism,** the principal exponents of which were John Locke (1632-1704), Jeremy Bentham (1748 – 1832) and John Stewart Mill (1806-1873). Utilitarians believed that nothing in nature had an intrinsic value but only an instrumental value since God had created nature and stocked it with things that his chosen creation, man, could enjoy. Hence, the desirability of any action had to be judged by the overall impact it produced on both mankind and nature at large, and any action that enhanced human happiness was preferable to one that reduced it. Equally importantly, Utilitarian philosophy preached that "the forms of life that were unable to experience anything akin to either enjoyment or discomfort are denied of moral status because it is impossible to increase happiness or reduce the suffering of something that cannot feel happiness or suffer." If one were to follow this dictum, then pleasure or pain caused to sentient beings like humans and animals would alone qualify for consideration in human actions. The rest of nature would be deemed insentient and would merit little concern. In the 20th.century, Peter Singer was to put this more tersely when he wrote "It would be nonsense to say that it was not in the best interests of a stone to be kicked along the road by a schoolboy. A stone does not have interests because it cannot suffer. Nothing that we could do to it could possibly make any difference to its welfare". An extension of this doctrine was that the merit of any state action should be judged by the number of people who would benefit from that action. That is, the greatest good of the greatest number alone mattered. Utilitarian philosophy didn't stop there. Not being content with expressing happiness or unhappiness qualitatively, Utilitarians proceeded to put their theory on a quantitative foundation by developing a methodology called **_hedonic calculus_** for evaluating happiness – if one may call it welfare – and unhappiness.

It is not difficult to gauge the extent of moral justification that Utilitarianism provided to the ecological and environmental degradation that western societies were to experience as the Industrial Revolution rolled on. To boot, the spillover effect on the rest of the world, both in the immediate and long-term, was devastating. As Susan Leeson chose to comment on Locke's philosophy "[It] legitimated virtually endless accumulation of material goods; helped equate the process of accumulation, with liberty and the pursuit of happiness; helped implant the idea that with ingenuity man can go beyond the fixed laws of nature, adhering only to whatever temporary laws he establishes for himself in the process of pursuing happiness; and helped instil the notion that the "commons" is served best through man's pursuit of private gain, because there will always be enough for those willing to work". In short, in Western thought, human intervention with nature created something of value out of something that was valueless. In some form or the other, this belief persists to this day.

The march of Europe's industrialization blessed by a favourable politico-economic climate was spurred on by the phenomenal growth of science and technology in the second half of the nineteenth century and in the early decades of the twentieth. The discovery of electricity, the invention of telephony and the development of long-distance communication, the discovery of mineral oil, and the invention of the oil-powered internal combustion engine changed the face of the western economies and the consumption patterns of their citizens, as never before. And contrary to popular apprehension, the new developments were helpful to the labour classes by ensuring them round-the-year employment in place of the seasonal employment they were accustomed to. Even the fear of population growth outstripping food supply was met with the development of a commercial chemical process to "fix" atmospheric nitrogen into soils to yield bountiful harvests. Both nature and adversity seemed to have been conquered that by the middle of the twentieth century, despite two world wars and the market meltdown of the late 1920s, the West had come to nurse a feeling of sustained economic and social bliss.

Growth of Western Economies

It would be interesting to look into the economic progress made by western colonial powers in comparison to China and India in the centuries before and after the Industrial Revolution. According to Angus Maddison, barring Italy, all the others started at almost the same level and continued to remain in step and in stagnation till 1825. Come the Industrial Revolution and within half a century, Britain, France, Germany, and Spain pulled up sharply and away from the

Asian powers. Britain recorded the highest growth of them all by the middle of the twentieth century. Japan's change in fortunes took a little longer, coinciding with the Meiji Restoration of 1860. China and India languished all along.

Many reasons have been advanced for the sharp differences in per capita GDP between the colonial powers of Europe on one hand and China and India on the other since the nineteenth century. According to one view, the divergence was not due to differences in wages but due to a rise in real incomes caused by a fall in prices. Robert Allen *et.al.* go on to identify the following factors as having been responsible for the economic growth of Europe:-

(a)   earlier urbanization;

(b)   role of textile productivity;

(c)   agricultural productivity; and

(d)   man/land ratio.

According to Allen *et.al,* "Northwest Europe led in the development of non-agricultural productivity concentrated in the capital goods and knowledge-based sectors". This, according to them, seems to be the most likely proximate cause of Northwest Europe's growth before 1870 (Peter Lindert). One would like to supplement this conclusion by highlighting the role of the colonies in Europe's growth. Europe's high industrial production levels could not have been sustained without its raw material requirements being met by imports from colonies. Further, the growth of industry and mechanization of agriculture led to the migration of labour from rural areas resulting in a fall in the rural population. This led to the mechanization of agricultural operations and higher agricultural productivity. Boosting these already substantial gains was the high profit earned from trade with the colonies. Of passing interest is the fact that slave trade accounted for 7% of the annual profits of the European trading companies. Their governments, in turn, benefited from higher tax revenues. The vast tracts of vacant land in the newly settled territories were farmed to grow cotton and tobacco for consumption in Europe and this helped free up land in Europe for industry. Mines in New World colonies were exploited for their silver and the metal was traded in large quantities to China. One may conclude that the colonies played a singularly important role in the early industrialization of the West resulting in the latter's wealth and global political and economic power.

Life Expectancy and Welfare

West's economic growth spurred by advances in science, technology, and medicine brought in its wake improvements in nutrition, public health, sanitation, and water supply. At the post-natal and infancy stages, the administration of immunological care through vaccination to prevent Small Pox alone was to save thousands of lives in Britain and Europe. These benefits were reflected in rising life expectancies at birth (Table below). Life expectancy went up dramatically during the Industrial Revolution. The percentage of children born in London who died before the age of five fell drastically from 74.5% in 1730-1749 to 31.8% in the period 1810 – 1849 (Tim Lambert)

Table

Life Expectancy of Men and Women at birth (years)

Century	16th. – 18th.	20th (1900-1930; 1930-1950)	21st (2015)
Great Britain	35-40 (both)	(1900-1930) 47 (men); 50 (women) (1930-1950) 60-65 (both)	79 (men) 83 (women)
France	25-30	45 (1900) (both) and rising	78.5 (men); 84.9 (women)

In stark contrast, developing countries lagged far behind the developed all along with India bringing up the rear. India managed to cross the fifty-year bar for life expectancy long after the others, including Latin American countries, did. One possible reason for India's slow growth in comparison with Latin America could be that India became independent of foreign rule long after the latter countries. Low life expectancy was colonial rule's unsolicited gift to a colony.

Growth of Western Economies and Society

The invention of electricity generation by burning coal, the discovery of mineral oil deposits in many parts of the world, and the invention of the internal combustion engine all occurring in the late 19th. century were events of surpassing value to human society. Coal mining on a commercial scale, an activity known to Britain and the rest of Europe for centuries, received a fillip with heavy demands for the mineral from enterprises engaged in the generation of electricity. This new form of energy to be harnessed for man's benefit came to exert an enormous influence not only on the industry but on society as a whole. The discovery of oil and its use in the internal combustion engine transformed public and private transportation in a profound way. Hardly, any other development in human history has had such an impact on the global economy and human lifestyles as the use of coal for power generation or of oil for transporting men and material over land, sea, and air.

Though the economic experience of the colonial powers at home was happy indeed, their local environment and social life were less so. In Europe and England, the Industrial Revolution brought with it dark skies laden with acrid smoke and waterways fouled by toxic discharges from industries; to boot, the steady migration of rural populations to the sprouting industrial hubs in search of livelihood gave birth to urban slums that were to prove the breeding grounds of epidemics and crime.

The appalling conditions, both within and outside the industrial establishments demanded countermeasures in the form of pollution control, ensuring industrial safety and labour welfare. The British, particularly concerned with the consequences of unchecked urban growth, responded with legislative and administrative measures to refashion town and country planning and urban administration. The urban middle class, a new social phenomenon, sought solace in the belief that pollution was a necessary accompaniment of industrial growth and in the march to prosperity. The Industrial Revolution thus had a double effect on the West, that of ravaging the "commons" and of giving birth to the pernicious doctrine of pollution being a necessary feature of growth and prosperity.

Ecological Impact of Colonialism

The impact of colonial rule on the natural environment of the conquered lands was disastrous, to say the least. Minerals in huge quantities were dug out of the earth leaving behind vast areas of derelict land; timber, mostly of lush tropical species, was extracted well beyond the regenerative capacities of the forests that yielded them leaving behind widespread barrenness; native populations were driven out of their long-held lands and, worst of all, made mass victims of European diseases like *typhus* and *syphilis* to which they had little resistance.

As the western economies grew in the centuries following the onset of the Industrial Revolution, the economies of the colonies saw a steady decline. This came about through a clever mix of political, legislative, and administrative measures adopted by the colonial rulers. Exports of finished goods from the colonies were discouraged and goods produced indigenously in the colonies for local consumption were replaced by cheap, mass-produced imports from abroad. Cumulatively, the effect was one of the colony becoming a plantation or a captive mine that supplied cheap raw material to the industry in the land of the colonial master and a vast importer of products of the latter's manufactories, from safety pins to textiles and industrial machinery. There is a school of thought composed of both Indian and foreign scholars that the Industrial Revolution in England "itself was a consequence of the plundered wealth of India." They conclude that "during the first half of the nineteenth century, India lost the proud position of supremacy in the trade and industry of the world, which she had been occupying for well-nigh two thousand years, and was gradually transformed into a plantation for the production of raw materials and a dumping –ground for the cheap manufactured goods from the West." (Majumdar, Raychaudhuri, Datta).

In the colonies, the natural environment and the people it supported were the worst sufferers. The dense forests, seemingly silent and impenetrable, were home to native populations. The people and the forests were not separate identities with the former preying upon the latter. The two melded into a harmonious whole. But this idyll was disturbed to an irreversible measure by the intrusion of the colonizer. The resulting impact on the natives, their habitat, and the whole ecosystem that housed and nurtured them was catastrophic. Africa saw a brisk trade in slaves which, besides being inhuman, denuded native lands of able-bodied labour. Trade in animal skins and ivory encouraged the poaching of wildlife on a large scale. The introduction of large landholdings, in preference to extant small parcels, to promote the raising of commercial crops for export led to the marginalization of the small landholder.

Of the two forms of colonization, "exploitation" or "settler", it was not that one was preferable to the other. Both were aggressive in nature in driving out the natives from their landholdings and in the process sowing the seeds of decay of native cultures and loss of native dignity. As put pithily by a writer, the psychological impact on the native populations was "as lasting as it was lethal." In the New World, the situation was no better. Writing about the North American experience, Frederick Jackson Turner observed more than a century ago that from the 1490s settlers went on to extend their frontiers through forest clearance, decimation of wildlife elbowing out in the process the "weak races" of peoples, plants, and animals. The extension of the frontiers was thus a transforming process resulting in "deep and irreversible ecological and human disjuncture, a trauma from which indigenous human, plant, and animal communities can never fully recover."

The utterly cruel and remorseless way in which European powers acted in concert to exploit newly explored lands and impoverish them is best illustrated by the experience of West Africa. The second half of the 19th Century began with European nations carving out their spheres of influence and dominion in West Africa. Thirteen of them led by the then mighty Germany with its "Iron Chancellor" Bismarck crystallized their control over their areas of "effective occupation" under authority conferred on them by the Berlin Protocol signed at the Berlin Conference in 1884. Congo, claimed by Belgium, became the personal colony of its ruler, King Leopold II through the subterfuge of handing it over to a body called the Congo Society" controlled by none other than Leopold himself. With this began the systematic impoverishment of Congo of its gold, copper, precious stones, and timber. It is of interest that the United States was a participant in the Berlin conclave.

By the end of the 19th Century, the entire African continent had fallen under the occupation of the European powers. Just as West Africa saw the emergence of European colonies blessed by an understanding among the colonizers, the rest of the Continent, particularly the southern and central parts were claimed by powers like Britain and Portugal on the specious ground that one who controlled the coasts controlled the hinterland too. All this was done in the name of ending the practice of slavery and the slave trade. The Western powers put on the fig leaf of ending slavery through political intervention with the rule of native African and Islamic powers which, supposedly, were indulging in the practice. Africa was the sad victim of both 'exploitation colonialism' and 'Settler colonialism', a situation that continued well into the middle of the 20th Century.

The situation in India, though free of slave trade, was no better. Both man and beast were treated savagely in their own native land, the first for economic gain and the second for sport. "To ensure a regular and abundant supply of cotton goods, the Company [East India Company] entered into forward contracts with the weavers to supply stipulated quantities of cloth at fixed dates .... Armed with the authority of the Company, they [the Company's servants] forced the poor weavers, on pain of flogging, to sign the most iniquitous bonds. The latter were paid for their goods much less than their usual price, sometimes even less than the cost of materials, while they were forbidden to work for any other party on pain of corporal punishment". The Indian subcontinent's lush timber forests were cut and the timber was auctioned to raise revenue for the government or was exported to Britain. However, it must be said in fairness to the British rulers, that they put Indian forestry on a scientific footing making the management of the subcontinent's forests a model in conservation-inspired management. The extensive rail transportation network they built, though at the cost of forest area, was commendable. They were equally benign to the subcontinent's floral wealth. But with fauna, they were less considerate, reducing fauna to 'game', 'wildlife' or 'vermin'. Organized official orgies of wildlife massacre were common.

The spirit of colonialism inspired by trade considerations lives on. The adverse impact of colonialism on the economy and ecology of the Third World is generally glossed over. The US stand, in the words of its Chief Negotiator at the Paris Climate Conference, 2016 was "There's one thing we don't accept, and we won't accept in this agreement [the Paris Climate Agreement, December 2016], which is the notion that there should be liability and compensation for loss and damage". The technologically advanced nations view environmental concerns as a huge trade opportunity. Way back in 1996, the then US Secretary of State, Mr. Warren Christopher in his address at Stanford University declared that the intention of the United States was to highlight care for the environment as a part of US trade promotion policy. This sentiment echoes in the words of the current US Chief Climate Change Negotiator Mr. John Kerry thus, "This [mitigation and adaptation to climate change] is the most extraordinary opportunity [for trade and commercial relations] in the history of mankind." That being the stand of the rich, it is little wonder that the rich-poor divide should continue to widen.

Select References

"An Advanced History of India", R.C. Majumdar, H.C.Raychaudhuri, Kalinikar Datta, Macmillan India.

"Environmental Ethics"; Robin Attfield, Polity Press, 2014.

"Contours of the World Economy, 1 – 2030 AD"; Essays in Macro-economic History, by Angus Maddison, Oxford, Oxford University Press, 2007.

"Preliminary Global Price Comparisons, 1500-1870" by Robert Allen et.al. in "Towards a Global History of Prices and Wages" ed. by Peter Lindert

"The Wealth of Nations", Adam Smith

"Between law and history: the Berlin Conference of 1884-1885 and the logic of free trade", Mathew Craven: London Review of International Law, Volume 3, Issue 1,2015, 31-59, OUP.

"A History of Life Expectancy": Tim Lambert

Chapter III

Growth of Nature Conservation and Human Welfare Concerns in the West

A scientific study of man-nature interrelationship began with the coining of the term 'Ecology' – derived from the Greek word 'Oikos' meaning a place to live in – by the German Zoologist, Ernst Haeckel in 1866. This scientific study was not confined to man and his relationship with the plant and animal life and the non-living physical matter surrounding him but could be applied to interactions of plants and animal communities with each other and with the surrounding non-living matter. The concept of an 'ecosystem', referring to the natural setting accommodating plant and animal life of unique or varied description peculiar to a physical area and interacting with each other, owes its introduction to the British ecologist, A.G. Tansley (1935). Environment, perhaps the most commonly used word in daily life today, denotes all living and non-living matter that surrounds an organism and with which it is constantly engaged in an exchange of energy and matter. Finally, the grand stage on which all this interaction takes place is called the Biosphere which, in combination with a thin layer of the atmosphere is termed the Ecosphere. Without exchanges of matter and energy with the non-living environment, life on earth in any of its forms, human, animal, or plant, cannot survive, a conclusion that the great religions of India had arrived at intuitively eons ago.

Although scientific inquiry into man's relationship with nature began only in the late 19th. Century, concern for nature and human welfare had been engaging the attention of social reformers in the West since mediaeval times. As western economies began to grow from the beginning of the 15th.century, these concerns became more and more visible and audible demanding effective intervention by the state. Response and redress did follow, though varying in nature and degree from country to country. After passing through several crises and learning many a painful but rewarding lesson from them, nations of the West steadily achieved standards of physical and civic well-being far higher than the rest of the world.

A study of the history of civic issues and protection of natural resources in developed countries would reveal that at the start of their industrialization and for more than two hundred years thereafter their concerns were just the same as those obtaining in today's developing world. At the start and well into later years, protection of nature and the pristine countryside from the onslaught of industry and human habitation held sway to the point of opposing such developments vehemently. However, this confrontation mellowed down when governments began addressing the problems associated with industrial development and urbanization like water and air pollution, potable water supply, lack of sanitation and community hygiene, solid waste management, and planning of human settlements. These problems, though similar to what developing countries experience today, differed in their magnitude in the West. In marked contrast to the East, neither the size of the population nor its growth over time was ever an overarching concern in the West for two reasons. In countries like the UK, France, Spain, and Belgium, the rural versus urban confrontation was greatly softened by the fact that industrialization and urbanization could proceed apace without exerting much pressure on agricultural lands as the foreign territories over which their influence spread made land available in plenty to raise food grains or rear cattle for meat or cultivate agro-industrial raw materials like cotton, jute or rubber for their industry and transport these to the homeland. Merchant fleets protected by strong naval forces made ocean voyages practically risk-free. At home, the flourishing industry created jobs in large numbers to absorb the labour that came in search of employment from the countryside. Where labour was scarce as in the newly colonized Americas, slave trade met the requirements. The issue that really mattered to the colonial powers was an internal one, that of rural-urban migration which called for physical and spatial planning of settlements and provision of sanitation and other public health services of an acceptable standard to the local residents and the incoming rural masses.

Since the basic environmental problems of yesteryears in the Western World were similar to the problems facing the developing countries today, it would be worthwhile to see how these problems were met with and overcome in the West and whether the developing world could learn any lessons from the former's experience. For this, one should look into the roles played by the state, civil society, and individuals in identifying and shaping responses to the felt environmental challenges. What emerges is, as we shall see, a revolution in public policy and responsible action underscored by the consent and cooperation of all the stakeholders in the process, the executive, the legislature, and the citizenry.

For the purpose of our study, we may divide the environmental concerns of the west following the onset of the Industrial Revolution into three categories, namely "Nature – Preservation and Conservation; Sanitation, Pollution, and Public Health; and Urban Planning."

Nature – Preservation and Conservation

The modern environmental movement in the West could be said to have begun with efforts to protect nature primarily for its aesthetic value. Assigning only aesthetic value meant, in practical terms, letting nature remain in its pristine form. Under this passive approach, which could be termed 'preservation', harnessing nature for economic gain was considered crass and secondary. However, the requirements of timber to support war efforts and civil construction and the availability of knowledge to make forests meet these demands sustainably paved the way for looking at forests as an economic resource also. This interventionist strategy, called 'conservation', meant resorting to active management of forests for economic gain without forsaking their long-term health and capacity to provide goods and services needed by man on a sustainable basis.

The preservation ethic dating back to the eighteenth century was championed by poets, nature lovers, and philosophers whereas conservation was espoused by scientifically trained naturalists. Preservation rested on the premise that nature had a right to exist in its pristine state undisturbed by man and brooked little intervention with it or its processes. In contrast, the conservationists with their scientific background considered the varied uses to which nature could be put to and believed that some degree of interaction and intervention with nature's ways was necessary and justified in the interests of nature itself. As the US National Park Service puts it "Conservation and preservation both have admirable aims. Conservation takes a more flexible outlook when it comes to human interaction with resources, while preservation is a very strict mindset determined to keep human impacts to an absolute minimum." The preservationist was emotional and the conservationist was rational.

In the West, conservation scored over preservation as it was in alignment with the Utilitarian political economic thinking of the eighteenth century and the flourishing mercantilist milieu of the day. It is a matter of interest that given the choice of strategy, preservation or conservation or both, each European country charted its own path to nature care mirroring its national culture and heritage. Romanticism and preservation ruled in England; science and conservation laced with atavism in historical might and glory in Germany; and economics in France. Larger national considerations like defence needs were, of course, always in the background in all European nations guiding overall national policy. With this background, it would be useful to take a look at the early approaches to nature care and how they found their way into the New World and the colonial world of yesteryears.

United Kingdom

The beginnings of the nature preservation movement in Britain go back to the 19th Century, a period coinciding with the early decades of the Industrial Revolution. Pristine in form and unspoilt by hand of man was the way in which the British craved to see the sprawl of nature around them. The belching smokestacks and the growing slums that accompanied the Age of the Machine jolted British sensitivity and served to intensify the longing for the quiet countryside with its spread of greens dotted with cottages and brooks with rushing water. Romantics like William Wordsworth (1770-1850), John Ruskin (1819-1900), Elizabeth Barrett Browning (1806-1861), Keats and Shelley, to name a few, came out strongly in favour of preserving nature as it was and had always been. Ruskin went to the extent of opposing the laying of a railway line to the Lake District as he feared a threat to the tranquillity of the place from the tourists whom railways may disgorge on it. Others like William Morris (1834-1896), an architect by profession, longed for the times when "the factories would disappear" and the "gardens to reappear". Edward Carpenter (1844-1929) was demonstrative in his fondness for the quiet countryside by setting up a farm near the steel city of Sheffield to mark the contrast between the grimy, smoke-filled town and a patch of inviting green close by. The 'amenity movement', as preservation came to be called by later writers, had begun in Britain.

The amenity movement set in motion a host of initiatives led by local bodies and the British Parliament to green the country. Urban development authorities aspired to recreate in the urban setting the bucolic calm by laying out parks and gardens. To protect areas of scenic beauty, bodies like the Lake District Defence Society (1877), the Scottish Rights of Way Society (1843), and The National Trust (1895) were formed. However, the formulation of a comprehensive national policy to protect areas of outstanding floral or faunal interest had to wait till 1949. That year saw the establishment of an agency named the Nature Conservancy under a Royal Charter. The agency formulated the "Nature Conservation Policy 1950-1980" which enabled the designation of appropriate sites as Nature Reserves and Sites of Special Scientific Interest (SSSIs). In the Reserves, no new form of land use was permitted whereas in SSSIs extant land uses like agriculture could coexist with forestry signifying that certain benign forms of land use were not incompatible with the ongoing natural processes at the Sites. However, some habitat loss did occur even with benign changes in land use and this deficiency was addressed by the Wildlife and Countryside Act of 1981.

France

France was more evolved than Britain in its approach to nature conservation. The Frenchman's love of nature was no less intense than that of the Britisher but the French view was that nature was as much an economic resource as an aesthetic one. To the French nation, embroiled in wars with neighbours, forests provided the timber needed to sustain the war efforts. Assured availability of quality timber in quantity was a necessity to keep the army and navy strong and in readiness. To meet this critical need indigenously, forests had to be tended to scientifically and their productivity enhanced and sustained. To this end, the French introduced a Forest Code in the fourteenth century followed by a stricter Forest Ordinance in 1669 both applicable to forests on the state as well as on private lands. As demand for timber grew during the Napoleonic Wars in the early nineteenth century and sourcing timber from colonies proved difficult due to cost, time and uncertainty of arrivals, insistence on indigenous sourcing grew. Supply was maintained by employing sound sylvicultural practices in forest management. Happily, the demands of war could not obliterate the finer sentiments in the hearts of the French; their love of greenery was reflected in the leafy avenues and boulevards they created in their nation's capital and other cities. A load of common sense laced with some sentiment marked the French approach to matters of nature.

Germany

Nature management in Germany reflected the nation's longing to relive its fabled past and its urge to explore how this longing could be fulfilled by emerging science. In practice, this meant a strong attachment to land and the traditional occupation of agriculture and a willingness to experiment with an open mind on new ideas thrown up by science on agricultural management. Guha observes that "in the German romantic tradition, environment was united with patriotism, such that peasants, forests and the nation came to constitute an organic whole." As industrialization set in and began to display its coarser side in the form of smoke and dirty water, the 'back to land ' movement became so strong in Germany that peasanthood came to be identified with 'Germanness' and patriotism. Thus, Germany worked itself into a coalition of love for nature and modern scientific management of its natural resources, a feature that marks the green influence on German politics even today.

Even before landmark discoveries came about in the field of Chemistry of natural products in the second half of the nineteenth century and forests came to be looked upon as a source of timber and chemicals for commercial exploitation, German foresters had worked on the principle that forests could be managed without forsaking either their ecological role or their economic utility. This, they claimed, could be achieved by replicating natural processes and avoiding practices like clear felling which laid bare nutrient-poor forest soils to erosion. As a German government publication claims "Much of these early practices paved the way for later forestry developments, including an increasing proportion of structurally diverse mixed strands, long rejuvenating periods and natural rejuvenation methods. Many valuable old forests both in terms of timber and biological diversity result from these initiatives. In 'plenter [variable/multiaged] forests' trees of different age classes stand side by side and rejuvenation takes place on a more or less continuous basis. Selective cutting or group selection cutting allows for natural regeneration to develop or existing regeneration to be used in the spaces opened up by cutting". Here one finds strong evidence to support the claim that conservation through scientific management of forests is necessary in the interests of forest ecosystems. Adopting a hands-off approach and consigning forests to the mercy of nature's destructive forces like lightning or fires or parasites as canvassed by some is not desirable either in the interests of society or in the interests of the forests. Sustainable forest management could thus be said to have begun in Germany almost three hundred years ago. We will have occasion to revert to this preservation–versus–conservation debate in a later Chapter.

Due to its scientific and practical approach to forest management, Germany became a world leader in forestry. The German government established a Department of Forestry in 1864 headed by Dietrich Brandeis who was to become later the first Head of the Forestry School in India. The principles evolved by German foresters were to prove a guide to forest management all over the globe, from the New World to Australia. These trained foresters adorned the offices of forest management in many other countries like US and India. Among them, as notable as Brandeis, was the Prussian, Bernhard Fernow who became the first Chief of the Division of Forestry in the US Federal government in 1879.

In Germany's eastern neighbours, on a political level, the impress of German practices was felt in the formation of agrarian political parties with the avowed purpose of defending the peasant from exploitation by the urban dweller. In Scandinavia, the influence of the 'Peasanthood' movement was equally strong, setting in currency "ruralist" ideas.

The New World

Unlike in Europe, the nature preservation movement in the US was confined in its application to select areas of extraordinary scenic beauty or those considered a national heritage because of their historic significance for protection from outside interference. But for forests, in general, scientific conservation and not preservation was accepted as the proper mode of management. This came about thanks to the publication of a seminal work on forest management by a man of many parts, George Perkins Marsh. His book "Man and Nature; or Physical Geography as modified by Human Action" (1864) was singularly effective in influencing US policy towards its forests. Sociologist Lewis Mumford acclaimed Marsh's book as "the fountainhead of the conservation movement".

To understand why the publication of "Man and Nature" became a turning point in the US attitude towards nature, we need to go into the personality of the writer himself and the message of the book. First, Marsh was not a romantic but a man of the world having been a lawyer, a businessman – though not a successful one – and a diplomat. He was also a Classics scholar and a polyglot who could find his way through ancient, mediaeval, and modern texts on the history of foreign lands written in their national languages. This background made him look upon forests and the wilds as objects of aesthetic appreciation as well as assets of economic value. As a result, "Man and Nature" did not preach a hands-off approach by decrying human intervention with nature in any form nor advocated blind, debilitating exploitation of nature. The book also dismissed the notion that nature, even if grievously disturbed for a long period of time, would restore itself to its original state once the disturbance was removed. Marsh asserted that for restoration to happen, human intervention was necessary.

It was natural for statements like the above to be highlighted and misunderstood. According to Lowenthal, the book's bold conclusion was that "Nature was not sacred; man must rebel against its limits, subjugate it, impose order; for whatever he fails to make himself her master he can but be her slave." Marsh did mention that relinquishing "dominion over nature would mean regression to amoral misery ruled by hunger, fear and superstition. Short of total global collapse, such a relapse was unimaginable. Every human act alters nature; every technical advance augments the potential for harm. The resultant damage might be contended, not by ceasing to alter nature but by taking greater care in doing so. Growing human might called not for abating, but intensifying global manipulation. We inherit a world indelibly marked by being both managed and mismanaged; it is up to us to manage it better."

Despite presenting such views of intervention with nature and that too in forceful language – an act bordering on heresy – the aim of "Man and Nature" was not to spread a rapacious, laissez-faire, atheistic attitude towards nature but to present a practical, sustainable approach to its protection keeping the interests of both man and nature at heart. A cautious and informed scientific intervention and not unthinking meddlesomeness was presented as the way to go forward in keeping the forests healthy and sustainable and playing their role as forests. This would be borne out by the impact the book had on the conservation policy and programmes of the United States. Marsh's biographer Lowenthal rightly described Marsh as the "Prophet of Conservation ".

"Man and Nature" motivated the American Association for the Advancement of Science to petition the US Congress in 1873 to establish a national forestry system and the creation of forest reserves. The declaration of an area as a national park meant its insulation from human interference except for scientific purposes, limited tourism, and leisure activities. Here was an example of nature care in practice and spirit, a remedy suggested ever since to guard rare and endangered species even in totally different climes and settings like the populous countries of Southeast Asia. One cannot, however, overlook the need to evaluate the appropriateness or otherwise of introducing such management concepts at any specific geographical location. In India, such protection provided to rare and endangered species by the law is at the base of the debate over the policy of settling traditional forest dwellers on forest land or of resettling them elsewhere and extinguishing their usufructuary rights like the collection of minor forest produce and fishing. We shall have occasion to look into this debate more closely later. Be that as it may, the US practice of preserving the habitat as a whole to preserve species, rare or endangered, has become an accepted part of modern conservation strategy. The Tiger Reserves of India are good examples of habitat protection to secure species protection.

United States struck a fine balance between preservation and conservation in the management of its forest wealth, thanks to the practical approach and farsightedness of not only foresters like Marsh but also political leaders like President Theodore Roosevelt. Roosevelt provided strong leadership in putting into practice what his technical advisors commended to him. Among them, two, John Muir and Gifford Pinchot, were the most notable. Arguing for a rational approach to forest management, Muir wrote in 1897 "In the settlement and civilization of the country, bread more than timber or beauty was wanted, and in the blindness of hunger, the early settlers claiming Heaven as their guide, regarded God's trees as only a larger kind of precious weed, extremely hard to get rid of". This callous attitude towards forests changed thanks to the crusading work of Muir and Pinchot and changed completely with the formation of the US Forest Service in 1905.

Pinchot, a forester by qualification and training, became the first head of the US Forest Service with his appointment as Chief Forester. To him goes the credit for anchoring forest management in the US on a sound, scientific basis. Like other conservationists, he believed in the instrumental value of forests, a value that could be unlocked on a sustainable basis "without compromising the long [term] health of the ecosystem." He was in close touch with the German forester, Dietrich Brandeis, who had by then proceeded to India to take over the reins of management of the subcontinent's extensive forest area. Through that correspondence emerged a blueprint of robust, scientific management of North America's forests. Significantly enough, forests were looked upon not in isolation from their environment but as a part of a dynamic ecosystem of interacting parts which individually or together engaged with the non-living environment through the exchange of matter and energy. In marked contrast with parcels of agricultural land managed by individuals, all forests, including sizeable tracts held in private ownership, came to be governed by state regulations and uniform management practices.

No account of American forestry or wildlife management would be complete without a reverential mention of Aldo Leopold (1887 – 1948) and his call for introducing an ethical dimension to the subject. A graduate of Yale School of Forestry, Leopold was a member of the US Forest Service for many years with his thinking anchored in Pinchot's views on scientific forestry. He promoted the idea of setting aside areas rich in wildlife as wilderness reserves. Based on his experiences, he developed a philosophy of game management modelled closely on the principles of scientific forestry, with game replacing timber as the product which needed to be harvested on a sustained yield basis". In later years, Leopold came under the influence of Muir and adopted the credo of "an intelligent humility towards man's place in nature". Outlining his thoughts on conservation in his classic work "A Sand County Almanac ", he wrote movingly thus: "It is inconceivable to me [that] an ethical relation to land can exist without love, respect, and admiration for land, and a high regard for its value. By value, I of course mean something far broader than economic value; I mean value in the philosophical sense." Leopold rejected the view that only those constituents of nature that made economic sense mattered for protection and others did not for the reason that man was not the best judge to make such a distinction. He went on to add that if man were to take on the role of a judge and pronounce "just what and who is valuable, and what and who is worthless in community life" it would turn out that "he knows neither, and this is why his conquests eventually defeat themselves." To Leopold, conservation was as much a matter of compassion and faith as of science and reason.

In any discussion on the management of natural ecosystems, one has to take note of the ecological niche of avian populations. The credit for ushering in the avian conservation movement in the United States goes to the Ornithologist, John James Audubon (1785-1851). His contribution to the protection of avian habitats was reflected in the formation of Audubon Societies in about 27 states in the US by the turn of the 19th Century with the first one set up in Massachusetts in 1896. Mention of Audubon would be appropriate for another reason too. Three-quarters of a century later, his work was to inspire Rachel Carson to come out with her classic 'The Silent Spring', a work of tectonic impact on global environmental discourse.

The outcome of the success of conservation policies and action in North America was to influence their replication in Africa and Asia. The London Conference of 1900, attended by the colonial powers of Europe, though derided as the "Repentant Butchers Club", did produce some desirable results. Its deliberations led to the formation of the "Society for the preservation of the Fauna of the Empire" in 1903 and the establishment of several game reserves and protected habitats in Africa and Asia. The Kruger National Park in South Africa and the Matops in Southern Rhodesia are good examples of these efforts. But here again, as it happened in the United States, the belated conservation efforts of the colonial masters were glorified as their heroic effort to save the natural heritage from despoliation by the subdued races. Sadly, even to this day, this racial mindset pervades international exchanges on protecting the natural environment.

Sanitation, Pollution and Public Health

As the twin schools of preservation and conservation were driving policy and action on forest and wildlife protection and were recording success, cleansing the urban environment of smoke, water pollution, mushrooming slums and dumping of domestic and industrial wastes on land and in water continued to prove to be challenges of a higher order calling for political will, legislative action, substantial finances, and public cooperation. Even if all these could be mustered, the question that still remained was one of weighing the costs and benefits of state intervention in managing public goods to ensure their availability at accepted levels of quality and quantity. From the beginning of the Industrial Revolution, this issue engaged the minds of urban policymakers and planners in Europe and it took almost a century for the issue to be resolved in favour of public welfare.

United Kingdom

Britain was an early starter in addressing matters of public sanitation and water pollution. The year 1388 saw the enactment of a law forbidding the disposal of filth and garbage into ditches, rivers, and other water bodies. The town of Cambridge was the first to enjoy the protection of urban sanitation. It may come as a surprise that some parts of England and Wales had the luxury of piped water supply and sanitation facilities as early as the 15th. Century. By the sixteenth, the discharge of untreated domestic and industrial effluents into rivers was a matter of concern serious enough to merit legislative action. In1535, Parliament enacted a law prohibiting the discharge of domestic wastewater into the Thames. But this measure was of hardly any effect considering the magnitude of the problem. Sanitary conditions became severe enough for the government-appointed Poor Law Commission of 1834 to bring the issue to the centre of public debate. In 1845, in the preface to his work "Conditions of the English Working Class", Frederich Engels lamented that "A large class, like a great nation, never learns better or quicker than by undergoing the consequences of its own mistakes." His words were to prove prophetic. In 1858, an unbearable stink emanating from the wastes discharged into the Thames pervaded the London air. The notoriety it brought to the city forced the Government to commence work on a modern sewerage system the very next year and complete it by 1866. The system consisted of a network of 1000 miles of street sewers to collect wastewater and 82 miles of intercepting sewers. Only treated water of acceptable quality was allowed to be discharged into the river.

A string of legislations came into force in the second half of the 19th. Century to ensure the protection of not only the Thames but other rivers like Lee too. The metropolitan area of London, in particular, received special attention for it had acquired the stature of an international hub of trade, commerce, and finance. The Metropolis Water Act of 1852, the Thames Conservancy Acts of 1857 and 1864, the Lee Conservancy Act of 1868, and the Metropolis Management Act of 1855 may be cited as examples of the legislative effort to control environmental pollution in the UK in the 19TH. Century. Together with the enactment of the Alkali Acts whose aim was to control industrial air pollution, this legal framework survived till developments in the 20th century demanded the enactment of more comprehensive legislation in tune with the demands of the time.

To satisfy the demand for a basic need like drinking water, England had to wait till water supply was taken care of by private enterprise. An interesting aspect of the modern-day British approach to the problem of water supply and distribution has been its tilt toward privatization. By 1989, meeting the water requirements of the entire country had been entrusted to private ownership.

Germany

On the Continent, with the exception of France, urban sanitation was no better than in the UK in the eighteenth and nineteenth centuries. Berlin acquired the unenviable distinction of having the worst sanitary conditions in the whole of Europe. Incensed with the all-pervading squalour, the German Socialist politician August Biebel (1840-1913) remarked that "As a metropolis, Berlin did not emerge from a state of barbarism until after 1870" when the Imperial German government resolved to make Berlin a model city. As a result of this resolve accompanied by action, Berlin became an example of "the most modern application of science, order and method of public life" and "a marvel of civic administration, the most modern and most perfectly organized city that there is." Hamburg acquired its comprehensive sewerage system in the mid-nineteenth century followed by Frankfurt. The impact of these schemes was highly noteworthy in terms of improvement in urban health. Statistics has it that in the two decades following the commissioning of the sanitation system in Frankfurt, deaths due to Typhoid fell dramatically from 80 to 10 per thousand of the population.

In Germany, unlike in the UK, public water supply is still mostly under the joint ownership of the government and private enterprise. Wholly privately owned supplies account for the needs of a meagre 3.5% of the population.

North America

In newly colonized lands, agriculture had always been the primary occupation of the settler-colonizer. So it was with North America. Even up to the middle of the nineteenth century, agriculture accounted for the economic activity of as much as 92 percent of the US population. Industry was late to arrive and hence the negative effects of industrialization were also late in manifesting themselves. Rural-urban migration also began late, almost towards the end of the 17th Century, but when it did begin it was quite torrential. Almost all negative aspects of human settlements and industrialization, in a significant form, appeared in the US in the last 150 years. 19th Century witnessed serious outbreaks of Cholera due to water pollution caused by the discharge of untreated domestic effluents into water bodies that were the sources of water supply. Surprisingly, in a nation that was to emerge later as the world leader in industry, science, and technology, the modern germ theory of diseases carried little credibility till late into the nineteenth century. The theory, already well established in Europe, that harmful bacteria thriving in unclean water gained ingress into the human system and caused morbidity and mortality was considered fanciful.

United States

America's history of piped water supply could be said to have begun in Chicago and New York in 1842 followed by Boston and Washington DC in 1853. Chicago was also the pioneer in building a sewerage system to handle domestic wastewater in 1842. However, despite the growth of industry and urban agglomerations, no specific legislation existed to control the disposal of domestic and industrial wastes into river courses. What all that was in force was a little-known of peace of general legislation, namely, the Refuse Act which formed a part of the Rivers and Harbors Appropriations Act of 1899. Realising this inadequacy, the US Congress came out with the Federal Water Pollution and Control Act in 1948, an effort that was to prove ineffective for a variety of reasons, not the least being that the Act did not target specifically the issues involved. As a result, about 2.5 billion tons of raw sewage found its way into inland water bodies.

The Clean Water Act of 1972 which replaced the 1948 legislation was to prove more effective. The new legislation set before itself the goal of eliminating all forms of water pollution by 1985. Its supplement, the Safe Drinking Water Act of 1974 set standards for water quality, both for municipal and industrial discharges. To promote the availability of safe, potable water, subsidized loans were made available to local bodies under a Revolving Fund established by the Water Quality Act of 1987. This was supplemented by the State Revolving Fund in 1996. The creation of these funds underscored the government's intention to move away from the earlier practice of extending direct federal financial support to state efforts to control water pollution. Instead, States were encouraged to take up initiatives on their own by being provided with access to funds from a statutory financing body. This also gave the opportunity to private enterprise to enter the public water supply business. US was, perhaps, the first country to recognize that water had a price, no matter who paid it, the state or the citizen.

The Great Lakes which straddle US and Canada and constitute the largest freshwater bodies in the world came under the protection of a bilateral Agreement between the neighbours in 1978, an arrangement that was given legal muscle by the Great Lakes Critical Programs Act, 1990.

Control of Industrial Pollution
United Kingdom and Europe

We had noted earlier in Chapter I that in Europe, particularly in the UK, economic progress that came in the wake of the Industrial Revolution turned out to be not an unmitigated blessing. The reasons for this development were twofold. Prosperity fostered not only rural-urban migration within the country but also immigration from abroad as could be seen from the fact that the population of England and Wales went up phenomenally from 8.9 million in 1801 to 32.5 million in 1901. Migration from rural to urban areas also witnessed a marked rise that by 1851 some 50% of the country's population was urban. Unlike agriculture whose demand for labour was seasonal, industry needed the services of labour year-round. It was, therefore, natural for rural labour to move closer to industry. This movement had a snowballing effect in that availability of labour in abundance attracted greenfield industries to the new centres and encouraged others located elsewhere to relocate themselves to these centres. The spurt in local populations led to the mushrooming of squatter and shanty settlements much to the detriment of the local environment. Further, the feeling that some degree of environmental degradation was a sign of economic progress and that the "commons", namely, air, water, and land were inexhaustible and available free for everyone's use contributed significantly to a fall in environmental quality. While polluted water led to frequent outbreaks of epidemics like Cholera, air pollution resulting from uncontrolled releases of gaseous emissions by factories like those manufacturing Soda Ash caused more than bearable discomfort throughout the year.

The growing menace of air pollution led to the passage of the Alkali Act of 1863 and the establishment of an agency known as the Alkali Inspectorate for its enforcement. The Act proved quite successful in achieving its objective as could be seen from the fact that it reduced industrial gaseous emissions from 14000 tonnes per annum to a mere 45 tonnes. To incorporate the lessons learnt during its implementation, the Act was amended twice, once in 1874 and again in 1876, and was later replaced by the Alkali & Works Regulation Act, 1881. Changes were called for even in the new legislation and accordingly, amendments were introduced in 1892 and 1906. More than eighty years later, a comprehensive Environment Protection Act was passed in 1990 with provisions to control air and water pollution and solid waste management.

It may be seen from the above account that the Alkali legislations of the eighteenth century remained operative in some form or the other till late into the twentieth century. This was mainly due to the fact that the collegiate manner in which they were enforced had a positive impact on the mindset of the industry towards environmental pollution control. The amendment made to the 1863 Act in 1874 required that 'best practicable means' (BPM) be adopted by an industrial unit to control emissions. Unlike a rigorous command and control regime which compelled industry to control its pollution regardless of the costs involved or the non-availability of appropriate technology, the BPM approach created an atmosphere in which the government and the industry saw themselves as partners in a campaign to promote a worthy cause and did not look upon themselves as antagonists. An industrial unit to which the law applied was willing to accept the suggestions of the Alkali Inspectors since the suggestions for pollution abatement were tailor-made to that unit and were not 'one-size fit all' solutions. This approach of the enforcement agency made economic sense to the industry. The sensible BPM approach and its successor, BATNEEC (Best Available Technology Not Entailing Excessive Cost) to do what was doable as opposed to the conventional approach of demanding the ideal but unaffordable and unattainable was to guide latter day legislations in Britain to a great measure.

The Alkali Acts were essentially meant to deal with air pollution emanating from industry in an age when the use of coal for power generation had just begun. But increasing coal-based electricity generation aggravated the peculiar atmospheric condition that prevailed over England most of the time causing severe air pollution. During the days in which such conditions prevailed, the burning of sulphur-rich British coals resulted in the emitted gases being trapped by the cool ambient air leading to high levels of sulphur dioxide concentrations at ground level. On four such consecutive days starting from the 5th of September 1952, a dense smog enveloped London affecting the entire population of the city, especially the old and those with impaired respiratory conditions. This partly natural and partly man-made disaster claimed four thousand lives and led to the British Parliament passing the Clean Air Act in 1956. The Act was modified in 1968 following the occurrence of yet another tragedy in 1962.

The 1968 legislation prescribed the erection of tall chimneys at larger point sources of air pollution like coal-burning power stations. This stipulation had its positive as well as negative outcomes. The positive result was that nearby areas were spared of the smoke and flue gases laden with health-damaging fine particulate matter and sulphur dioxide as the tall chimneys ensured wide dispersal of the emerging stack gases. The negative consequence was that the sulphurous emissions travelled over the sea to shower acid rain over Scandinavia. Norway, in particular, reported considerable damage to its marine fisheries. Such airborne transboundary pollution was also encountered in the Baltic countries due to the operation of industries in Europe.

United States

Awareness of industrial pollution as a public health concern of a grave nature was simply non-existent in the US till the Cuyahoga river in Ohio caught fire in 1936, a fire set off by volatile industrial wastes dumped into the river. There was a repeat of the mishaps in 1952 and 1969 that incensed the public so much that it led to the birth of "grassroots activism" in the US directed against industry in general. In fact, this incident could be said to have ushered in a new era globally in the common man's fight in defence of the environment. The slow ecocide that can be caused by prolonged exposure to toxic substances emanating from industry was forcefully demonstrated by yet another incident known in American environmental history as the "Love Canal accident." The mile-long canal was a part of an abandoned navigation project and was in the possession of a chemical company that reclaimed it and started using it as a dumping ground for its toxic wastes. Later, the site became a residential neighbourhood. Consumption of the contaminated groundwater by the residents set in a process of poisoning leading to their developing carcinoma and their children being born with birth defects. As the horrors came to light in 1970, the resulting public revulsion and protest demanded preventive action in the form of strong legislation. These developments synergized the prevailing demand for control of municipal effluent discharges and led to the passing of the comprehensive Clean Water Act, 1972 referred to earlier.

In the context of control of industrial water pollution in the US, some more words need to be said about the Clean Water Act of 1972. This piece of legislation marked a comprehensive approach to address water pollution problems created by major sources, domestic and industrial. Water quality standards were prescribed for receiving water bodies and the federal EPA (Environmental Protection Agency, set up in 1970 by the President of the US through an executive order) and state authorities were called upon to determine the "total maximum daily loads" of pollutants that these bodies could assimilate without violating the water quality standards. Recognizing that discharges of polluted water from non-point sources like run-off from public spaces were much more in volume than those from point sources like residences and individual industrial units, the new law laid emphasis on the formers' regulation through the imposition of conditions like zero discharges into rivers. To crown it all, an ambitious target of making all waters of the US "fishable and swimmable" by 1985 was set. The federal government assured the states to meet 75% of the costs of construction of needed control facilities. Though they failed to achieve the water quality targets they had set for America's rivers, the 1972 Act and its amendments made it in subsequent years and were quite a success in other ways too. Over 40,000 polluting sources of significance were regulated and this prevented almost 700 billion pounds of pollutants from finding their way into rivers.

Marine pollution arising out of oil spills was yet another environmental problem causing short as well as long-term damage to marine ecosystems. For the US, a country that had for long been a significant onshore and offshore producer and importer of oil, such accidents were important enough to be responded to immediately. The Torrey Canyon disaster off the English coast in 1967 that released 1,20,000 tons of crude oil into the sea triggered action in the US in the form of a Presidential Declaration authorizing the drawing up of a National Oil and Hazardous Substances Pollution Contingency Plan (NCP) in 1968. This Plan was later supplemented by the Robert T. Stafford Disaster and Emergency Assistance Act, PL 100-707, which empowered federal authorities to intervene with response and relief activities in the event of an accident being declared a national disaster by the President. The Contingency Plan found one immediate application in January-February 1969 when the Santa Barbara Channel off the coast of California was affected by an oil-well blowout that released almost 100,000 tons of oil into the marine environment killing 3500 sea birds and causing major damage to the marine ecosystem.

In the United States, it took much longer than in the UK or Europe for air pollution to be recognized as a health hazard as serious as water pollution. This could, perhaps, have been due to the fact that whereas the adverse health impacts of water pollution are fairly immediate, those of air pollution take longer to manifest themselves and hence tend to get dismissed as no more than a nuisance. So it was with the perpetually dark, smoke-laden skies of some industrial hubs like the Steel City of Pittsburgh till conditions became serious enough to demand immediate intervention. On 29th. November 1939, a Tuesday, conditions became so critical that the day passed into US environmental history as "Black Tuesday". Still, it took almost a decade for public attention to get focused on the problem but when it did, the result was a landmark development in US public health administration.

As a grim reminder of Pittsburgh's Black Tuesday, came the Donora incident of 26th October 1948 when the small town of Donora situated in a valley in the Appalachians was engulfed in the smoke emitted by a Zinc smelter for full five days. Nature compounded the man-made problem as the cause of the smoke trap was an atmospheric condition known as 'temperature inversion'. The smoke affected half of the small town's population of 14,000 and claimed twenty lives. The tragedy attracted national attention and resulted in the promulgation of a state ordinance in 1946 to avert the recurrence of such happenings in the State of Pennsylvania. The Division of Air Pollution Control created under the Ordinance proved to be quite effective in that in the six years that followed visible air pollution fell by 97%. More importantly, the incident contributed to the rising swell of public disquiet in the US over the lack of adequate measures to avert avoidable public health problems through timely and comprehensive legislative and executive action.

The Federal Air Pollution Control Act of 1955 was the first national response to the growing problem of air pollution in the United States arising out of industrial activity and a phenomenal rise in personalized transport. The Donora incident and the possibility of the London smog of 1952 replicating itself in the US brought home the urgency of air pollution control in industrial locations and in large cities prone to congestion due to poor modes of public transport. The reaction was the passage of a landmark legislation, the Clean Air Act, 1970 which overhauled all previous enactments on the subject. This comprehensive piece of legislation dealt with the phenomenon of acid rain, toxic emissions and other forms of air pollution. Its amended version which came into force in 1990 added further teeth to air pollution control measures in the form of introducing a National Permits Program which allocated pollution entitlements to industry. A novel feature of the 1990 law was that it provided for introducing market-based instruments like emissions banking and trading. The cumulative impact of these vigorous measures was a huge drop of 70% in pollution levels in 2015 compared to 1990.

The year 1970 was to witness the initiation of more measures to clean up the environment. A high-level federal regulatory body, the US Environment Protection Agency (EPA) was created by President Nixon through an executive order. The Order affirmed that the EPA was to be "a strong, independent agency… to make a coordinated attack on the pollutants which debase the air we breathe, the water we drink, and the land that grows our food." An adequately funded and well-staffed expert agency, EPA was to emerge soon as an effective authority in setting national ambient air quality standards, point source standards, air quality indices and in disciplining errant industries to adhere to the norms set. EPA has taken on the challenge of global warming too by initiating vigorous policy measures to discourage the use of fossil fuels for electric power generation thereby giving a boost to renewable energy. Hardly any other body in the world can be compared with the US EPA in its coverage and control of polluting activities and their sources or in its technical expertise. In recent times, however, efforts are afoot to prune its authority and financial allocations, a setback to the US and global environmental cause.

Solid Waste Management

The problem of waste management has yet to be met with a totally effective solution anywhere in the world, except perhaps in the European Union. It needs little effort to divine the causes of such failure. Simply put, waste is too varied in its composition and magnitude of generation from source to source and too numerous in its sites of origin. Because of these factors, wastes do not lend themselves to uniform treatment either in their disposal or in processes to recover useful materials from them. Despite these inherent challenges, western countries have been able to record more than a fair measure of success in the last two centuries in their efforts to deal with the problem. Western experience in solid waste management is all the more interesting because in the last fifty years it has undergone a qualitative revolution in that waste is no longer looked upon as a nuisance to be got rid of but as a resource that can be exploited to good effect. As Walter-Stahel put it "The wastes of today are the resources of tomorrow at yesterday's prices." This is true of all wastes, municipal, industrial and commercial and an economy that sets store by resource recovery from waste has come to be known, aptly, as a "circular economy".

United Kingdom

Earlier, we had made reference to the importance attached in the UK to the amelioration of the living conditions of the working classes in the 19th. Century. In 1840, a Commission was set up to recommend changes in the then-prevalent Poor Laws. The Commission, headed by Sir Edwin Chadwick (1800-1890), a social reformer of his time, drew special attention to the deterioration in the quality of potable water brought about by the disposal of untreated domestic wastes into water bodies and by the disposal of animal and vegetable wastes on open land. Identifying these factors as the main cause of sickness and mortality among the poor, the Commission went on to observe that "of the 43,000 cases of widowhood and 112,000 cases of destitute orphanage.... the greatest proportion of deaths of the heads of families occurred "from poor sanitation and foul domestic air." Though the Commission's conclusions were wrongly based on the then-current miasmic theory of disease propagation, they held good when weighed against the bacterial theory developed later.

The Chadwick Report was a milestone in waste management in Britain and may well be said to have introduced the country to the "Age of Sanitation". It called for entrusting the responsibility of waste collection and disposal to a centralized authority in large cities. Its recommendations led to the installation of incinerators for disposing off waste that, hitherto, was being burnt in the open. Following the Chadwick Report, the Nuisance Removal and Disease Prevention Act came into force in 1846 which saw the creation of the Metropolitan Board of Works in London, the first centralized authority for managing waste disposal in large urban conurbations. The Public Health Act that followed in 1875 made it compulsory for households to deposit their weekly wastes in "moveable receptacles" to be collected by municipal authorities. The waste came to be transported in closed trucks instead of open vehicles as was the practice till then. More effective steps were to follow.

UK's Environmental Protection Act of 1990 mandated the drawing up of a National Waste Strategy. Waste disposal operations were to be so carried out that they did not endanger either peoples' health or the environment. The core of the Strategy was to establish "an integrated and adequate network of waste disposal installations, taking into account best available technology not entailing excessive cost. Special attention [is] to be paid to disposal of hazardous wastes." The results of the enforcement of the Strategy were quite dramatic. Since 1996-97, composting of waste quadrupled and the volume of waste that was sent to landfill sites diminished by 9% between 2000-01 and 2004-05. This successful measure for handling waste was further refined by the Waste Strategy of 2007 and the Waste Management Plan of 2013.

European Union

The European Union, the largest economic agglomeration in the world, has a population of 550 million. Its annual per capita consumption of materials estimated at 15-16 tonnes produces 4-5 tonnes of waste per capita. Of the total quantity of about 2750 million tonnes of waste thus generated per year, households account for 250 million, manufacturing for 360 million, construction activities for 900 million and lastly energy generation for 95 million. About 100 million tonnes of total waste are considered hazardous due to the presence of toxins and heavy metals in them. Management of such huge quantities poses innumerable problems not the least of which is the limited availability of land and high population densities of many member states, factors that militate against the adoption of conventional methods of waste disposal like landfilling or incineration.

Over the last thirty years, the EU has evolved a common approach to waste management in its member countries. The approach can be described as a need to change humanity's view of waste as something of no value to a resource at the wrong place. Hence, waste needs to be looked upon as an input having economic value and attempts should be made "To reduce waste and manage it safely as a resource" (Federal Ministry for the Environment, Nature Conservation, Building and Nuclear Safety, Germany). This pithy statement and its operative version "reduce, recycle and reuse" have vast significance for they seek to bring about a sea change in the mindset of governments, local bodies and citizens on how the problem of waste needs to be looked at. A world faced with diminishing resources like oil, minerals and metals, can ill afford to throw away anything of economic value as waste. Further, mankind has to realize that the waste assimilating capacity of air, water or land is not infinite and that some wastes are hazardous to human, animal and plant health even in minute quantities.

Prior to 2005, the EU had a Waste Framework Directive. Its Sixth Environment Action Programme (2002-2012) identified waste prevention and management as one of its top priorities. The focus was on waste reduction as the EU economy grew. The 2005 Policy revision set a target of recycling 50% of municipal and 70% of construction waste by 2020. According to available statistics, recycling of municipal waste increased from 19% in 1998 to 38% in 2007. The recycling industry handled waste worth Euro 137 billion per year which was over 1% of the EU's GDP. In the process, it created two million jobs. An estimate puts the prospects of employment going up by at least half a million in the EU if the member states recycled 70% of their wastes.

EU has an impressive record of waste management indeed. As an industrial body, EuRIC puts it "recycling has a role to play in achieving a genuine EU industrial renaissance." Transition to a zero waste economy is underway in the EU, a process marked by recycling 150 million tonnes of a variety of materials annually accounting for a turnover of 95 billion Euros. These initiatives are worth following by newly emerging major industrial economies like the BICS (Brazil, India, China and South Africa).

EU's three-part strategy on waste management can be summed up in the words "reduce, recycle and reuse". The three parts are "Life Cycle Assessment" (LCA), "Design for Environment" and "Product Stewardship". LCA, also known as "cradle to grave" analysis, enquires into the plausible environmental impact of a product from the stage of procurement of inputs to the manufacturing stage and finally to its end-use and disposal. The first stage involves an assessment of the impact of the technology employed in the sourcing of the inputs like mining and processing before they are fed into the manufacturing process. The second involves conceptualizing the least environmentally harmful process methodology and the third is the responsibility of the provider of the good towards minimizing the adverse effects of the spent product on the environment. The last part is also known as "Extended Producer Responsibility (EPR). Both products and processes can be ranked for their environment and resource friendliness by adopting this approach. This enables both businesses and society to make informed choices on production technologies and consumption patterns. The 3Rs approach has now come to be accepted the world over as an essential component of the 'Best Business Practices' which an ethical, environmentally aware and socially responsible business should adopt.

United States

In the United States, awareness of the problem of disposal of municipal solid wastes was simply non-existent until late into the 18th Century. The problem had a comic but very real component in the form of nuisance created by draught horses that pulled coaches transporting men and material. As Joel Tarr reported in the American Heritage Magazine in 1971, by 1900, the US had about three and a half million horses in its cities and another seventeen million in the countryside making up their not-too-insignificant contribution to the problem. Management of municipal solid wastes was hamstrung by a lack of finances to undertake capital works necessary for the purpose. The lack of fund flow from federal and state sources made municipal solid waste management (MSWM) the responsibility of local authorities. But that did not eliminate the participation of private enterprise in shouldering some of the burden. New York was the first city to take up the challenge. Thanks to the adoption of a scientific approach of looking at unit operations involved in MSWM, like "street sweeping, refuse collection, transportation, resource recovery and disposal" and attending to them, New York blazed the trail in setting up a system that became an example for the rest of the country to follow. Mechanisation of street sweeping and collection and transport of waste by self-loading carts to disposal sites became an accepted practice since 1855. A decade later, a group of private entrepreneurs banded themselves together to form the New York Sanitary and Chemical Compost Manufacturing Company for "cleansing the cities, towns, and villages in the United States". With such initiatives getting into full swing, almost all US cities with a population of over thirty thousand were introduced to MSMW by 1880.

The common methods adopted for waste disposal from the beginning were either incineration or dumping in landfill sites. These practices, though undesirable from an environmental point of view, did not change even till the 1980s. More than 90% of the waste collected was treated thus with little effort made to recover anything of value from it. During the '60s and '70s, less than 7% recovery was affected. It was only after the 1980s and rising environmental consciousness that landfilling became a less and less preferred option, declining to around 54%. Encouragingly, the proportion of resources recovered went up to more than 34% of the waste handled in 2012. This significant development could be ascribed to the enactment of a piece of legislation known as the Resource Conservation and Recovery Act of 1976 (RCRA) which banned the dumping of wastes in the open and called for the drawing up of regional plans for MSMW. Although MSMW is largely looked after by local authorities, involvement of private enterprise is not barred.

To deal with threats posed by sudden or threatened releases of hazardous wastes at any site within the territory of the US, a law popularly as 'Superfund' came into force in the US in late 1980. This enactment, the Comprehensive Environmental Response, Compensation and Liability Act (CERCLA), vested federal authority with powers to take action in the form of short or long-term steps to deal with releases or threatened releases of hazardous substances that may pose danger to public health or the environment. CERCLA provided for the prescription of standards for maintaining closed disposal sites and for prohibiting threatened releases of hazardous substances that may pose danger to public health or the environment. A trust fund was created to provide financial assistance to take needed action at any site where those responsible for maintaining the site cannot be tracked. The law also introduced a tax on the chemical and petroleum industries to augment the finances of the trust fund. CERCLA underwent amendment through the coming into force of the Superfund Amendments and Reauthorization Act, 1986. With all these measures, US may be said to have taken bold and effective steps to tackle the problem of management of municipal and industrial wastes of all descriptions.

Urban Planning

Besides access to clean water, pollution-free air and waste-free surroundings, well-planned and well-regulated landuse governing human settlements is another requirement of an acceptable quality of life. The need for land use planning and management is all the more relevant where population densities are high as in towns and metropolises. It is now well accepted that settlement planning taking into account people's health, recreation and commuting needs goes a long way in promoting sustainable towns and cities. A detailed look at the West's experience in managing the environmental problems of urban settlements over the centuries would prove useful to countries of the developing world even though some of them like China and India have had a history of such management right from ancient times.

Europe

The founding of new cities and rebuilding of existing ones has had a long history in Europe stretching back to the pre-Christian era. Monarchs and nobles vied with one another to erect structures of great majesty and splendour to display their rising power and fortune or to commemorate their expansion of national borders and victories in battle. Towns were only rarely founded by the inhabitants themselves. Whatever the reason, the common man had little influence in shaping matters affecting his daily life. New cities thus came up as expressions of celebration and commemoration. Occasionally, less welcome events like the plague pandemic that swept Europe in the 13th and 14th centuries or the Lisbon earthquake (1755) or as happened with the city of London, the Great Plague epidemic (1666) that claimed

100,000 lives and the Great Fire (1666) were also responsible for city redevelopment or relocation of the city at a new site.

Whatever the proximate cause, the strongest motive of rulers to build new cities or redevelop existing ones was to carve out a place for themselves in history. For the nobles and the rich who owned large tracts of land and dwellings in the towns and cities, this narcissism of the rulers opened up avenues for money-spinning and consolidating their influence by giving either land or dwellings on rent to the newcomers. Boerefijn observes that "From the 12th to the 14th century more and more landlords, great and small, lay as well as clerical, got convinced of the idea that the franchising of nucleated settlements could be an effective instrument for the consolidation of their power."

With the arrival of the Industrial Revolution in the last quarter of the 18th. Century, in marked contrast to the above situation in earlier periods, the growth of cities was influenced not so much by individual vanity, greed, or natural calamities as by public clamour for the essentials of a healthy life. The Revolution set off a rush of rural population into the towns causing "the luxuries of wealth and the meanness of poverty [to live] in juxtaposition ". The result, as we saw earlier, was the outbreak of public health problems provoking strident demand for better sanitation, wholesome drinking water, clean air and removal of filth. The "Progressive Movement" in the UK which championed social causes stood up for finding solutions to the health and sanitation problems of the poor. A new factor, namely commuting to place of work within a reasonable time became as important as health and sanitation. This called for locational and spatial planning of human settlements like zoning of residential and non-residential developments.

The trend towards concentration of populations engaged predominantly in non-agricultural occupations has been a non-stoppable one ever since it began in Britain and the Continent in the late 18th century. A century following the birth of the Industrial Revolution, a Catalan engineer, Ildefons Cerda, who planned and built the extension to the city of Barcelona, christened this demographic feature as "urbanisation", a term that is embedded in the minds of planners, sociologists and economists today. The disease infested, congested walled city of Barcelona where outbreaks of Cholera were frequent moved Cerda to suggest bringing down the walls and adopting "a new form of urban planning" that accorded "the contained" (the people) priority over the "container" (the stones or gardens)". To him the needs of the city dwellers could be summed up as "sunlight, natural lighting and ventilation in homes, greenery in [their] surroundings, waste disposal including good sewerage and finally the seamless movement of people, energy and information. These new considerations, the desire to make cities grand always lurked in the background.

Cerda's extension of Barcelona on an orthogonal layout with land divided into grids called the 'Eixample' inspired the expansion of other cities not only in Spain but in the rest of Europe too. Here was a good example of the display of the Continental yen for functionality and utility in urban planning in contrast to the British nostalgia for the bucolic. Cerda's principle of 'eschance' (expansion) was aimed at catering to high population densities that resulted from the process of urbanization and ensuring the sustainability of the increased economic activity. However, in fairness to the British approach to urbanization, it must be conceded that it was to influence urban development in the New World as much as the European concepts, particularly Cerda's, did.

France, Germany and Britain could be said to have been the leaders in influencing settlement planning in Europe in modern times.

In France, under Royal command, Baron Haussmann relaid the avenues, boulevards and parks of Paris in the second half of the 19th century, permitting in the process, limited mixed land use in the city zones. In Germany –Prussia as it was known then – the abolition of serfdom in 1810 led to the mass migration of rural populations into the cities, notably Berlin. The planning of Berlin by James Hobrecht (1825-1902) envisaged the construction of two ring roads with arterial roads running into the city. The space between the arteries was divided into rectangular grids catering to mixed land use. The Jansen Plan that followed in 1910 gave a boost to green spaces in the City by providing for a smaller inner ring road and a wide outer ring of forests, parks, and gardens. The gap between the two rings was also developed into gardens. The greening of Berlin continued under the "General Space Plan" of 1929 as well as under the post-war reconstruction of the city. However, in the two decades following 1960, as the population of the city and its environs soared to almost three million, the green spaces shrunk. Fortunately, the Landscape Programme introduced in 1990 reversed this trend successfully.

Among the European nations, UK can boast of the longest experience in town planning and country planning dating back to the 19th century. Earlier in this Chapter, while on the subjects of sanitation, public health, and pollution control, we had encountered the Chadwick Report (1842) on the living conditions of the labour classes in the UK and the Acts passed by Parliament in the last quarter of the 19th century to ameliorate their sufferings. Chadwick's report and the laws that followed established a basic principle of urban development, that is, it needed to be people-oriented. The Report led to amendments to the Poor Laws. During the Victorian era, both government and people came to realize the importance of sanitation and general improvement in the living conditions of the working classes in boosting labour productivity and in reducing public expenditure on the poor's healthcare.

Despite the clear message of the Chadwick Report and the objectives of the legislation, the next development that took place in the UK proved to be in marked contrast with them. In place of improving sanitation and living conditions of the working classes in existing towns and cities, it took the form of establishing "Garden Cities" catering to the better-off sections of the community. In a hark back to the British yearning for nature at their doorstep, Sir Ebenezer Howard (1850-1928) championed the idea of developing small towns that would be self-sufficient in all their requirements, self-supporting, and managed by the residents themselves. Each town, set over an area of 6,000 acres, was to have a population of not more than 32,000 and ample greenery all around. Two such towns, Letchworth (1903) and Welwyn Garden City (1920) came up but the movement could spread no further because technological developments like the invention of the automobile changed the character of urban development in a manner unforeseen by Howard.

The 20th century saw a surge in governmental action to tackle the problems arising out of increasing population densities in urban areas through the instrument of physical and spatial planning. The Town Planning Act of 1909 authourised local authorities to prepare town planning schemes to govern all land use in towns and cities. The Housing Act of 1919 made it mandatory for the design of houses to be approved by the Ministry of Health before construction began. Most important of this raft of legislations was The Housing Act of 1930 which stipulated that all slum housing proposed in designated improvement areas should receive prior clearance. The Barlow Commission set up in 1938 looked into ways of dispersing population and industry to relieve the existing congestion in the towns that had been experiencing rapid growth since the Industrial Revolution. Further reforms in housing and urban planning, however, had to wait till World War II was over.

Reconstruction of war-ravaged towns was a matter of high priority for the government. An urban planning group called the "New Townsmen" headed by Frederick Osborn recommended the establishment of a number of towns to come up on new sites or as satellites of existing ones instead of perpetuating the high population densities of the older areas. The main objective, as with the Barlow Commission recommendations, was to disperse the populations of many of the large cities into new settlements to reduce congestion in the older locations and thereby achieve the twin objectives of ensuring a high quality of life for the citizens in both the old and new areas. Enabled by a new law, the New Towns Act of 1946, twenty-seven such towns were established.

The foregoing account of urban planning in the UK would point to the richness of the British experience in human settlement planning and the valuable lessons one can draw from it. In a nutshell, even in a small, densely populated, industrialized island nation, spatial planning could optimize land use successfully. It should be much easier in a large country, provided the state and the citizen play their roles responsibly. In a tribute to Britain's environmental planning and execution, The Guardian UK wrote in 2014, "The British invented [urban] planning in its modern form, then implemented it with such ambition and skill" that it made Britain the "global leader".

United States

For a sparsely populated, young colony in the 17th century, it was natural for the United States, as it became later, to take its first lessons in settlement planning from its colonial masters. Initially, urban planning in the US was much influenced by the models of Europe and the UK. But the country was to learn soon that implanting the exotic overlooking the local social and economic milieu had its limits. Philadelphia, perhaps the earliest city to be founded in the US, offers a good example of such realization. In 1682, William Penn founded the city and drew up plans for its development in the form of grids with identified land use interspersed with open spaces, parks, and gardens. But the residents who valued their economic interests much more than the quality of their habitat tended to cluster around the port which offered them jobs and livelihood. Penn's plans went awry. Somewhat similar was the experience of Washington DC whose plans drawn up by Pierre L' Enfant in 1791 based on European models was not acted upon till 1902.

The dilemma facing town planners and those in authority in the US was best summarized by a British planner in 1898 who posed the question, whether cities were for people or it was the other way. Addressing the delegates at the First Urban Planning Conference in New York, he enquired rhetorically "whether he and his colleagues were striving for beautiful people or beautiful cities. Is urban planning about physical design or about making things easier for the people who live in our urban spaces." Elaborating on this conflict, Amanda Erickson writes "by the beginning of the 20th century, there were three schools of thought on what cities should look like, as architects, public health officials and sociologists thoughts differed from each other. For the architect, the town or city was simply a built environment to look as grandiose as possible; for those connected with public health, provision of adequate infrastructure... And lastly the social workers wanted to use the city to improve the lives of the people working there. They wanted cleaner tenements, spaces for immigrant children to play and more light and fresh air for residents". But as events turned out "Urban planning's intellectual history ended up grounded in architecture."

The developments that led to this end are worth speculating. The first could have been that the US, unlike Britain or the Continent, was bereft of the legacy of history (ancient or mediaeval), tradition and a distinct native urban culture. Second, none of the forces that shaped the growth of cities in Britain or Europe, that is, the authority of the monarch or the church, as in the Continent, or strong public opinion, as in the UK, was available in the US to shape public policy on human settlements. In the absence of such forces, it was natural for commerce and personal gain to fill the vacuum. The result was that expediency and lack of forethought dictated urban development. The ready course to give practical shape to impulsive thinking was to divide the city space into neutral grids and put up the grid parcels for sale. The result, as Clifford Ellis concludes, was that "The city became a checkerboard on which players speculated on shifting land values."

Industrialization helped promote the commercial trend. First, it brought to the cities a surge in population as farm labour flocked into the towns in search of employment swelling the city population manifold. New York's population of around 300,000 went up to 47, 00,000 and Chicago's from a meagre 4,000 to 21, 85,000 during the period 1840 – 1910. Many smaller cities saw their population going up six times during the period 1850-1910. This surge of people into the cities, big and small and quite unprepared to handle the influx, meant insanitation, inadequate water supply, and poor housing, a fertile ground for fostering morbidity, mortality, and a general loss in what may be called quality of life and deterioration in civility in public behaviour.

The bigger American city that emerged was one that greatly differed from the European or British models. It was characterized by a central business district in place of the royal palace or the magnificent mediaeval church and close by were the factories and warehouses that led to the growth of labour clusters. Shopping centres, entertainment houses and railroad stations arrived soon in the business district completing the checkerboard that was the new, bustling America of steel and concrete. The arrival of the automobile gave a new organ to the body of urban America in the form of the suburb. The suburb provided all the privacy one needed and the automobile along with the road network gave the comfort of smooth travel to the place of work. The automobile revolution and the urban sprawl led to the creation, in course of time, of a continuous belt of towns and cities, the megalopolises as they came to be called. In the 20th century, these agglomerations of steel, concrete, and asphalt became 'heat islands' compounding the miseries of global warming.

Despite the criticism that has been levelled against them, it must be recorded in fairness to the US urban planners that they were not totally oblivious to aesthetics and the outdoors in designing the urban landscape. Two influences that promoted this form of design, one foreign and one home-grown, did leave their impressions on American urban planning. These were the Garden Cities movement of the UK and the indigenous City Beautiful movement. Washington, DC was an early example of the first followed by parts of New York, Boston, Cleveland, and the states of New Jersey, Maryland, and Virginia. The 'City Beautiful Movement' had a short span of acceptance between the 1890s and the 1920s. Promoted by two leading architects of the time, Frederick Law Olmsted Sr. and Daniel H. Burnham and a journalist, Charles Mulford Robinson, the Movement addressed itself to encouraging "civic virtue and the waning of social ills." Its influence was noticeable in cities such as Cleveland, Chicago, and Washington, DC.

A more notable and lasting concept of urban design in the US has been 'zoning' and ''subzoning' dividing a city into parts and permitting only a specific form of land use in each zone or subzone. The move was aimed at remedying the general fall in the quality of life arising out of mixed land use practised earlier. While the cities of Los Angeles and New York had already started practising this concept since the early years of the 20th century, the process was facilitated all over the land by the issue of model regulations by the federal government in 1924. The regulations could be modified by the states to suit the local context.

Summing Up

The experience of western countries in meeting the environmental challenges arising out of economic growth holds many pointers to the developing countries of today. In the West, industrialization, the engine of growth, though bringing with it many ills, ushered in prosperity as never seen before. This raises several issues for debate like whether environmental deterioration should necessarily accompany industrialization; whether a clean form of development is possible; and whether it is desirable to strike a trade-off between environment and development. What emerges from a study of the West's environmental history is that societies can ill afford to give up either environment or development but should strive to reach a workable and affordable compromise between the two. Forsaking one for the other is not an acceptable solution. Most importantly, any debate on the issue should be governed by reason and not emotion. A nation's good lies as much in its economic development as in the sound health of its natural environment. Western experience, as it evolved over the past centuries, has much to guide the thinking of the developing world in the debate on environment and development.

It is worth drawing attention to the fact that the traditional conception of environmental concerns as being limited to nature preservation alone, first came to be extended to welfare matters like public health, sanitation, and settlement planning. This development has now undergone profound expansion and inclusion. The expanded conception with a focus on social issues like education and gender empowerment and facing up to threats like global warming transcends national boundaries. In an integrated world dominated by discussions it is of little surprise that they orchestrate all discussions on these matters. This raises the nettlesome question of the extent of responsibility of the rich and the poor in overall global efforts. It is indeed difficult for any single developing nation, however significant like India, to establish justice and equity in these efforts by acting alone. The global issues and how they arose form the subject matter of the next Chapter.

Select References

"The American Forests", John Muir; The Atlantic, August Issue 1897.

"A Brief History of American Conservation Philosophy" – USDA, J.B. Callicott.

"Prophet of Conservation", Lowenthal.

"A Sand County Almanac", Aldo Leopold.

"Environmentalism: A Global History", Ramachandra Guha, OUP, 2013.

"Man, Nature and Morality from George Perkins Marsh to the millennium", David Lowenthal, Journal of Historical Geography, 26, 1 (2000) 3-27.

"A Brief History of the Birth of American Planning" Amanda Ericson, Aug.24, 2012, The Atlantic Cities, Bloomberg City Lab.

"Report on the Sanitary Condition of the Labouring Population of Great Britain" Edwin Chadwick, 1842, House of Commons, Sessional Papers.

"The Victorian Web: Chadwick's Report on Sanitary Conditions" by Laura Del Col, West Virginia University.

"A historical context of municipal solid waste management in the United States", G.E.Louis, Waste Manag Res. 2004 Aug. 22(4) Res.

"Collection – Old style/ Resource efficiency and Waste", 'Waste Management' European Environment Agency 2020.

"A History of Life Expectancy", Tim Lambert, Local Histories – Tim's History of British Towns, Cities.

"History of Cities and City Planning: Evolution of Cities", Cliff Ellis, URI:http//hdl.handle.net/11070/ 1/5916 Date 2014-02-26

Chapter IV

The Twentieth Century (Part I)

Only One Earth

The twentieth century was remarkable in many ways. It saw global strife in the form of two World Wars, the emergence of oil and nuclear power as new energy sources, and the profuse flowering of science and technology in fields as diverse as atomic energy and cracking the human genetic code to commutation, computation and communication and the emergence of space exploration. Of course, the more spectacular among them were two, the development of nuclear weaponry and man's landing on the moon. Events of interest on the geopolitical side were the redrawing of the map of the world due to the wars and the emergence of new nations following the end of colonial rule. The nascent nations were home to sizeable populations full of aspirations. Globally, ideologies, political and economic, bloomed, some to wither away soon and some to guide human destiny ever since. Despite strong assertions of political sovereignty, nations found it necessary and expedient to come together under the aegis of a world body, the United Nations Organization. International trade and commerce expanded manifold governed by a single body, the United Nations Commission on Trade and Development (UNCTAD), and later the World Trade Organization (WTO). The old concept of nation-states with full sovereignty born out of the Treaty of Westphalia (1648) had to accommodate a limitation on its scope in so far as international relations were concerned. The world seemed to expand and diversify but shrink and become uniform at the same time as nations came together on common issues under the aegis of the United Nations Organization (UNO) and its constituent bodies.

Earth in the Balance - Population, Pollution -Resources Exhaustion

One would have thought it unlikely that In the midst of such epoch-making events any other development would emerge to command serious global attention. But, belying the unlikelihood, a watershed of change did emerge as the 20th. Century entered its second half. The change came in the form of serious doubts being cast on the future of life on the planet for a reason other than the familiar ones of a catastrophic war or a natural calamity like an earthquake or a pandemic like the Great Plague or the Spanish Flu or the recent COVID curse. While the reason for this change could be stated in simple terms, the message underlying it was profound and highly disturbing. Man was inflicting irreparable damage on the natural environment that had been sustaining him so far and life on earth was suspended delicately between existence and doom. Al Gore was to put this situation pithily in the title of his book, "Earth in the balance", written years later.

How did this "existential threat" come about? Strange as it may sound, it was the result of introspection over the modern-day paradox of impressive economic growth in the developed world being accompanied by a falling quality of life. Man had all along believed – and quite rightly – that the desired outcome of growth was always an improvement in his living standards which basically meant an improvement in his income and quality of life. Quality of life, in turn, had been understood in terms of freedom from hunger, disease, and crime, access to adequate shelter, and social and cultural progress. Therefore, as the 20th. century progressed, it appeared incongruous that despite their economic growth, rich nations should see a fall in the quality of life of their citizens.

To explain the paradox, a thesis was advanced that growth that relied on the overuse of earth's natural resources was necessarily accompanied by pollution of the natural environment in more ways than one resulting in conditions that led to a lowering of the quality of life. Further, such vigorous growth was unsustainable because neither the natural resources which powered that growth were inexhaustible nor was the resilience of the natural environment to excessive damage caused to it by high and rapid growth. Terming the situation arising out of the hitherto prevailing notion that the earth's capacity to meet human needs and wants was unlimited as unsustainable, economist Kenneth Boulding (1966) compared it to a "cowboy economy". Over utilisation of natural resources strained nature's capacity to assimilate wastes in the quantities generated. Long-term sustainability of life on this "Only One Earth" under conditions of unchecked growth came under doubt.

Silent Spring - The Population Bomb - The Limits to Growth

The fear of unsustainability of growth raised many uncomfortable questions. Did it mean that the economic growth path, characterized by high volumes of production and consumption and high waste, adopted by developed nations and being copied by the developing ones, needed to be abandoned? If so, what would be the alternative path to follow? These issues were the tinder that stoked the fire of the 20th. Century's environmental revolution. All that was needed to set the tinder afire was a spark. Unlikely as it may sound, the spark came in the form of three publications and an event of geo-economic significance. The publications were **"Silent Spring"** (1962), **"The Population Bomb"** (1968), and **"The Limits to Growth"** (1972), all emanating from the US and the event was the first global oil crisis of 1973.

If a poll were to be held to pick the most influential among the books that shaped global introspection over the future, the runaway winner would be **Silent Spring** by Rachel Carson. The **Spring** highlighted the devastation caused to bird populations in New England by the widespread spraying of trees with an organochlorine insecticide, DDT, in the 1950s. It was noticed that as the years rolled by, bird arrivals in New England in springtime began to dwindle. Carson, a well-qualified biologist, attributed this near absence of birds, particularly Warblers, to the spraying of Dutch Elm trees with DDT in earlier years to protect them from rust attacks. According to Carson, the insecticide residues on the leaves travelled up the natural food chain from the worms that fed on the leaves to the birds that preyed on the worms. The build-up of the chemical and its break-down products in bird systems resulted in thinning of the egg shells making the eggs prone to cracking before they were hatched. This led to high mortality of chicks and consequently in a fall in bird populations.

Despite the fact that the science behind Carson's explanation of dwindling bird populations was questionable, the impact the book had on the public mind was resounding. The insecticide DDT that was effective in protecting vegetation against pest attacks and had been hailed as the saviour of 400,000 combatant lives during World War II and millions of civilian population in developing countries later suddenly became an environmental poison leading to its ban in the US in 1972. The wave of sympathy towards nature spread over the Atlantic and the Pacific causing similar steps to be taken in Europe and Japan. United Kingdom abolished the use of DDT in 1984 and by 1991, 26 more countries followed suit. Even India couldn't remain immune to these developments and the use of DDT became restricted to Malaria eradication only. With the publication of the **"Spring"**, banning of chemicals that could harm the environment gained public support and care for the planet became the slogan of the times.

Even from before the campaign against DDT began, there had been a simmering feeling of distrust against chemical industry thanks to some industrial accidents in the developed world. The death of 900 people in Japan in 1956 due to the consumption of blowfish caught in the Minamata Bay was attributed to the slow build-up of mercury in the fish and human systems. Mercury, a neuro – poison, present in the effluents released by an industrial unit into the Bay was first ingested by blowfish and then found its way into consumers' food. The large number of deaths was enough to arouse distrust against chemicals in general. Similarly, industrial accidents, again in Japan, leading to Cadmium poisoning in humans in the form of bone softening – a condition called **Itai Itai** – also served to create a climate against increasing use of chemicals in daily life. Even the application of chemical fertilizers in agriculture came into question. Thus, concern about possible harm to the environment that may be caused by chemicals in common use soon became an obsession with the developed world. This obsession became the Environmental Revolution.

While concern over the impact of chemicals on the environment was essentially a twentieth – century development, there was another that man had been nursing since the eighteenth century, namely the fear of his own numbers. Did not Reverend Malthus express concern over the mismatch between the rapidly growing population and slow growth of food production? Did he not warn of the impending doom due to this asymmetry? Despite the fact that his foreboding never came true, it had commanded the attention of academic circles and enjoyed several rebirths. The year 1968 was to witness one such in the release of "**The Population Bomb**" authoured by Paul Ehrlich and Anne Ehrlich.

The message of the **Bomb** was unsettling, to put it mildly. In brief, whereas world population took two hundred years to reach 200 million by 1850, only eighty more years were required for it to touch the 400 million mark and a mere 35 years to double itself further to 800 million. In the 20th.century, doubling times dropped to as low as 20 to 30 years in developing countries. To maintain living standards in developed countries at levels already reached and to raise the standards in developing countries to minimum acceptable levels, a quantum jump was needed in food production, energy supply and physical infrastructure. Accomplishing the task was admittedly difficult even for a rich nation like the US, leave alone the less and the least fortunate ones of the global South.

The **Bomb** went on to caution that failure to step up food production to desired levels would result in mass starvation and heavy loss of life by the year 1970 in many of the poor countries particularly those in Sub-Saharan Africa. Thankfully, the world was spared of such a situation. But, the possibility of occurrence of such a situation could not be discounted lightly. Yet, quite uncharitably to the authors, the non-occurrence of a global catastrophe was used by critics to question the validity of the **Bomb's** message. But, it must be pointed out that the **Bomb's** apprehensions about population growth were not off the mark in that between 1950 and 1985, world population grew by 1.9% per annum compared to 0.8% in the period 1900 to 1950, the increase occurring mostly in Asia, Africa and Latin America. In defence of such honest prognoses it must be said that failure of the feared contingency to materialize cannot be taken as a reflection on the merit of the analysis or of the message. The **Bomb's** predictions were not an intuitive guess but a conclusion based on genuine projections. Despite the cold reception it received from the cognoscenti, the book turned out to be hugely successful in raising public awareness of the population problem. That daring was enough to justify its publication.

The **"Spring"** has often been called emotional and evangelical and the **"Bomb"** pessimistic and needlessly scary. The third work, the **"Limits"**, however, was quite different from these two. Its authors were hard core academics at the Massachusetts Institute of Technology (MIT) engaged in Systems modelling and drawing probabilistic conclusions from such models. Their study, titled **"The Limits to Growth"** was commissioned by the Club of Rome, a multinational group of enlightened individuals drawn from diverse walks of life. The Club was interested in a project called "The Predicament of Mankind" as it was deeply concerned with certain developments witnessed all over the world that seemed to threaten the very existence of mankind. In the words of the Club, these concerns were "poverty in the midst of plenty; loss of faith in institutions; uncontrolled urban spread; insecurity of employment; alienation of youth; rejection of traditional values; and inflation and other monetary and economic disruptions." The Club of Rome was apprehensive of the "basic behavior" of the world system, that is, "exponential growth of population and capital, followed by collapse."

As Phase I of the **"Predicament"** project, MIT was asked to examine the five basic factors that in the opinion of the Club determined and hence limited "growth on this planet". These factors were "population, agricultural production, natural resources, industrial production, and pollution." The study concluded that:

"1. If the present growth trends in world population, urbanization, pollution, food production and resource depletion continue unchanged, the limits to growth on this planet will be reached sometime within the next one hundred years. The most probable result will be a rather sudden and uncontrollable decline in both population and industrial capacity;

2. It is possible to alter these growth trends and to establish a condition of ecological and economic stability that is sustainable far into the future. The state of global equilibrium could be designed so that the basic material needs of each person on earth are satisfied and each person has an equal opportunity to realize his individual human potential;

3. If the world's people decide to strive for the second outcome rather than of the first, the sooner they begin working to attain it, the greater will be their chances of success."

The "**Limits**" was worried over the possibility of growth in population or decline of any other factor taking an exponential turn instead of a linear one. A rise in growth of population in a reducing timeframe would lead to an overcrowded planet with limited resources and a fall in the quality of life. A rapid fall in population growth, on the other hand, would lead to an overaged population and a reduced number of able bodied citizens to support them and make the economy grow. As for resources, a steep rate of their exhaustion with little availability of substitutes would make the world poorer with all its social and political consequences. The only way to avert a crisis, according to "**Limits**" was for the global economy to make a conscious transition from a perpetually growing one to one at equilibrium with its environment. In other words, the economy should reach a steady state. The authors of "**Limits**" outlined the features of this "equilibrium" state and how global economy could make a transition to it. Refreshingly, in doing so, they stressed the role of social factors in bringing about such a transition. According to them, high energy and resources consumption were as much due to social and behavioural patterns as to economic forces.

The conclusions of "**Limits**" have been challenged ever since the work was published. The continued availability of oil and mineral resources and that too in enhanced quantities, despite talk of "peaking" of supply, has been held out as negating its conclusions. The book's scepticism over science and technology emerging as saviours has been countered by the discovery and development of new oil and gas deposits and by availability of techniques to exploit sources hitherto considered uneconomic. Despite all these developments, the strong message of the book that society needed to change track from an environment unfriendly growth path to one that was in equilibrium with the environment has remained unshaken and has formed the basis of all later global discourse on environment and development. The call for "Sustainable Development" of human society can be said to be the direct outcome of the **"Limits"**. Therein lies the work's lasting merit. We shall have occasion to revisit the issue of earth's limits at a later stage in the discussions on "Planetary boundaries" and sustainable development.

Though the persuasive logic of **"Limits"** made a deep impression on the minds of the intelligentsia, the world at large needed a grassroots movement to pave the way for the larger revolution to arise. The baby boomers of the US, as the generation of American youth born in the period 1948-64 was called, enjoying the benefits offered by a generous welfare state, could afford to indulge in anti-conservative and non-conformist movements like flower power and in shows of resentment against the state that supported the industry. America's involvement in Vietnam and loss of American lives was a favoured cause of disaffection among the youth. To divert their attention, Senator Gaylord Nelson of Michigan persuaded President Reagan to declare 22nd March as the Earth Day to be celebrated all over the US. The declaration of the Earth Day and its first celebration in 1970 marked the beginning of official recognition of the movement for care of the planet and was the precursor to the World Environment Day (5th June) declared by the UN later.

As these dramatic developments were unfolding and commanding public attention, the UN was silently at work to find a solution to a larger problem affecting humanity, the rich-poor divide. In 1961, UN launched the First Development Decade to "accelerate projects toward self-sustaining economic growth and social advancement in the developing countries." It was expected that each developing country would set its own target to achieve "a minimum annual growth rate of aggregate national income of 5% at the end of the Decade". Towards this end, in December 1961, the UN General Assembly, through Resolution 1710 (XVI), recommended that the flow of international capital and assistance to developing countries should be about 1% of the combined national incomes of the economically advanced countries.

The expectations of the UN on the size of funds transfer from the rich to the poor never materialized. Despite this, poor countries registered a fairly acceptable economic growth rate of about 4.6% but much of this was neutralized by population rise resulting in the growth rate falling to 2%. One of the reasons identified by the UN for the shortcomings and slow progress of the efforts was the "absence of a framework of international development strategy." That this important lesson was not missed by the UN would be revealed by developments since then. Strategy and institutional mechanisms have been the built-in features of latter day international agreements.

Founex (1971) and Stockholm (1972)

Few events in human history have had such a monumental impact on present and future generations as the United Nations Conference on the Human Environment (UNCHE) held in 1972. UNCHE was the initiative of the developed countries and not the developing ones. As to why this was so, one may go back to Chapter II which traced the economic growth of European powers – the bulk of today's developed countries – through industrialization of their economies. Their industrialization and growth were made possible by exploitation of natural resources of their colonies at little cost and exporting finished goods back to the colonies at high prices. This practice of double exploitation of the poor had gone on for nearly two hundred years and well into the twentieth century. However, as the late 1940s and the beginning of the 1950s witnessed more and more colonies becoming independent, a fear gripped the western world of shortage of raw materials hitherto sourced from the colonies at cheap prices . This fear was compounded by the apprehension that the newly independent nations would exploit their natural resources rapaciously to feed their own growth and this development would lead to deterioration of local and global environments. Thus, there was a strong mix of economics and self-interest in the West's environmental concerns which were sought to be legitimized by giving them a global relevance needing global intervention.

The voice of the West's fears was not any of the former colonial powers or the US or the fast growing Japan but a totally unexpected one, Sweden. The unlikely champion, however, had the right credentials to don the mantle of the speaker of the developed world. Sweden's industrial rise, though delayed till the late 1870s, picked up strongly in the closing years of the 19th century and in the early twentieth thanks to private initiatives and governmental encouragement. This happy development continued till the end of World War I. These years of growth have been dubbed the "Golden Age" of Swedish industry. World War II did not affect Sweden as the country remained neutral, though some accused it of having been accommodative of Nazi policies and actions. Swedish firms established themselves abroad as makers of quality products in their respective industrial segments like paper and newsprint, steel, cutting tools and electrical goods. At home, promoting social welfare was adopted as the all – important duty of the state.

As the 1960s rolled on, Sweden, backed by impressive achievements at home and abroad, found itself in a position to assume the moral high ground on many issues in the international arena. Given the conditions of the 1960s, with Europe, US and Japan enjoying robust economies and the welfare state having been adopted as the avowed goal of governments, there was no better way to capture public attention than highlighting the possible negative outcomes of prosperity. Care for the environment was a slogan that was tacky and timely to adopt and was made much of by the proponents of the 'Welfare State'. In 1968, led by its newly elected radical Prime Minister, Olaf Palme, Sweden seized the opportunity for furthering its global recognition by suggesting to the Economic and Social Council (ECOSOC) of the United Nations Organization (UNO) to convene a conference on global environment and development. The move met with favourable response and the next year the UN General Assembly (UNGA) passed General Resolution 2398 to hold such a conference in Stockholm in June1972. That Sweden had been critical of the involvement of the US in the Vietnam War lent spice to the choice of the Swedish capital as the venue of the Conference.

The first step in delineating the contours and content of the subjects to be deliberated at the Conference was to prepare a well authored background document. For this purpose, a high level expert committee, mostly of economists drawn from the world over, was constituted in 1971 and this committee held its discussions in Founex, Switzerland in June of that year. India was represented on the committee by Pitambar Pant, member in charge of Perspective Planning in the erstwhile Planning Commission of India.

The Founex Report, while lauding the concern for protecting the environment, cautioned the developed nations of the possible consequences of applying fetters to the economic progress of developing countries in the guise of such concerns. The Report considered environmental improvement not in isolation but in a broader setting of economic development, international trade and finance, and technology transfer. It assuaged the fears the developing nations had over the purpose of holding the Stockholm Conference. The Founex

Report made a strong plea for additional aid flows to developing countries to help them address their main environmental concerns and to safeguard their exports to developed countries from environment-related trade restrictions. In addition, the Report cautioned against cost escalations that development projects, in general, may experience due to the need to comply with stricter environmental standards. It sought to secure a level playing field for the developing countries in global environmental exchanges.

The Stockholm Conference on the Human Environment (UNCHE, 5-16 June 1972) was hailed as one of the major international conferences of the twentieth century for more reasons than one. It brought out effectively what ailed the rich and what ailed the poor in so far as the quality of life of their citizens was concerned. The rich were seen as suffering from the effects of overconsumption, an accusation that rang true as, for example, the United States with just 6% of the world population at the beginning of the1970s consumed 40% of the goods produced in the world. On the other hand, the plight of the poor nations was due to an antipodal reason summed up brilliantly in the Founex Report thus: "Millions continue to live far below the minimum levels required for a decent human existence, deprived of adequate food and clothing, shelter and education, health and sanitation. Therefore, the developing countries must direct their efforts to development, bearing in mind their [development] priorities and the need to safeguard and improve the environment."

It augured well for the developing countries that the Secretary-General of the Conference, Maurice Strong of Canada, sensed their mood correctly while observing that "Developing countries were considering boycotting the Conference. They thought that the concern for 'environment' was one for the rich and would detract from their [developing countries'] main concerns which were the relief of poverty and continuing development". Strong could sense what could mar the Conference and how best to avoid It. And he steered the proceedings successfully.

The developing world had a pugnacious leader in the then Prime Minister of India, Mrs. Indira Gandhi who led the Indian delegation to the Conference. Referring to the poor as the "disinherited majority" of the world she argued that "Poverty was the biggest polluter." In a ringing address, she brought home to the affluent nations that the environmental problems of the poor like lack of sanitation, degraded habitat, high morbidity and mortality stemmed from economic underdevelopment and cautioned that any excessive concern for the environment as overriding developmental imperatives would be unacceptable to the poor. While reiterating that "Environment cannot be improved in conditions of poverty" Mrs. Gandhi did agree that the poor too had a responsibility to become environment conscious and contribute to arrest environmental degradation. In that context she reminded the global audience of the man-nature harmony which India's ancient culture and religious texts preached.

The comprehensive Declaration that came out at the end of the Stockholm Conference was to inspire all subsequent discourse on environmental issues in national and international fora. Despite the political manoeuvring the rich nations indulged in to play down the right of the poor to development, the Declaration highlighted the developmental needs of the latter. The Declaration exhorted everyone, rich as well as the poor, to take note of the fact that development could not remain sustainable for long without being environmentally compatible. The preamble to the Declaration reminded the international community that "Man is both the creature and moulder of his environment..."and "Both aspects of man's environment, the natural and the man-made, are essential to his wellbeing and to the enjoyment of basic human rights – even the right to life itself." A point to note here is that by recognizing the fact that the environment around us is not all natural but a good part of it has been impacted by man over thousands of years, the Declaration did not subscribe to the back to pristine nature philosophy, much to the chagrin of the ardent Greens who had flocked to Stockholm. Stockholm took a balanced and pragmatic view of pursuing economic development and safeguarding the environment.

The Stockholm Declaration contained 26 Principles to guide future action both at national and international levels. Mindful of the needs of the poor, these Principles looked at environmental concerns from the angles of economics, equality, freedom, fund flows and ease of access to knowledge and technology. Principle 1 of the Declaration proclaimed that "Man has the fundamental right to freedom, equality and adequate conditions of life, in an environment of a quality that permits a life of dignity and well-being...". That is, an acceptable standard of living coupled with acceptable environmental quality is of the stature of a fundamental right to a human being as is his freedom. As to what would be needed to ensure "adequate conditions of life" in an environment of acceptable quality, Principle 8 highlighted that "Economic and social development is essential". This would mean that there is no such thing as an acceptable quality of environment in the absence of economic and social development as that would not ensure a life of dignity and well-being. Addressing the main concern of the developing nations that economic development was vital to them, Principle 11 was specific in that "present or future development potential of developing countries" should not be adversely affected by the environmental policies of states." It is a matter of regret that though these Principles were accepted over fifty years ago globally, the environment and development imbroglio continues to rage to this day. It is of greater regret that such a debate should go on in a developing country like India.

Only One Earth

The deliberations at Stockholm were marked by a sense of special concern for the natural resource needs of future generations. "**Only One Earth: The Care and Maintenance of a Small Planet**", an official publication brought out on the occasion, authored by the French microbiologist Rene Dubos and the British Social Anthropologist, Barbara Ward, dwelt on the limitations of the planet to continue to support the world population, a part of which was enjoying high standards of living and a much larger part struggling to meet basic human needs and nursing high aspirations for as plentiful attainments as the former. If the exploitation of natural resources continued unabated at high levels to satisfy the wants of the present populations, then future generations would stand deprived of them. Hence, Principle 2 of the Declaration cautioned that natural resources like "...air, water, land, flora and fauna and especially representative samples of natural ecosystems, must be safeguarded for the benefit of present and future generations through careful planning or management...". This was fortified by Principle 5 which exhorted nations to exploit non-renewable resources of the earth in such a way as to guard against the danger of their future exhaustion..." The theme of these two Principles is referred to as "Intergenerational Equity".

Stockholm proved to be an institution builder too. On its recommendation, the UN General Assembly (UNGA) established the United Nations Environment Program (UNEP) in 1974 with its headquarters in Nairobi, Kenya to act as a specialist agency to evolve global programmes of action and facilitate their implementation. The day the Stockholm Conference began, that is, 5th June, was declared by the UN as the World Environment Day.

In the following decades, UNEP was to notch up notable successes in many areas of environmental concern like the thinning of the Ozone layer, arresting the loss of earth's biodiversity, regulating transboundary movement of hazardous wastes, global warming and climate change.

It is a matter of deep irony that while speaking up for the poor, Stockholm created a somewhat adverse climate for them, namely the setting in motion of a trend to globalize issues arising in the developed countries and arriving at international compacts imposing obligations on the poor nations too. The impact of this trend on the poor's national development strategies and their national sovereignty in charting public policy has been tremendous. A good example is provided by the Vienna Convention on protecting the Ozone Layer and the Montreal Protocol on Phasing out of Ozone Depleting Substances, both of 1986 and the hotly debated Paris Agreement on climate change. These issues will be discussed a little later in this Chapter. A large number of countries including India whose use of Ozone Depleting Substances was miniscule compared to their consumption in the North had to comply with the Protocol terms to phase out completely the use of these substances. This had a significant economic impact on many developing countries, quite some of which had to rely solely on these chemicals for protecting their export oriented agricultural products. Another example is the Paris Agreement on Climate Change (2015) which has treated the rich and poor nations alike in shouldering responsibility to combat global warming, overlooking the historical fact that the rich, industrialized nations are solely responsible for creating the problem.

Vancouver, Canada 1976

Stockholm could be hailed as marking the birth of an era in global environmental history. With the welfare of both man and his physical environment having been recognized as necessary conditions for survival and sustainable development of life on earth and the elevation of these issues to the centre of global political agenda, it was time to set in motion steps to realize the objectives. The next step was the convening of the UN Conference on Human Settlements (HABITAT Conference) in Vancouver, Canada in 1976.

Stockholm, while highlighting the challenge of economic development in the face of growing environmental degradation, had called for urgent attention to be paid to the problem of urbanization, a problem common to both rich and poor countries. The phenomenon of rapid urbanization leading to environmental degradation and social strife was not confined to the affluent North. It swept the entire global South from Latin America through Africa to Asia. As the then Secretary-General of the UN Kurt Waldheim observed "One third or more of the entire population of the developing world lives in slums and squatter settlements. The poor had not only the immediate compulsion of meeting their basic needs of food, clothing and shelter but also answer the inner call of aspiration for a better life."

There were several aspects to the problem of urbanization. First, there was the varying nature and magnitude of the problem from one hemisphere to the other and from one country to another. Differing legal regimes governing human settlements necessitating solutions to be tailor-made to a country was another. Not the least was the capacities of countries to address the problem, both technically and financially. What was common among them, however, was a lack of will on the part of their governments to deal with the problem head on. Habitat (1976) was the first international initiative to address these issues organized by a newly created UN agency of the same name having its headquarters in Nairobi, Kenya.

Habitat made the world acutely aware of the ballooning population and its fallout, a big slide in the quality of life for most of its people, particularly in developing countries. Surely enough, global population rose two fold in the next twenty years and continued to grow. If one-third of global population lived in urban areas in 1976, this share rose to one-half in 2000 and is expected to account for two-thirds in 2050. The brunt of the vastly increased population has fallen naturally on the urban environment and on the quality of life of the citizens. Hence, a significant improvement in the quality of the urban environment "is a requisite for the full satisfaction of basic needs, such as employment, housing, health services, education and recreation." This underscores the point that improving living conditions in human settlements must be seen as "an instrument of development" as well as an "object of development".

International Union for Conservation of Nature and Natural Resources (IUCN)

Nature conservation had been engaging the attention of the UN community for long, from years prior to the rise of the environmental movement. The International Union for the Protection of Nature was established in 1948 in Fontainebleau, France. It was renamed the International Union for Conservation of Nature and Natural Resources (IUCN) in 1956 and has its headquarters in Switzerland. IUCN's principal contribution has been to convince the world to look upon nature as made up of ecosystems, as a collection of dynamic spatial and biological entities engaged in a constant process of exchange of matter and energy with each other and with their non-living environment. Man cannot survive in isolation of other living species and the non-living environment, be it soils, rocks, air or water. Making humanity aware of this message and act upon it has been the principal occupation of IUCN all along. For its pioneering work and the worldwide attention its messages are receiving, IUCN has come to be called the "world's oldest and largest global environmental network."

In pursuance of its mandate, IUCN brought out a World Conservation Strategy in 1980 that highlighted the role of natural ecosystems like land, forests, fresh water bodies and the marine environment in sustaining life on earth and presented the following precepts for national and international observance:-

> "to maintain essential ecological processes and life support systems like soil conservation and soil regeneration, the recycling of nutrients and the cleansing of water;
>
> to preserve genetic diversity of plants, domesticated animals and microorganisms; [and] sustainable utilization of species and ecosystems."

The Conservation Strategy urged the world community to respond by adopting an international convention to give legal status to the strategy. A little known fact about the strategy is that the now oft used expression "sustainable development" first found mention in it. Similarly, the term 'conservation' got a comprehensive definition as "the management of human use of the biosphere so that it may yield the greatest sustainable benefit to present generations while maintaining its potential to meet the needs and aspirations of future generations" (Eblen and Eblen). This pioneering effort of IUCN and its espousal of sustainable development influenced many historic developments in the years to come. Most notably, it influenced the preparation of the document **"Our Common Future"**, popularly known as the Brundtland Report released in 1986 which went on to dictate the script of the Rio Conference on Sustainable Development (1992). The adoption of the UN Convention on Biological Diversity (CBD) at Rio could also be attributed to IUCN's World Conservation Strategy.

Vienna Convention (1985) and Montreal Protocol (1986)

Earlier in this Chapter, we had noted that following the Stockholm Conference (1972), a spirit of international cooperation emerged in meeting environmental problems of a common nature. There are, indeed, many such problems whose cause could arise anywhere but their effects could be felt everywhere. A good example is to be found in depletion of the Ozone layer in the stratosphere (7-15 km above the earth) by a family of chemicals known as chloro-fluoro carbons (CFCs). These chemicals collectively known as Ozone Depleting Substances (ODS) were in extensive use in household and industrial applications like air conditioning, refrigeration, fire retardation and crop protection. During their application, they wafted their way into the stratosphere and with the help of sunlight reacted with the Ozone layer and depleted it. The Ozone layer acts as the earth's shield against ultraviolet radiation emanating from outer space and its depletion has a damaging effect on humans in the form of higher incidence of skin cancer and Cataract and mutations in human, animal and plant cells.

In the backdrop of these developments, United Nations Environment Programme (UNEP) began addressing the issue of framing an international agreement in 1981 and its efforts led to the adoption of the Vienna Convention on Phase-out of Ozone Depleting Substances in 1985 followed by the Montreal protocol in 1986 to operationalise the terms of the Convention. The Montreal Protocol was to become a model of international cooperation in meeting threats to human life and the environment. The Protocol has been amended four times to keep it relevant to changing contexts arising out of discovery of new ODS.

Although the annual consumption of ODS by developing countries and Least Developing Countries (LDCs) was less than 0.3 kg per capita in the 1980s and was of no comparison with their use in the developed countries, governments all over the world joined in the global effort to combat the problem, of course with assistance, financial and technical, from agencies like the Montreal Protocol Fund and the World Bank. Bilateral assistance also became available. The developed countries began implementing the phase-out schedule in 1984 and completed it by 1994. Others were given an extended time limit to schedule their phase-out beginning from 1994 and to be completed by 2010.

The success of the Montreal Protocol could be attributed to many factors. The first was a rare commitment shown by all nations to address the challenge. To make the deal acceptable to all, the principle of "common but differentiated responsibilities and national capabilities" was accepted as the premise to start action. Since the Protocol was founded on the principle of equity in the form of 'common but differentiated responsibilities', it met with little opposition. Second, the grant of an extended time limit to the developing countries to comply with the provisions of the Protocol and making available finances for implementing the phase-out programmes were really meaningful concessions. Last but not the least was the availability of substitutes in the market for the ODS being phased out and the facilitation of technology transfer by the Protocol Secretariat. The influence of the Vienna Convention and the Montreal Protocol on later green compacts like the UN Framework Convention on Climate Change (1992) was total.

At this juncture, we cannot overlook the influence of commercial interests in environmental matters of a global nature. US chemical Industry, much affected by falling consumer demand for ODS and goods using these chemicals, tried to stall the phase-out initially by debunking the science of Ozone depletion but fell in line later as it could develop the substitutes indigenously. The forging of a Protocol opened up a huge export market too. The economic gain to the US by internationalizing the issue as against handling it as a national one was appreciable as can be seen from the Table below:-

Costs and benefits of Montreal Protocol to the United States (US$ Billions, 1985; US EPA)

No Control	Montreal Protocol	US Unilateral Implementation of Protocol
Benefits	3,575	1,373
Costs	21	21
Net benefits	3,554	1,352

US ascendancy in global environmental exchanges could be said to have begun with the adoption and implementation of the Montreal Protocol. From then on, US promoted only those initiatives that were in its overall economic interest and was either opposed to or lukewarm in extending support to other measures. In this Chapter, we shall see one more example of this disturbing trend in the form of US opposition to joining the Basel Convention on the Control of Transboundary Movements of Hazardous Wastes and Their Disposal (1989). The battles – royal over the UNFCCC and its adjunct, the Kyoto Protocol (1997) and over the Paris Climate Agreement (2015) would be looked into in the next Chapter.

Basle Convention (1989)

A concomitant feature of industrial development and rise in standards of living in the developed world over the last 250 years has been the generation of solid wastes in great quantities. Of this, much of the solid waste from industry is also of a hazardous nature. Collection of wastes, their transportation and disposal in an environmentally sound manner poses a big challenge to national and local governments, civic authorities and to the industries themselves. The problem assumed urgency in the second half of the last century for two reasons, one, the quantities to be disposed of had grown to unmanageable levels and two, the absence of solutions to the problem with available technology and at an affordable cost.

In the last quarter of the 20th. Century, new challenges emerged in the form of stringent regulations governing disposal of metallic and plastic scrap. Further, the growth of the semi-conductor industry with its fast product obsolescence led to the generation of hazardous waste needing scientific disposal adhering to strict environmental requirements governing such wastes. To tackle the problem, US enacted the Resource Conservation and Recovery Act in 1976. Because of the costs involved in complying with the law, US industry looked to cheaper ways to dispose of wastes by exploring their exports to developing countries, particularly those whose governments were unaware of the hazards posed by the wastes. This gave birth to what came to be called "Toxic Colonialism". The issue came to the fore in 1976 when a vessel named ***Khian Sea*** carrying 14,000 tons of incinerator ash from Philadelphia dumped 4,000 tons of it on the shores of Haiti by misrepresenting the material as 'fertilizer' and disposing off the rest of the cargo on high seas. The public outrage the incident created led to initiation of steps to frame an international convention to control and regulate trans-boundary movement of hazardous wastes and their disposal called the Basle Convention (1989). The Convention came into force in 1992.

The coming into force of a multilateral agreement on exports of wastes from one member-country of the agreement to another was surely a welcome step. This paved the way for countries poor in metals and mineral resources to import them in the form of reclaimable wastes at prices quite low in comparison to the price of primary metals. Because of this, world trade in both and non-metallic wastes grew tremendously since Basle. The availability of such reclaimable material reduced considerably the foreign exchange outgo of many developing countries, including India. Further, the availability of comparatively cheap labour in developing countries contributed to low costs of production of primary metals from metallic wastes. This enabled downstream industries to gain an edge in their export competitiveness. From the angle of environmental impact too, reclamation of primary metal from metal wastes was a far less polluting operation than winning the metal from the naturally occurring ore.

EU countries and many other members of the OECD (Organization for Economic Cooperation and Development, a group of rich nations) are parties to the Basle Convention. A point of interest here is that as of February, 2018, while 185 countries had ratified the Basel Convention, the US and Haiti had not done so. Despite the backing of two Presidents and approval of the Senate, US administration advanced inadequacy of the national legislative framework to implement the provisions of the Convention as the reason to keep away from it.

As for availability of reclaimable wastes, particularly of steel, the case of imports of discarded ships for breaking could be quoted. Ever since the days of the **Torrey Canyon** and **Exxon Valdes** disasters, a need had been felt to make oil transportation through ships highly safe by making the ship hulls more strong and sturdy. Ships with double hulls replaced existing fleets rendering a large number of single-hulled vessels to be consigned to the scrapyard. Since the breaking of the discarded vessels was a labour intensive activity and labour costs were high in the developed world, the vessels were exported as scrap to developing countries where labour costs were low. Starting around 1980, a flourishing ship-breaking industry grew up in countries like India, Bangladesh, Sri Lanka and Thailand giving employment to thousands of people. On the flip side, these ship-breaking units became notorious for lack of occupational safety measures for their labour force resulting in frequent casualties. What made economic sense did not make humanitarian sense in the way ship-breaking was practised. Worse still, lack of occupational safety measures in ship-breaking industry cast its shadow on recycling industry in general. Most unfortunate was the fact that the shipbreaking industry was portrayed as environment unfriendly as it released asbestos into the marine environment, even though the quantities of asbestos released formed a miniscule part of the total tonnage of the scrap handled.

A Momentous Period

The first three quarters of the 20th century will go down as a momentous period in world history not simply for the two great wars but also for successful efforts to restore and guard world peace. With the return of peace, attention came to fall upon human living conditions particularly in countries of Africa, Latin America and Asia. A geopolitical economic entity peopled by the world's poor emerged. Its priority was economic development and meeting its basic environmental requirements like housing, sanitation and, drinking water for its people. The efforts of the UN system in helping developing countries in this direction were augmented by international financial institutions like the International Bank for Reconstruction and Development (World Bank) and regional development banks but the Overseas Development Assistance as promised by UNGA Resolution of December 1961 did not materialise to the expected levels. Despite the efforts of the UN system and the development financial institutions, the rich – poor divide widened on both economic and environmental fronts and their relationship hardened. Efforts to promote understanding often met with friction, debate and unconscionable delay. The situation got more complicated with the arrival of new concerns of a truly global nature like global warming and climate change, and loss of biodiversity. The global system was under test.

Select References

"A Program for International Economic Cooperation (I)", UNGA Resolution 1710 (XVI) 19 December 1961, Dag Hammarskjold Library;

UNGA Resolution A/RES/2626 (XXV), 24 October 1970; Dag Hammarskjold Library;

"Silent Spring" Rachel Carson, Crest Books, Fawcett Publications CONN;

"The Predicament of Mankind: Quest for Structures, Responses to Growing World – wide Complexities and Uncertainties: A Proposal, 1970, Future World's Resource Center.

"The Limits to Growth" Donella Meadows *et. al.*; Potomac Associates;

"The Population Bomb" Paul Ehrlich and Anne Ehrlich, 1968, Sierra Club, Ballantine Books;

"The Economics of the Coming Spaceship Earth", Kenneth E. Boulding, 1966, http://www.geocities.com/RainForest/3621/ BOULDING. HTM, 7.3.2003;

United Nations Environment Programme Executive Series, "In Defence of the Earth – The basic texts on Environment: Founex – Stockholm – Cocoyoc" 1981.

"Only One Earth: The Care and Maintenance of a Small Planet", Barbara Ward and Rene Dubos, The UNESCO Courier: a window open on the world, XXVI, 1; Penguin Paperbacks, January 1972.

"The World vs. The United States and China? The Complex Climate Change Incentives of the Leading Greenhouse Gas Emitters" – Cass R. Sunstein, 55 UCLA Review 1675 (2008).

Chapter V

The Twentieth Century (Part II)

Our Common Future

Ever since the holding of the Stockholm Conference in 1972 and the expression of its aspirations in the form of a Declaration on the Human Environment, a strong need had been felt to mobilize the energies of the world community towards translating these aspirations into practice. It was natural to assume that the developed world would take the lead in this effort since the poor could not be expected to do so as their first task was to rise above abject poverty requiring the commitment of all their resources to that task. To boot, the success of the poor in adopting an environmentally sustainable development pathway was also contingent upon a steady, substantial flow of funds and technology to them from the rich.

Rich - Poor Divide

The exercise in tempering economic growth with due regard to the environment, as the unfurling events showed, turned out to be a difficult one with mixed results, the most glaring of which being the widening of the rich-poor divide. As a result, even almost two decades after Stockholm, its vision and expectations remained largely unrealized. This is not to deny that there was no success at all for the UN system in any area of environmental concern during these years. On the contrary, the UN had led effective global action in protecting the earth's Ozone layer from thinning caused by Ozone depleting substances (ODS) and in setting up an international legal regime to protect the marine environment from oil pollution. The Vienna Convention (1985) on phasing out the use of ODS within a specific timeframe and the Montreal Protocol (1986) to operationalise the provisions of the Convention were spectacular efforts indeed. Barring such instances, little else could be done by the UN system, in general, to prevent member states from reneging on their environment-related obligations and commitments, a practice that became more the rule than an exception with some developed countries.

The record of the UN system in ensuring the flow of Official Development Assistance (ODA) from the rich to the poor to the tune of 0.7% of the former's GNP (Gross National Product) as envisaged in the UN General Assembly Resolution 2626 (xxv) 24 December 1970 was poor indeed. Barring the Scandinavian countries, most others, including many former colonial powers, fared poorly in funds transfer with their contributions falling well below fifty percent of their targets. On the other hand, the demand for funds grew at an accelerated rate. As more and more countries became independent following the end of World War II and moved towards economic growth, the need for financial and technical assistance grew, a call the rich failed to answer. At the bottom of all these concerns was a procedural factor that discouraged the flow of assistance from the rich to the poor. Under the prevailing dispensation of one country – one vote, the stand of the developing countries based on their vastly large numbers prevailed over the vote of the developed ones on any issue put to vote in UN fora. This became a source of irritation to the developed countries.

Given this emerging adversarial scenario, it could be said that from the 1970s, a climate of chill had set in in the relations between developed and developing countries. Further, the post-war world dominated by two mighty, armed powers and divided by two conflicting politico-economic ideologies saw the formation of new alignments among nations. Tilting the scales in favour of the poor was the entry of China into the UN fold marked by its participation in the United Nations Conference on Environment and Development in Stockholm in 1972. Most of the developing nations preferred to remain non-aligned and banded themselves together under the banner of G-77 which with the entry of China became G-77+China. The numerical strength of the developing countries ensured that their position prevailed in any UN vote, a situation that was galling to the developed group which bore the brunt of UN expenditure.

Global Warming

In addition to the geo-political developments and the concern of exhaustion of natural sources, there emerged in the 1980s an urgent challenge to life on earth in the form of the phenomenon of global warming. It had come to scientists' attention that global temperatures had gone up by more than half a degree Celsius since the beginning of the first Industrial Revolution in 1775. This temperature rise, akin to warming in a greenhouse, was attributed mostly to increasing concentrations of certain gases like carbon dioxide, methane, nitrogen oxides and chlorofluorocarbons in the atmosphere. These Greenhouse Gases (GHGs), as they came to be referred to, being chemically very stable, have a long residence time leading to their build-up in the tropospheric region lying between 6 – 11 kilometres above the earth's surface. Their increasing concentration resulted in the formation of a blanket or an umbrella that trapped the heat released by the earth and reflected it back to the earth's surface. This phenomenon, called 'radiative forcing,' raised temperatures on the earth. This temperature rise continues to this day raising the average global temperature by about 1^0 Celsius compared to what it was around 1775. For interest, it may be noted that the temperature rise is reported to be 1.18 degrees Celsius in 2022.

Climatologists sounded an alarm that if this observed warming trend were to continue unabated and the temperature rise soared to a level of two degrees Celsius – now revised to 1.5 degrees Celsius – over preindustrial levels, the earth's climate would reach a point of no return and touch off several disastrous consequences. The consequences may range from changes in seasons and weather patterns, changes in movements of ocean currents affecting global climate, rising sea levels threatening coastal populations and property, warming and acidification of oceans destroying marine life, heavy rainfall and floods over some parts of the globe and scanty precipitation over some others causing droughts and famines. The melting of polar ice caps that would raise sea levels endangering coastal areas would be another distinct possibility. Hurricanes of increasing fury, though not more in number, would become a common occurrence.

The threat of global warming added a new dimension to the rich-poor confrontation in the form of sharing responsibilities in mitigating the problem and adapting to the changing climatic conditions. Mitigation of GHG emissions was anathema to the poor as it militated against their use of fossil fuels on which their entire economic development was based. They cast the entire burden of mitigation on the rich as the latter alone bore the responsibility for begetting the problem. The first Industrial Revolution began on the soil of the rich and benefitted them immensely in the two centuries following it. Looking to their wealth and technological muscle, the rich alone could afford to take measures to mitigate the challenges not only within their national boundaries but also globally. The rich, as expected, retaliated by repudiating any responsibility for their past and present actions. Climate action emerged as the new battleground furthering the North-South confrontation. More such new areas of discord were to follow.

Species Extinction – The Brundtland Report

In the last Chapter, we had occasion to note the immense impact the publication, **The Limits to Growth**, had on the world that was fast running out of mineral resources leading to the sober conclusion that growth that relied on high consumption of energy and natural resources was unsustainable. To this feared exhaustion was added another concern, the extinction of plant and animal species at an unprecedented rate, much of it being attributed to the destruction of natural habitats in the developing countries. Natural green wealth was being over-utilized in some countries in the tropics to earn foreign exchange and to discharge their staggering external debt burden. As was to be expected, this concern over the loss of green wealth and resulting species extinction was perceived by the poor as yet another ploy by the rich to thwart their growth.

Faced with the widening rich-poor divide on one hand and the urgent need to attend to problems of global warming and species extinction on the other, the UN set up a Commission in 1983 headed by Gro Harlem Brundtland, the then Prime Minister of Norway, to come up with a comprehensive study of the problem. The result was the Brundtland Report (1989) titled *Our Common Future* which highlighted the alarming rate of extinction of plant and animal species in modern times. To give an idea of faunal and floral species loss, the Commission drew attention to the stark fact of the disappearance of almost half of the world's tropical forests which were home to more than half the world's animal and insect species. Agricultural expansion accounted for further loss of forest lands. This crisis was compounded by a bigger one in the form of the loss of fertile topsoil that supported all agriculture. The Commission's finding was that once the global plant and animal diversity and the factors that nurture the diversity were lost, mankind's continued survival would be in jeopardy, a message of caution that deserved to be given urgent attention. Further, the Report warned that impoverishing the earth of its natural endowments would be a crime against future generations as they would stand deprived of the benefit of enjoying the fruits of these resources. Echoing the Inuit saying "We do not inherit the earth from our ancestors, we borrow it from our children", the Report pleaded for a change in the current highly resource-dependent and wasteful model of development to one of 'sustainable development.'

Sustainable Development

Sustainable development was defined by the Brundtland Commission as development **"that meets the needs of the present without compromising the ability of future generations to meet their own needs."** With the publication of the Brundtland Report, environmental sustainability became the main theme of global development. A point of interest about this definition is that it has a second part that is often overlooked. This part reads **"It [Sustainable development] contains within it two key concepts:**

- **the concept of 'needs', in particular the essential key needs of the world's poor, to which overriding priority should be given; and**

- **the idea of limitation imposed by the state of technology and social organization on the environment's ability to meet present and future needs."**

The reason for highlighting this second part is that in arguments over environment and development this part is generally lost sight of or glossed over thereby conveying a wrong impression to the lay public that exhaustion of natural resources like metals and minerals is just around the corner and hence, whatever is left should remain reserved for future generations. That is, sustainable development means non – interference with nature and natural endowments to satisfy even present human needs. A totally misconceived interpretation indeed!

The United Nations Conference on Environment and Development (3-14 June 1992) - Rio Summit

Seized of the challenges that had arisen to sustained development, the UN General Assembly passed Resolution (44/228) on the 22nd December 1989 to convene a Conference in Rio de Janeiro in June 1992 to chalk out a strategy to arrest global warming and universal loss of biodiversity. The Resolution required all countries to accept the urgent need to recognize the enormity and urgency of these challenges and pledge to take not only national action but also cooperate in global efforts.

The UN call for national action and international cooperation ran up against the ground reality of the widening rich-poor divide over their respective responsibilities in combating global environmental problems. The poor were quick to point out that since the rich were historically responsible for environmental ills like global warming and biodiversity loss, they needed to bear full responsibility for taking remedial action today in their own lands and facilitate the efforts in the rest of the world. The latter action consisted of assistance in the form of financial help, transfer of technology and desisting from the adoption of restrictive and protective measures like erecting trade barriers against imports, mostly commodities, from poor countries on health or environmental grounds. The rich struck back with the charge that the contribution of the new, emerging industrial economies like China, India, Brazil and South Africa to both global warming and loss of biodiversity in the last two decades of the 20th century was no less significant than theirs and hence these countries had as much responsibility as the former in shouldering the burden. Such accusations and counteraccusations forebode turbulence at the Rio Conference.

Rio Outcomes

The outcomes of Rio could be split into the following five parts:-

Rio Declaration on Environment and Development and Agenda 21;

UN Framework Convention on Climate Change (UNFCCC) – review and adoption;

UN Convention on Biological Diversity (CBD) – review and adoption;

Release of the Rio Declaration on Forests; and

Discussion on a Convention on Desertification.

Rio Declaration on Environment and Development and Agenda 21

Agenda 21 – the numerals indicating the need for a change in world development strategy in the 21st century – was the base document prepared to comply with UNGA Resolution 44/228 of 22nd December, 1989. The Resolution gave the call to convene an international conference to ensure "the acceptance of the need to take a balanced and integrated approach to environment and development questions". The approach was expected to be a "dynamic programme" meant to reflect "a global consensus and political commitment at the highest level on development and environment cooperation."

The Agenda was in the form of a list of "programme areas...described in terms of the basic for action, objectives, activities and means of implementation." Literally, it was a handbook on the "strategies, plans, policies and processes" to be adopted and followed up by individual nations to achieve the ends of the identified programmes.

The programme areas covered almost all natural resources from air, water and land to forests, mountains and the seas. Management of wastes, conventional and nuclear, and wastes of a hazardous nature also came under its purview. The roles of local, national and international agencies were listed under each one of these programme areas. Importantly, Agenda 21 was much concerned with the need for the flow of international aid and assistance to developing countries to help them play their part in the global endeavour. Noting that international trade had an important role to play in promoting the development of poor countries, the need for trade promotion was also highlighted.

It needs to be stressed here that the Rio Declaration consisting of 27 Principles and Agenda 21 were documents neither on safeguarding the environment at the cost of development nor an endorsement of development unmindful of its adverse impact on the environment. This would be amply clear from a reading of the Preamble to the Agenda which took serious note of the "perpetuation of disparities between and within nations, a worsening of poverty, hunger, ill health and illiteracy ..." along with the "continuing deterioration of the ecosystems on which we depend for our well-being." The Agenda addressed both development and the environment with an eye on maintaining harmony between the two. The same sentiment was echoed in Principle 1 of the Rio Declaration which recognized "Human beings are at the centre of concerns for sustainable development. They are entitled to a healthy and productive life in harmony with nature." Principles 3 and 5 of the Declaration reinforce this sentiment. Principle 3 stresses that the "Right to development must be fulfilled so as to equitably meet developmental and environmental needs of present and future generations" and Principle 5 emphatically states that poverty eradication should be an indispensable requirement of sustainable development. Thus, at Rio, the two seemingly contrasting threads of environment and development were woven together to form a single fabric called "sustainable development".

How do development and environment go together ensuring the sustainability of the former and the conservation of the latter? The answer is to be found in Principles 15, 16 and 17 of the Rio Declaration. These three Principles could be taken as the basic policy guidelines for ensuring harmony between nature and human development.

Principle 15, often referred to as the "Precautionary Principle", states that "In order to protect the environment, the precautionary approach shall be widely applied by states according to their capabilities. Where there are threats of serious or irreversible damage, lack of full scientific certainty should not be used as a reason for postponing cost-effective measures to prevent environmental degradation." A plain reading of this Principle would show that abundant caution must be exercised before embarking on any measure even if there is a mild suspicion of any serious or irreversible impact occurring to the environment as a result of undertaking the measure. Hard scientific evidence to the effect that such an impact is sure to happen should not be insisted upon to give up the measure or to build in cost-effective safeguards. By the same token, mere suspicion of harm to the environment unsupported by any evidence cannot be a ground for giving up the measure or executing it with safeguards at an unaffordable cost.

One should take care to note that Principle 15 should not be construed as a convenient tool to stall or derail project proposals by raising flimsy, imagined grounds of harm to the environment. Where the grounds of possible harm are worth being considered, one should explore the option of undertaking the project by incorporating such preventive measures as may be necessary and at an affordable cost. Insistence on technological or other safeguards where such safeguards are not available or available only at an unaffordably high cost should be avoided. The policy of incorporating "Best Available Technology Not Entailing Excessive Cost (BATNEEC)" – which we had encountered earlier in Chapter III while recounting the UK approach to pollution control – can be said to reflect the true spirit of the Principle. Principle 15 is not a provision to be used as veto power to thwart any project from coming up.

Principle 16, often referred to as the "Polluter pays Principle", has a pedigree in economic theory. The Principle states that the costs of pollution to society caused by an individual's actions should be borne by the individual himself. It is expected that such "internalization of environmental costs" would bring down the incidence of pollution. In Welfare Economics, an unintended side effect of an activity is called an 'externality'. An externality can be good or bad depending on its effect on societal welfare. Pollution is considered a negative externality as it minimizes welfare and hence is called an "economic bad" as opposed to an "economic good".

One common and readily adopted approach to deal with a negative externality referred to as the "command and control" approach, is to ban the production of the good since this would prevent the production of any 'bad' as well. Infractions of the ban could be punished by imposing a penalty. But such a step may not be desirable as the society will have to forego consumption of the 'good' which may have no economically viable and readily available substitute. Hence, economics suggests that in place of penal action, either a tax could be imposed on every unit of externality caused in the manufacture or in use of the 'good' over and above a prescribed limit or by extending an incentive to the producer for not exceeding that limit. The limit could be based on considerations of public health, pollution assimilating capacity of the environment, available technological options to reduce the incidence of the 'bad', and finally, the economic viability of switching over to a less polluting technology or product. Both theory and available experience commend extending incentives as a preferable approach to control negative externalities instead of imposing a penalty. A three-way test of technological feasibility, financial viability and environmental acceptability needs to be applied before embarking on any exercise to set pollution control standards and enforcing them.

An ideal way to avoid negative externalities arising out of any production process or lessen their impact could be to identify *a priori* the possible adverse impacts and build–in safeguards. This step, known as Environmental Impact Assessment (EIA), amounts to a study of local conditions of a site – physical, economic and social – and assessing the possible adverse impact the proposed development may have on local biological features and populations, both in the short and long terms. Where the cost of avoiding the adverse impact outweighs the benefits, the desirability of going ahead with the project will have to be assessed carefully. The project may either be given up or proceeded with by incorporating safeguards against the foreseeable adverse consequences. We shall have more occasion to consider these guidelines in Chapter XII where we take up the issues that often lead to friction between environmental protection and development.

The United Nations Framework Convention on Climate Change (UNFCCC)

We now turn to the problem of global warming, a subject to which we had made a reference earlier in this Chapter. As we saw earlier, this problem described by Ban Ki Moon, a former Secretary-General of the UN, as an "existential threat" to mankind is, primarily, a manmade one. Even at the time of Rio, it had been well understood that though warming may arise out of natural causes, its rapidity since the days of the Industrial Revolution was attributable mainly to anthropogenic activities that released Greenhouse gases (GHGs) into the atmosphere.

As stated earlier, the fear of the occurrence of disastrous consequences of global warming was the possibility of the suddenness of their occurrence. Climate scientists drew attention to the fearsome prospect of humanity reaching certain levels called 'tipping points" which may touch off irreversible changes in climate. Such changes could be in the quantum and rate of precipitation leading to deluges or droughts, loss of biodiversity, sea level rise and submergence of coastal areas, fall in marine fish catch, and increasing intensity of storms and cyclones.

Since the build-up of GHGs in the troposphere (6-11 km above the earth) began with the harnessing of coal and oil as fuel for generating energy to power industrial operations and for transportation of men and materials in the UK, Europe, the US and the developed world in general, it was accepted at Rio that the developed countries should bear a much greater responsibility than developing countries in bringing about cuts in these gaseous emissions. That is, countries have "common but differentiated responsibilities' in meeting the challenge of global warming and consequent climate change and hence needed to act according to their "respective capabilities and their social and economic conditions" in arresting them. Also, in the interests of justice and equity, the developed world had to take the lead in these efforts and aid the developing countries to meet the challenges climate change posed.

The UN Framework Convention on Climate Change (UNFCCC) that was adopted by the Conference of Parties to the Convention in May 1992 at Nairobi came up for review and signature by the Parties at Rio, a month later. The aim of the UNFCCC was to bring down the greenhouse gas concentration in the atmosphere to the levels prevailing in 1990 mainly through the efforts of the developed countries. For this purpose, these countries were grouped under two annexes to the Convention. Annex I listed all of them including the "economies in transition", that is countries that were earlier a part of the Soviet Block. Annex II consisted of the developed countries most of which were members of the OECD. All the rest fell under neither list and came to be referred to as "Non-Annexe I Countries." The call for bringing down the GHG emissions to the 1990 levels was directed only at the Parties in Annex I. The rest were given a general exhortation to bring down their emissions of Greenhouse gases. They also got an added protection in that the efforts they were expected to make in this direction and in adapting themselves to adverse climate change would be contingent on the aid they would receive for the purpose from the developed countries.

The discord that arose at Rio over the UNFCCC could, to a large measure, be attributed to the US stand on the relative responsibilities of developed and developing countries in causing the problem of global warming and in taking steps to reduce their emissions of gases that led to such warming. The US, while accepting the historic role of developed countries in bringing about the perilous situation, was opposed to paying any compensation to the developing countries for the damage caused. Further, the US stand was that some of the developing countries like China and India had emerged as significant emitters of Greenhouse gases and hence could not remain without any obligations being cast on them to reduce their emissions. In this context, the US economic situation in the mid and late 1980s and in the 1990s needs to be kept in mind.US trade deficits were growing due to the rise of China as a major industrial power with access to the huge US market for its exports. The quiet industrial advancement of South Korea and the rise of Asian economic Tigers were added factors of concern not only to the US but to other rich countries as well.

Given the state of global trade and the differing positions of leading exporting and importing countries on market access, border controls, and taxes, measures to arrest global warming by limiting emissions of

Greenhouse gases were apprehended to make industry in the developed World, particularly in the US, less competitive in comparison with the industry in developing countries like China. In addition, the supposedly lax environmental restrictions on the industry in the developing world giving them a cost advantage was another fear that haunted industry in the developed world. President Bush (Sr.), a Republican, observed quite laconically that" We are exercising prudence, but not becoming hysterical about this problem."

While the autarchic mindset of Republicans in the US was well known, it was surprising that even Democrats joined the fray by maintaining that countries exempted from quantitative obligations to cut emissions under the Climate Change Convention and its adjunct, the Kyoto Protocol (1997), could not expect to prosper by exporting their way to the US. Hence, for the US, accepting any responsibility to reduce emissions of these gases without corresponding action by China and India amounted to accepting trade and economic sanctions imposed on it. Thus, due to purely trade and economic reasons, the climate impasse continued for over two decades till the successful passage of the Paris Climate Agreement in December 2015.

Convention on Biological Diversity (CBD)

The CBD had the following three aims for being negotiated and adopted:-

Conservation of biological diversity;

Sustainable use of biological resources, plant, animal and soil; and

fair and equitable sharing of biological resources.

Third World countries had much cause to be happy over the adoption of the CBD. Many of them have immense plant and animal wealth the occurrence and utilities of which have been preserved either in texts or through oral tradition. The CBD, as it emerged after much debate, fully reflected the spirit and content of the Principles of Agenda21. The Convention recognized the 'sovereign right of states, that is, Parties to the CBD, to exploit their natural resources pursuant to their own environmental policies' (Article 3). This right carried with it the authority to 'determine access to genetic resources' subject to national legislation (Article 15). The contracting Parties were called upon to create conditions to facilitate access to their genetic resources for environmentally sound uses only. Conservation of plant and animal species, both *in situ* and *ex-situ* was encouraged (Articles 8, 9).To minimize the adverse impact of development measures on natural ecosystems, Article 14 of the Convention laid down that before taking up any such work, an assessment of possible environmental impact be made and safeguards built in to minimize the impact.

On the sensitive issue of Intellectual Property Rights (IPRs) over natural resources and their extracts and the possibility of exploitation and piracy of the biodiversity wealth of poor nations by others, the CBD provided that states could regulate the sharing of results of any research and development undertaken by the latter as well as the sharing of benefits of any commercial uses of such research and development through legislative, administrative or policy measures (Article 15). Further, under Article 16(5), the Convention cautioned that IPRs should not run counter to the objectives of the Convention, the principal one among them being that in the conservation of global biodiversity the whole of humanity had a stake even though individual states may have the sovereign right to exploit their natural resources and control access to them by others.

The CBD was followed by three adjuncts, the Cartagena Protocol (2000), the Aichi Protocol (2005) and the Nagoya Protocol (2010). The objective of the first was "to contribute to ensuring an adequate level of protection in the field of the safe transfer, handling and use of living modified organisms resulting from modern biotechnology that may have adverse effects on the conservation and sustainable use of biological diversity." With growing populations and food shortages accentuated by phenomena like global warming and the rediscovery of the medicinal values of many a plant and microbial species, the scope for the introduction of genetically modified crops in agriculture or for production of pharmaceuticals had increased greatly. So was the threat of bio piracy to the plant and animal wealth of Third World nations. Facilitation and protection of such deviant practices through conferral of Intellectual Property Rights on the predatory discoverer from the North would hurt the world at large, not to speak of the impoverished resource provider be it a country or an indigenous tribe or community.

The CBD imbroglio offers an interesting insight into the extent to which the two principal political factions in the US differed and continue to differ in their perceptions over such issues given the same facts and conditions. Barring the notable exception of President Richard Nixon, a Republican, other Heads of the US Executive had always been less keen on any initiatives, global or local, that necessitated more federal regulation or circumscribed the authority of the constituent states of the nation. The attitude of the Republicans was best captured by Senator Bob Dole, a Republican, according to whom the US had laws and regulations governing "nearly every aspect of life... we regulate almost to the point of being absurd..." meaning thereby that the US had enough legal cover to protect its biodiversity and did not need to subject itself to any international legal regime in this regard. It was clear that apprehension of loss of US national sovereignty over law making on national issues was at the root of the Republican opposition. Republicans always had a doctrinal aversion to any threat, real or imagined, to their national law making authority.

Opposition to becoming a Party to the CBD was only a manifestation of that mindset.

The same basis of adequate national legislation being available to protect the nation's biodiversity was used by the Democrats in the US to desist from becoming a party to the CBD. President Clinton, a Democrat, observed that "There are hundreds of state and federal laws and programs and an extensive system of federal and state wildlife refuges, marine sanctuaries, wildlife management areas, parks and forests. These existing programs and authorities are considered sufficient to enable any activities necessary to effectively implement our responsibilities under the Convention [CBD]." Therefore, President Clinton argued that the US was in a position to discharge its obligations under the CBD even without becoming a Party to the Convention.

Besides nursing an aversion to international agreements governing issues of national relevance, the US had another reason for opposing the CBD. This was a purely a commercial one in the form of protection of intellectual property rights (IPRS) over knowledge acquired on the economic and therapeutic values of natural resources like plants and microbes. Science had got over the limitation of reproduction of species from being a biological one to one of non-biological intervention like asexual reproduction. In the early 1990s, conferral of IPRs on processes and products of such biotechnological advances was the subject of intense discussion under the title of "Trade Related Intellectual Properties (TRIPS)" at the talks held under the aegis of the World Trade Organization (WTO). India, a biodiversity – rich and scientifically advanced pharmaceutical manufacturing nation feared that TRIPS would result in bio-piracy on a large scale and pave the way for the birth of an era of neo-colonialism, a fear that haunts India to this day. Hence, India and other developing countries welcomed the CBD with its assurances of the sovereignty of nations over their genetic resources. On the other hand, the US argued that the basic tenets of the CBD and of the WTO agreement being negotiated were asymmetric with each other.

Rio Declaration on Forests

Rio provided the forum and an opportunity for the world community to demonstrate how the loss of global biodiversity and global warming were related to each other and how mitigating one would contribute to mitigating the other too. The Declaration of a "Non-legally Binding Authoritative Statement of Principles ..." to govern the "Management, Conservation and Sustainable Development of All Types of Forests" was the result of hectic efforts to secure this objective. While emphasizing the vital role of forests in supporting "all forms of life" on the planet, the Declaration asserted that "Forests are essential to economic development" and "Forest conservation and sustainable development policies should be integrated with economic, trade and other relevant policies." [(Para 13 (g) of the Declaration]. The Declaration cautioned that since forests have multiple uses, they need to be managed "sustainably". The Principles recognized that since the benefits of forest conservation in any country accrued not only to that country but to the entire world community, the latter should share the costs of conservation equitably. The objectives of the Rio Principles on Forests were quantified by the Aichi Protocol of 2005 (an adjunct to the CBD) which aspired to reduce the rate of loss of forests by at least half and where feasible, to be brought down to zero by the year 2020.

UN Convention on Desertification

Desertification in Africa, mostly created and perpetuated by nature, was in part a man-made problem too as the African Savannah was cut and laid waste by the colonial masters in the centuries gone by. Following the growing concern for the environment generated by

Stockholm, UNGA passed a Resolution (31/108) in 1976 paving the way for convening a UN Conference to deliberate on the problem of desertification and its resolution, with particular reference to the situation in the Sudano-Sahelian region of Africa. The next year UNGA approved a Plan of Action to combat desertification and followed it up with a Programme of Action for African Economic Recovery and Development in the period 1986 – 1990. However, from the beginning of the 1980s, as the call for deliberations over problems like the Thinning of the Ozone Layer, accelerating loss of global biodiversity and climate change came to occupy the central stage of global concerns, African nations felt that the issue of desertification was being lost sight of and hence insisted on its inclusion in the Rio (1992) agenda. Following this impetus, negotiations on a desertification convention began in 1993 and a Convention was adopted in June 1994. It came into force two years later. That it would address the problems of Africa on priority was highlighted by its long title "United Nations Convention To Combat Desertification in Those Countries Experiencing Serious Drought And/or Desertification, Particularly in Africa".

With all the attention paid to it at the time, one expected the Desertification Convention to emerge as a success story. Alas, it was not to be so. The rich nations showed little interest in the Programme of Action as reflected by their disinclination to allot funds for "effectively and equitably managed, ecologically representative and well-connected systems of protected areas." To the rich, desertification was a problem in distant lands which held little economic interest to them. Hence, the Convention remained "the most underinvested of all conventions" (William Dar).

Rio Summit – An appraisal

A question that has often been raised about the Rio Summit is whether it was a success or a failure. This ambiance of doubt is in contrast to the scene of all-round accolades showered on Stockholm. The answer, perhaps, lies in comparing two world gatherings that, though on the same theme, had different scopes. The first highlighted how development, as understood and practiced since the beginning of the First Industrial Revolution, and population growth had brought about environmental degradation and the global need to arrest the trend. The second showed the way to achieve development without adversely affecting the environment and keep the development sustainable. Stockholm was, by its very nature, full of generalities and pious statements which, as is normally the case, go down well with governments and the lay public. On the other hand, specifics, as dealt with at Rio, tend to get shrugged off. Stockholm erected the guidepost, Rio laid the guide path. Generalities are easy to agree with, but specifics are not. The two require different criteria to evaluate their merits.

The conviviality that marked Stockholm earned it the badge of success. With Rio, on the other hand, the gloom that preceded it and the acrimony that marked it led to it being pronounced a failure. Even those who saw much good to have resulted from Rio preferred to remain circumspect in their overall evaluation as typified by the remark of Blomquist (a former Foreign Minister of New Zealand) that "Overall, however, skepticism is prudent". Similarly, a major compact like the Convention on Biological Diversity adopted in the teeth of opposition from the US was termed as "being too timid" by Jacques Delores of the European Union, a group that should have appreciated a strong protective wall erected against arrivals of genetically modified food products from across the Atlantic. Strange are the ways in which developments in the international arena are perceived by different nations! Each country looks at them from its own limited perspective.

Post -Rio developments - Kyoto Protocol (December 1997)

While the UNFCCC drew humanity's attention to the urgent need to check global warming, it was couched more in terms of a statement of intention and exhortation than as an operational document. While it cast responsibility primarily on the rich to shoulder the greater part of the burden of mitigation, it remained unspecific in detail on the expected contribution of each one of them and the modalities of measuring their efforts, methods of reporting and verification of the results reported. An adjunct to the UNFCCC in the form of a protocol attending to these details was, therefore, considered necessary. The result was the Kyoto Protocol negotiated between 1994 and 1996 and finally adopted in Kyoto, Japan in December 1997.

The Kyoto Protocol was applicable to a list of 41 countries of which 27 fell under the description of "developed" and 14 were former "command economies" then making a transition to "market economies". The Protocol identified a list of four distinct gases (Carbon dioxide, Methane, Nitrous oxide and Sulphur hexafluoride) and two families of gases (Hydrofluorocarbons and Perfluorocarbons) as having global warming potential and hence to be targeted for reduction of their releases into the atmosphere. The overall objective of the Protocol was to bring down global GHG emissions by 5% from their 1990 levels as envisaged in the UNFCCC. Emission reduction targets were thus prescribed for 36 countries to be achieved in the period 2008-2012 A novel feature of the Protocol was to create a market for emission reductions achieved by a Party over and above its commitment (Article 6). These carbon credits, subject to their approval by the Conference of Parties, could be sold to other Parties that fell short of their commitments. This was the first step to recognize clean environment as a good that could be traded at the market.

Did the Kyoto Protocol succeed in meeting its goals? It did not. The main reason for this failure was the refusal of the US, the then biggest emitter of Greenhouse gases, to ratify it. Despite the positive approach of the then US President Bill Clinton and Vice-President Al Gore, the US Executive stumbled at the Senate to get the ratification through. In July 1997, a period during which negotiations on the Kyoto Protocol were going on, the US Senate adopted the Byrd-Hagel Resolution that foreclosed the possibility of the US becoming a party to the Protocol or any agreement under the UNFCCC "unless the protocol or agreement also mandates new specific scheduled commitments to limit or reduce greenhouse gas emissions for Developing Country Parties within the same compliance period". This was a direct reference to countries like China and India being left out of commitments and being vested with a perceived competitive advantage in world trade. This became amply clear when the Senate Resolution went further and forbade the US from becoming a party to any agreement or protocol under the UNFCCC that "would result in serious harm to the economy of the United States". A "detailed explanation" of the legislative or regulatory steps that would be required to be taken in the event of the US joining any protocol or agreement "accompanied by an analysis of the detailed financial costs and other impacts on the economy of the United States" was also insisted upon by the Resolution. Passed by a 98-0 vote in the US Senate, the Byrd-Hagel Resolution precluded any possibility of the US becoming a party to the Kyoto Protocol.

What was worth noting was the ground truth of the working classes in the US being against the introduction of any restrictions on industries dependent on coal and coal mining. These industries formed the backbone of revenues of some states and employed large numbers of labour. The mood of the Senate was either one of denial of the phenomenon of global warming altogether, or if it did exist, then to explain it away as being due to natural causes with man having no role in it. Thus, while the young and the intelligentsia in the US desired curbs on GHG emissions, their lawmakers chose to swim with the mood of the working classes in opposing such measures, the Republicans out of conviction and the Democrats out of political expediency.

Refusal by the then biggest emitter of greenhouse gases, the US, to become a Party affected the Kyoto Protocol in two ways. One, it delayed the coming into force of the Protocol till 2005 and two, it encouraged some other developed countries like Canada to stay away and some others who became a Party, like Japan, to renege on their commitments to reduce emissions. A stocktaking done in 2016 of the progress made by Parties in achieving their emission reduction targets in the First Commitment Period to the Protocol (2008-2012) revealed that of the 36 countries that were assigned targets including the 18 countries of the EU as a block and the 18 "Economies in transition" had all achieved their targets partly through their indigenous efforts and partly by taking recourse to permitted devices like the purchase of carbon credits, joint implementation and CDM (Clean Development Mechanism) provided in the Protocol. For instance, the EU's average annual degree of emission reduction expressed as a percentage reduction of GHG emissions below 1995 levels, was only 11% compared to the target of 18% set by the Protocol, the shortfall having been made good by other means.

Some observations on how some nations achieved their targets in the First Commitment Period would provide interesting reading. For Germany, reunification in 1991 came as a blessing in that it led to the hectic closure of inefficient public industrial enterprises (about 7,000 in number) in the former Eastern part at the rate of twenty a day. The German government which would have pulled the shutters down on these units for solely economic reasons, now had a virtuous reason for doing so as the units, using coal or lignite as fuel, were emitting vast quantities of carbon dioxide. With their closure, reunified Germany could meet its Kyoto target and even exceed it. It could share the surplus with other EU nations in meeting the target set for the EU as a whole.

There were other gainers by default. Russia (erstwhile USSR) gained carbon credits due to the secession of many territories of its former Federation. Industries located in the former socialist Republics were notorious for their high carbon emissions. The selection of 1990 as the base year for emissions reduction in the UNFCCC favoured Russia and the "command economies" as their base year emissions were so high due to obsolete plant and technology that they could meet their Kyoto targets with little effort like closing down the plants. In the process, they could also earn high carbon credits which could be traded with the countries of the EU to enable the latter to meet not only their own targets but also help meet the targets of the EU as a community. These sales of "hot air" proved lucrative. Later, when the EU introduced a system of allocation of carbon credits to its constituent countries to be reallocated to their industries, the same set of emission permits was transferred more than once from one buyer to another leading to multiple uses of a single permit.

The course of climate discussions spread over more than a decade brought home many a lesson on how to find a solution to a global problem, the chief among which being the voluntariness of individual country targets and a pledge to fulfill them. The US attitude to Kyoto revealed that it would not be possible to make much headway in global emissions reduction without the US taking part in the campaign and that prescription of targets for the Parties by an external body –which may even be the UN – was not the best approach to combat the problem. The problem was decidedly global but its alleviation lay in national action by the major emitters. Hence, the efforts expected of individual countries must be voluntary with the caveat that their efforts should be ambitious enough to arrest global warming within the timeframe dictated by science. Further, the mode of implementation of the voluntarily accepted targets should be left to be decided by the countries themselves. This approach of common but differentiated responsibilities guided by national capabilities and ambition came to govern all future negotiations starting with the Bali Action Plan (December 2007) and culminating in the Paris Agreement on Climate Change in December 2015.

Select References

"Our Common Future: The Brundtland Report", Brundtland Commission, 1987, Oxford University Press

"Agenda 21, UN Conference on Environment and Development", Rio de Janeiro, Brazil, 3 to 14 June, 1992, UN Department of Economic and Social Affairs (DESA)

"The United Nations Framework Convention on Climate Change", United Nations 1992

"Kyoto Protocol To The United Nations Framework Convention on Climate Change" December 1997

"The Convention on Biological Diversity (CBD)" 1992

"The Byrd-Hagel Resolution" 25 July 1997, US Senate, Congress. Gov. S.Res.98

"Kyoto Protocol's Carbon credit scheme increased emissions by 600 m tonnes", Arthur Neslen in The Guardian, 24 August 2015

Chapter VI

Conceptual Foundations of Sustainability

Jam Today, Jam Tomorrow

Over the years following the release of the Brundtland Report and continuing to this day, sustainable development has been the subject of much scholarly analysis by economists, sociologists and political scientists. A substantial body of literature has been built around this concept but the nature of the subject is such that the last word has yet to be pronounced on it. Much of this debate is attributable, quite deservedly, to the somewhat cryptic definition of the concept itself as given in the Report of the Brundtland Commission. Over seventy definitions are said to be available of the concept. Basic questions have been raised on what is supposed to remain sustainable, whether it is economic development or the integrity of natural ecosystems and life-supporting systems, and for how long. This prompted sweeping criticism of the type that sustainable development is a contradiction in terms because "development and sustainability obey opposing logistics" (Abu Khairul Bashar). A harsher view has it that it is "no more than a "catchphrase than a revolution of thought "and a ruse to sustain the pursuit of business-as-usual." One who saw much merit in the concept initially but got disenchanted as things unfolded, commented "…it seemed that world leaders and development experts were attempting to atone for the negative side effects that unbridled economic growth unleashes. While sustainable growth had the potential to become the basis on which further positive economic and environmental reforms were introduced worldwide, it has in fact served to further justify and reinforce the very paradigm that it initially sought to deconstruct" (Hilary Howe). In general, critics, particularly economists, have engaged themselves in either welcoming the concept or in denouncing it.

Looking at critical reviews like the above, one would naturally be interested in plumbing their basis and provocation. Such views could have arisen either due to disappointment on the part of the believers of the concept of sustainable development over the way things turned out in practice following the lofty ideals talked about by world statesmen in the 1970s and 1990s in the Summits at Stockholm and Rio or due to the wide spectrum of subjects brought under the ambit of Sustainable Development reducing the concept to a vague wish list. More importantly, the concept itself had come up against sharp criticism on ideological and theoretical grounds from economists of repute.

Precept and Practice

As noted in the last Chapter, Rio (1992) ended on a positive note stressing the principle of sustainability to underpin development. But, the undercurrent of rich nations' interests that thwarted the attempts to arrest global warming or conserve global biodiversity or promote the SDGs left the world community in apprehension over the sincerity and extent of cooperation that could be expected from the rich in combating global environmental problems and in assisting the poor to meet their own needs. The record of some rich nations was too discouraging to be overlooked. The negative response of the biggest emitter of Greenhouse Gases at the time, the US, to the call to become a party to the Kyoto Protocol or the Convention on Biological Diversity or the Basel Convention on the Transboundary Movement of

Hazardous Wastes provided the handle for the hardening of the poor's apprehensions into distrust.

The Kyoto Protocol adopted in December 1997 had to wait till 2005 before it was ratified by the requisite number of 55 states together accounting for 55% of the global emissions of GHGs. Even after it came into force, major developed nations performed poorly in meeting their commitments to bring down their GHG emissions to levels specified under the Protocol. It was evident that these acts were indications of the rich refusing to abide by international agreements on the environment due to their national economic interests, international trade competitiveness, and an unwillingness to contribute to the development efforts of the poor. Having failed to discharge their commitments towards reducing their Greenhouse Gas emissions under the first phase of the Kyoto Protocol (2008-2012), many of them showed little interest in accepting any commitments for the second phase (2012-2020). As a result, nothing significant was achieved on the climate change front in the twenty years following Rio. Given this backdrop, it was natural for cynicism to set in over the true intentions of the developed nations towards efforts to arrest not only global warming but other pressing environmental problems as well.

Second, there was thinly veiled criticism that the concept of sustainable development as enunciated in the Brundtland Report and in Agenda 21 of the Rio Declaration was vague and too general to be translated into practice and needed modification to be applied to specific situations. As if anticipating such a comment, the Brundtland Report had conceded that "No single blueprint of sustainability will be found as economic and social systems and ecological conditions differ widely among countries. Each nation will have to work out its own concrete policy implications. Yet, irrespective of these differences sustainable development should be seen as a global objective."(P.51 of the Brundtland Report). The conclusion that is to be drawn from this passage is that the concept of sustainable development is not a ready recipe for development but is more a word of caution and clarification.

Third, an important reason for the rise of the critics' ire over the developed countries was the reluctance on the latter's part to share the enthusiasm of the UN in pursuing the Principles of Agenda 21 agreed to in Rio (1992). As a consequence of poor fund flow to kick-start action on Agenda 21, poverty rates remained high in developing countries with an estimated 2.8 billion people – almost half the world population at the time – earning less than two dollars a day per capita. Besides the abysmal living conditions, the incidence of HIV/AIDS worsened substantially among the poor. Rightly, the 1990s were called "a lost decade" (Das Gupta) though with a silver lining in the form of a rise in school enrolment and literacy in the least developed countries.

The overall situation on the eve of the Johannesburg Conference of the Commission on Sustainable Development in 2000 was one of gloom and this was a pointer to the Conference's poor outcome. It was not surprising that bodies like The World Resources Institute were unsparing in their criticism of the course of the deliberations at Johannesburg. Singling out the US, a representative of the World Resources Institute remarked "For months, the US denigrated the importance of this Summit, and fought to limit its agenda. The rest of the world gave in to that negative leadership. Issues were swept off the table. No binding agreements to improve the lives of the poor, value and protect biodiversity, create incentives to reduce the global economy's massive use of materials, or protect the Earth's climate was ever on the agenda." It would appear from critical remarks like these that they were actuated not so much by the practical difficulties in translating Agenda 21 into practice but more by the palpable disinclination of rich nations to help others to do so.

The Ideological Debate – Sustainable Development and Welfare Maximization

Apart from inimical practical developments whittling down faith in the merits of sustainable development, the concept became a subject of much academic examination too. The critique of sustainable development by economists has been quite varied and interesting. Barring some, most have been quite critical of the concept. The thesis of the critics is that sustainability and development are entities independent of each other and the twain shall never meet. Dingler categorically dismisses the unification of the two in the following words: "The economic subsystem is striven to be independent of the ecological subsystem. Economically [economic] resources are transported and processed very fast, ecologically these resources [ecological resources] are discharged slowly. Distances are economically bridged easily, ecologically more difficulty transported [transported with difficulty]. Economy tries to a large amount to unify singularities, to make them tradeable, whereas ecology depends on diversity." Dingler arrives at the conclusion that "the orders of both subsystems cannot go together and therefore would produce instabilities."

The pantheon of critics of sustainable development is a large one. Two titans of social cost-benefit analysis, Little and Mirrlees, see sustainable development as a contradiction in terms. According to them, sustainability, as one understands it, is essentially aimed at the welfare of future generations. It may or may not be supportive of measures to promote present welfare even if such measures are very much desirable. Therefore, they see sustainability as a poor criterion for the appraisal of projects intended for today's welfare. They mince no words when they say "Sustainability has come to be used in recent years in connection with projects.... it has no merit. Whether a project is sustainable (forever?-or just a long time?) has nothing to do with whether it is desirable. If unsustainability were really regarded as a reason for rejecting a project, there would be no mining and no industry. The world would be a very primitive place".

It is difficult to extend unqualified support to the above arguments. They are based on a limited understanding of development as a two-dimensional process involving economic and social aspects only and limited to the present day. They overlook the fact that events since the beginning of the Industrial Revolution had led to a fall in the quality of life and this pointed to a missing dimension to the growth process, namely, the environmental sustainability of the very process of development. Development should not only take place now but should also remain sustainable over time so that it does not end as a passing show. Hence, we need to move away from dismissive views on environmental sustainability and turn to reasoned discourse.

Four Forms of Capital

Sustainability of any form of capital means its continued existence and availability, that is, its assured inexhaustibility. Capital itself is of four types, Natural, Human, Social and Cultural, and Built capital. Natural or environmental capital refers to land, water, air, minerals, flora, and fauna and the capacity of nature to assimilate wastes generated by man. Natural capital provides both goods and services (including intangible services) to man. Social and cultural capital is made up of "social networks, political systems, trust and reputation" and "influence and power."

Given this fourfold division of capital, it is readily seen that the 'capital' whose 'sustainability' environmentalists are worried about is 'natural capital'. The Brundtland Report and Agenda 21 were both concerned with conserving natural capital as the world moved forward with economic development. Both advocated caution and wisdom in this exercise for a strong reason, namely that life on earth, today and tomorrow, depended solely on the continued availability of natural capital. It is noteworthy that some of this capital, like forests, is capable of renewal while others like metals and minerals are not. With this preamble, we can proceed to look at the different schools of thought on the relevance and soundness of the idea of sustainable development.

Nature First School

First, let us take the two extreme views, one a hands-off approach towards nature and the other a development-at-all-costs approach. The first is generally canvassed by green activists and philosophers of the 'Deep Ecology' school and has little concern with – rather it has scorn for – economic issues. This school would like natural resources to be left totally undisturbed so that they are available for enjoyment by future generations in much the same measure as they are enjoyed by us today. This argument could be extended to other forms of capital too like a heritage monument (an example of manmade capital) or even to preserve intangible gains to human beings in the form of amenity values arising from natural scenery. For instance, the protests against the construction of the massive Three Gorges Dam in China rested, among other things, on the site's scenic beauty which found special mention in Chinese literature.

The nature-first school has acquired considerable strength in recent times thanks to the recognition of what is called "ecosystem goods and services" and their value to man. This school looks at the natural environment as a complex web of species and their subspecies and a complex array of processes known and yet to be known to man. This web of entities, their mutual interactions and their exchanges with the non-living environment provide goods and services of enormous value to man. For instance, the natural process of pollination performed by bee populations results in a contribution of $ 700 billion to the global economy annually. If bees were to be affected by spraying crops with unfriendly pesticides, the world will be a big loser. Yet another estimate made in 1997 had it that "the economy of the services of all global ecological systems and the natural capital tasks that produce them" was, on an average of the order of "an astonishing $33 trillion a year". In comparison, the "Gross Global national product total" was 'around $18 trillion per year" (Constanza et. al). Given the economic significance of natural ecosystems for life today and in the future, it is axiomatic that the wise use of natural endowments must rank high in any strategy of economic development.

Substitutability, Complementarity and Sustainability

Welfare economists look at the deployment of different forms of capital with the object of maximizing society's welfare now and later. In doing so, they observe that some types of capital are substitutes for one another whereas some others act as complements to each other. Under substitutability, where one form of capital can be substituted by another, for example, coal (natural capital) in power generation by an array of solar cells (manmade capital), the depletion of natural capital (coal resources) does not affect welfare as substitute fuel and methods of power generation are available. In contrast, complementarity of capital means that for the deployment of one form of capital to promote welfare, availability of another form of capital is necessary. For example, for a paper mill (manmade capital) to function, continued availability of wood from a source in the form of a forest – which is natural capital – is necessary. The paper mill (manmade capital) and the forest (natural capital) providing the wood are complementary to each other and hence should coexist. This is possible through a judicious operation of the paper mill, matching its requirement of wood with the regenerative capacity of the forest.

In addition to substitutability and complementarity, economists look at another feature of capital, namely its sustainability. They draw a distinction between 'weak sustainability' and 'strong sustainability' of capital. Weak sustainability obtains where the availability of any form of capital is fairly large and hence it can be substituted by another form of capital to a good extent. For instance, if the availability of wood is substantial, then more and more investments would be made to set up paper mills. That is, natural capital in the form of forests would tend to get replaced readily by manmade capital in the form of plant and machinery. Hence, forests and the wood they provide are said to have weak sustainability. On the other hand, strong sustainability is witnessed where the possibility of substitution of one form of capital by another is limited or non-existent. If the fish stock (natural capital with no substitute) in a river is limited, deployment of more boats (manmade capital) may land more fish for a while but there may be no fish thereafter till the next fishing season. Hence, the fish get protection from overfishing and the fish stock can be said to have strong sustainability. Also, the fish population and the boats deployed are complementary to each other.

In the light of the fourfold classification of capital and the sustainability of its forms, one can conclude that, in general, any development process dependent on the use of natural capital would remain sustainable so long as the natural capital is limitless or capable of regenerating itself to keep pace with its exploitation but would be unsustainable otherwise. Technological developments may bring about greater efficiency in the process of substitution of natural capital and prolong its availability but this may not go on indefinitely.

Pro-growth School

None of the above arguments, however, seem to matter to the pro-economic growth school. To this school, maximization of the welfare of the present generation matters most and hence should be accorded a higher priority over the welfare of future generations. This school sees no difference between the concept of welfare maximization and economic development at the expense of capital having weak sustainability. That is, natural capital, in general, can be substituted by manmade capital at will to maximize welfare. Hence, to this school, welfare maximization today and sustainable development are one and the same thing. Therefore, it is argued that there is no need to purvey 'sustainable development' as if it were some radically new concept. What matters to the pro-growth school is that so long as total capital is left intact, whatever its composition, humanity is not worse off than before. On the contrary, future generations may end up even richer than the present one because the depletion of one form of capital and its substitution by another might have enhanced the total capital bequeathed to them. Therefore, there is no virtue in the present generation leaving natural capital undisturbed and as intact as it is found.

Daly's Rules of Sustainability

It would, indeed, be useful to discover a golden mean between the pro-growth and no-growth schools. For this, we need to look at the work of the American Economist, Herman Daly who depicted the dependence of man on natural resources in the form of a pyramid.

DALY'S PYRAMID

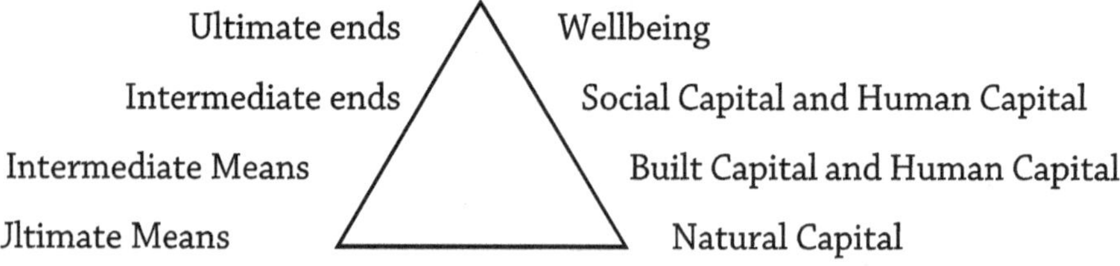

[Note: Daly's Pyramid was inspired by the earlier work of Donella Meadows]

Daly's Pyramid shows that the ultimate means to satisfy human needs and wants lies in natural resources only and since not all these resources are renewable, prudence would dictate that this limitation should govern natural resource-based human development. Daly went on to reduce this conclusion to three rules called "Daly's Rules of Sustainability" which may be stated as follows:-

- the withdrawal of resources cannot exceed the regeneration of resources;

- waste generation cannot exceed the ecosystem's ability to process waste; and

- in the long term, non-renewable resources cannot be utilized at all.

Daly argues that while welfare may remain the same when capital of weak sustainability is substituted by manmade capital, it would not be so when capital of strong sustainability is so treated. The Daly thesis rests on the ground that if two forms of capital are complementary to each other, then the two need to coexist to realize welfare maximization of the society at present and in the future. Daly cites the illustration of fish and boats to drive home this argument; if fish were in abundance, deploying more boats may net more fish, but there is little virtue in netting the fish to exhaustion as the society would soon stand deprived of fish and end up loaded with redundant boats, a situation of net loss in welfare. Given time and protection to spawn and hatch, fish are a renewable resource. If, however, they are netted during spawning season too, then over time the water source would be totally bereft of fish.

Daly's approach has much to offer in chalking out a strategy of sustainable development. It supports the practice of harnessing natural capital for human welfare with the caution that such harnessing should not lead to total depletion of the resource; second, the weaker the sustainability of the type of natural capital, the more one can afford to be liberal in substituting it with manmade capital with the caveat that the stock of the substituted capital left does not fall below a critical level. But where the sustainability is strong as it is with complementary forms of capital, it would be wise to recognize the complementarity and not attempt much substitution. For instance, where a water source caters to the drinking water needs of a community, there is hardly any gain to society's welfare by diverting the water to other uses.

Sustainable Production and Sustainable Consumption

What emerges from the above discussion is that sustainable development really means sustainable production and sustainable consumption "with limitations imposed by the present state of technology and social organization on environmental resources and by the ability of the biosphere to absorb the effects of human activities". Broken down into its components, it calls for efficiency and economy in resource and energy use in all forms of human activity, from agriculture to industrial production, transportation, communication, lifestyles, recreation, and leisure. Care for the environment is a built-in feature of this mode of development. This transformation, however, would be a slow process as it involves a change in mindsets and lifestyles, premature retirement of existing productive assets, an extra burden on current financial resources, and a drop in current national incomes, all of which would invite societal resistance.

To minimize social resistance, sustainable development should be understood in the context of a country's current level of development and the gap between this level, as indicated by its human development indices, and acceptable minimum standards, whether it be in the area of per capita energy consumption or nutritional requirements or education or health care. This would mean, as the Brundtland Commission clarified, that no single sustainable development strategy can be adopted by all countries nor any such strategy should be forced upon all. Differentiated approaches tailored to suit individual country contexts need to be arrived at. This implies that where the basic human development needs have been fully met, as in developed countries, sustainable development would mean addressing issues other than minimum development goals. These could be steps like emission reductions to combat global warming, material, and energy efficiency in industrial production and transportation, arresting biodiversity loss at home and abroad, and desisting from exploration and extraction activities to win oil, gas, and minerals in fragile ecosystems like the Arctic or the Tundra.

As for the least developed countries, the content of the list of sustainable development measures is clear. Attainment of minimum acceptable levels and standards of housing, drinking water, sanitation and public health would remain their primary goals of development for decades to come. Besides this, some of them like the small Island nations in the Pacific face the prospect of disappearance from the world map due to sea rise touched off by global warming. It is churlish to expect these climate-sensitive and other not-so-sensitive but nonetheless delicate members of the world community to undertake any degree of responsibility to combat global problems.

The situation of countries that were earlier called developing countries and which have emerged as major industrializing nations in the last three decades, namely Brazil, India, China, and South Africa (BICS), offers a big challenge to defining what sustainable development means to them. Despite their economic advancement in recent times, large swathes of their populations lack the satisfaction of basic human needs like food, water, shelter, and health care. A bitter colonial past had been a burden on two of them, India and South Africa, well into the twentieth century. Given the nature and size of the task of development, it is worth looking into the contribution expected of these countries in the efforts to combat universal issues like global warming. Also, looking inward, it is worth examining how far the substitutability of natural capital can be pushed in pursuing economic development in these countries, particularly in a large democracy like India. As we do this, we would profit immensely if we keep in mind the words of Dasgupta: "We are embedded in nature; we are not external to it. No amount of technological progress can make economic growth as conventionally measured an indefinite possibility. Ours is inevitably a finite economy, as is the biosphere of which we are a part."

Select References

"Our Common Future: The Brundtland Report", Brundtland Commission, 1987 Oxford University Press.

"Critiquing Sustainable Development: A Meaningful Way of Mediating the Development impasse", Hilary Howe, Undercurrent, Volume 1, No.1, 2004.

"The Value of the World's ecosystem services and natural capital", Robert Constanza et.al.1997, Nature, Vol.387, Issue 6630, Pages 253-260.

"Dasgupta, P. (2021), The Economics of Biodiversity: The Dasgupta Review", February 2021.

"Blue Planet Prize: A Better Future for the Planet Earth: Prof. Herman Daly, Interview, Summary"

"Indicators and Information Systems for Sustainable Development; Donella Meadows, 1998 – A Report to the Balaton Group, published by The Sustainability Institute, Hartland, VT.

Chapter VII

Sustainable Development – The Future We Want

Leaving No One Behind

The Three Transformations

In earlier chapters, we traced the history of the environmental movement in Europe and the US from the time of the Industrial Revolution to the first two decades of the 21st Century and the theoretical discourse on the concept of sustainable development. Perusing the chronicle of events, one would have noted that the movement underwent three distinct transformations over time. The first spanning the late 18th and the first half of the 20th. centuries was the gradual change from the movement being a predominantly nature conservation campaign to a human welfare movement encompassing issues of public health, sanitation, and spatial planning in human settlements in the then-emerging industrial societies of Europe and the New World. In the second phase, starting from the 1950s and up to the 1970s, it turned into a movement against pollution of air, water, and land caused by unchecked industrialization and was confined mostly to the richer nations. With the Stockholm Declaration on the Human Environment (1972) and the slew of international agreements that followed with their concern for the need for economic growth and its compatibility with social and environmental goals, the movement entered its third and current phase, namely Sustainable Development. A diligent observer of the environmental movement would not fail to note that the movement is no longer understood as an environment versus development tussle but a campaign for life with dignity today and tomorrow with minimal adverse impact on the environment.

The three transformations had widely different motivations, that of the first was improving urban living conditions benefiting the rich and the poor alike; the second was the fear of the arrival of an apocalypse in the form of a populous planet bereft of natural resources and healthy life supporting systems, a fear that haunted the rich more than the poor; and the third, a compromise ensuring equity among nations in terms of economic growth and welfare as the world proceeded to deal with environmental threats of a global order like climate change to which both the rich as well as the poor contributed. Each transformation left its mark on global thinking and action. The first saw public awakening to a high degree regarding living conditions in Europe, the UK, and the USA but hardly concerned itself with the colonies which constitute much of today's developing world. The second transformation was all pervasive casting fear in the hearts of the poor that the environment movement was a ploy of the rich to keep their own consumption levels high and keep the poor, poor forever. The poor felt, and not without justification, that the rich having already attained high standards of economic and social welfare could afford to return to matters of aesthetics and leisure like care for the natural environment at home and abroad. In the poor's reckoning, indulging in environmental concerns was a pastime of the elite.

The third transformation reflected the veering of the North-South dialogue to an agreed choice of development priorities for all. This called for a new development paradigm. Development had to be interpreted as a multidimensional effort encompassing economic issues like reduction in the numbers of people living in absolute poverty, narrowing income inequality among and within nations, betterment of welfare and social conditions like health care, housing, sanitation, education, and gender equality and finally, paying attention to environmental imperatives like protection of terrestrial and marine ecosystems and stabilization of global climate as these formed the life support system of the planet.

Our Common Future and **Agenda 21** were two bold and broad attempts of the last quarter of the 20th Century to bridge the environment and development divide. These two historic developments led to the formulation of specific operational milestones, namely the eight **Millennium Development Goals (MDGs)** and their sequel, the seventeen **Sustainable Development Goals (SDGs)** with as many as 160 targets to be achieved in the first two decades of the 21st. Century. Of course, one should hasten to add that sustainable development is a much larger area of human, social and environmental concerns than the number of goals identified as MDGs or SDGs. The MDGs and SDGs as spelt out marked only the beginning and not the end of the exercise of moving into a sustainable development mode of life and progress.

Johannesburg (2000) - Millennium Development Goals (MDGs)

Though the MDGs had their origin in Agenda 21 (1992) they had to wait for eight years to be translated into specific goals and targets. The reason for this delay was not hard to seek. From the developing world's point of view, though Rio '92 was a success so far as its decisions were concerned, the experience of translating the decisions into practice was not easy. This needed transfer of resources of a high order from the rich to the poor, a proposition which the former were never enthusiastic about. The reluctance was palpable. As a consequence, poverty rates remained high in developing countries with an estimated 2.8 billion people – about half of the world population at the time – earning less than two dollars a day per capita. Besides abysmal living conditions, the incidence of HIV/AIDS worsened in the African continent, home to a sizeable proportion of the world's poor. Barring a significant "improvement in school enrolment and literacy", the rest of the conditions in the poor world were such that the decade 1990-2000 was to them, as Das Gupta put it, "a lost decade".

Faced with this not-so-happy situation post-Rio, the UN General Assembly met in New York in September 2000 to adopt the Millennium Declaration to hold an international conference in Johannesburg later in the year. Despite the fanfare that accompanied the Declaration, the Johannesburg meet was expected to be a lacklustre one due to US disinterest and attempts to limit the Conference agenda. Belying the foreboding of turning out to be barren of results, the meet proved to be a success for both the UN and the poor in that it laid before the world community a set of goals called **Millennium Development Goals (MDGs)** of utmost relevance to the poor.

Millennium Development Goals

- To eradicate extreme poverty and hunger;

- To achieve universal primary education;

- To promote gender equality and empower women;

- To reduce child mortality;

- To improve maternal health;

- To combat HIV/AIDS, malaria and other diseases;

- To ensure environmental sustainability;

- To develop a global partnership for development.

The eight goals with 19 targets and as many as 60 Indicators had poverty alleviation as their foremost priority backed by a resolve "to halve" the proportion of the world's people whose income was less than one dollar a day or who were struck with hunger or did not have access to safe drinking water, all by the year 2015. Delivery of basic health services to all, reduction of environmental threats to health, increasing access to sanitation, reducing infant mortality and provision of public schooling were other areas of intervention in the list of MDGs. Thus, in a departure from the 20th Century Conference norm of expressing only lofty ideals, the 21st Century norm turned out to be one of action spelling out specific objectives (goals), targets, and schedules.

The MDGs were not unrealisable. A stocktaking done by the United Nations Development Programme (UNDP) in 2015 showed highly encouraging progress in the achievement of the goals. Fund flow had increased and this was reflected in good all-round performance. The number of people living in extreme poverty fell by half from what it was in 1990. Similar was the achievement in the population suffering from malnourishment. Mortality among children below the age of five went down by half and maternal mortality came down to 45% worldwide. Enrolment in primary schools went up to a staggering 91%. Detailing the achievements, UNDP observed that "even the poorest countries can make dramatic and unprecedented progress with targeted interventions, sound strategies, adequate resources and political will…" and that "the 15 year effort has produced the most successful antipoverty movement in history."

The successful implementation of MDGs, however, was marred by the fact that in many countries the reported benefits of economic growth were not evenly distributed. Further, rapid growth led to increased energy consumption and faster depletion of natural resources to such an extent that the environmental cost exceeded the economic and welfare gains. These shortcomings of the MDG effort were soon addressed by the UN system, as we shall see below.

Rio+20 - World Summit on Sustainable Development - "The Future We Want" (2012)

To overview the progress made in the direction of sustainable development in the two decades following Rio (1992) and keeping in mind the consensus on MDGs arrived at in Johannesburg (2000), the UN General Assembly adopted a Resolution in December 2009 (Res. A/RES/64/236OF 24 December 2009) to convene a conference in Rio in 2012. Popularly referred to as 'Rio+20', the conference had the inspiring theme **"The Future We Want"**. The theme highlighted the three pillars of sustainable development, namely economic growth, social improvement, and environmental integrity. The eponymous declaration that came out at the end of the conference noted the long way that still remained to be covered to reach the basic minimum development goal of poverty eradication in many regions of the world, particularly Africa (para 105 of the Rio+20 Declaration). Much stress was laid on "sustained, inclusive and equitable growth in eradicating poverty and hunger and achieving Minimum Development Goals" (para 106 of the Rio+20 Declaration). It was agreed that a set of sustainable development goals should be drawn up for consideration at the next UN Sustainable Development Conference in 2015.

Before passing on to the Conference of 2015, let's look at the deep distrust the developing countries had of any suggestion made by the rich. At Rio+20, the developed countries and many private institutions working in the area of economics and environment had an interesting suggestion to offer on how to implement and realise sustainable development. Noting that the movement that began with the Rio Summit in 1992 had not taken off on the scale expected, they suggested a new approach to the problem. The suggestion called "Green

Economy" was to make economies function with almost total reliance on green and renewable inputs under a market-based approach that favoured the production and consumption of such green goods. This would, it was suggested, lay down a level playing field and take care of the reservation that internalising environmental concerns in the production process was an imposition on the economy, making the goods produced uncompetitive. A 'Green Economy' that demanded only green goods would make green concerns an integral part of the goods and services provided by the market and thus make the environment a market force influencing demand and supply. To encourage green markets to come up, the EU suggested a level playing field for green goods and services vis-à-vis normal products by eliminating subsidies extended to the latter and by imposing eco-taxes.

Despite its appeal, the suggestion of promoting a Green Economy met with rejection by the developing countries on the ground that the technologies behind the production of green goods and provision of services were generally protected by Intellectual Property Rights (IPRs) held by private firms in the developed countries and hence the suggestion to promote a green economy was a ploy to keep the scientific and technological superiority of the developed nations intact and make them suppliers of goods and services to the entire world. Green Economy was looked upon as an instrument of commercial and trade colonialism. Despite this reverse, the idea of a 'Green Economy' continued to survive and make a comeback, as we shall see in Chapter IX.

UN Conference on Sustainable Development, New York 2015 - "Leaving No One Behind"

The task of drawing up a list of Sustainable Development Goals with targets and schedules as desired at Rio+20 was taken care of by the UN Conference on Sustainable Development that took place in New York in September 2015 coinciding with the 70th Session of the UN General Assembly. Taking guidance from the MDGs which had identified the objectives and goals of utmost relevance to the poor and after interviewing nearly 4.5 million people in different parts of the world, a set of 17 goals with as many as 169 targets was adopted to be achieved in the timeframe of 2015-2030. The effort elicited high praise with the UNDP describing the SDGs as "a set of universal goals that meet the urgent environmental, political and economic challenges facing our world" and a three-dimensional "plan of action for people, planet and prosperity". The drawing up of the SDGs was such a monumental step that the SDGs came to be referred to as Agenda 30.

Given the fanfare that heralded the adoption of the SDGs, a question that arises naturally is whether global progress is on course to achieve the SDGs by 2030. For this, we may look at the assessment report submitted by the UN Secretary–General to the UN Commission on Sustainable Development (UNCSD) in July 2019 based on the National Reports submitted by the member – countries. A summary of the Goals and Progress recorded in achieving them is given below.

Sustainable Development Goals (2015-2030) and Progress (2019)

SDG 1: No Poverty

Goal: To eradicate extreme poverty by reducing the number of people living below the poverty line – defined as income of less than $1.25 per capita per day – by at least half.

Progress: The share of the world population living in extreme poverty declined to 10% in 2015 from 16% in 2010 and 36% in 1990. However, the pace of poverty reduction was decelerating with 8.6 percent in 2018 and [projected] 6 percent in 2030. Eradication of poverty fully by 2030 did not appear to be possible.

SDG 2: Zero Hunger

Goal: To ensure all people access to safe, nutritious and sufficient food and end malnutrition by 2030. In doing so, the Goal called for ensuring sustainable food production systems with a word of caution to maintain genetic biodiversity of seeds, cultivated plants and domesticated animals and their wild relatives by 2020.

Progress: World population of the undernourished went up from 784 million in 2015 to 821 million in 2018. Of the former population, 22% falling in the age-group of Zero to five years was stunted. Among the stunted children, a significant number was affected by either wasting or obesity.

SDG 3: Good Health and Wellbeing

Goal: Bring down by 2030, the global maternal mortality ratio to less than 70 per 10,000 livebirths; reduce preventable deaths of new born and of children below 5 years of age; end epidemics like AIDS, TB, and Malaria; by 2020, halve the number of global deaths and injuries from road traffic accidents. [For those who view sustainable development as involving only green concerns, prevention of loss of lives in road accidents would surely come as a surprise and drive home the comprehensiveness of the concept!]

Progress: Child mortality dropped appreciably from 9.8 million in 2000 to 5.4 million in 2017; incidence of Tuberculosis among children fell by 20% between 2000 and 2017. In the same period, vaccination helped greatly in bringing about an 80% drop in deaths due to measles. Incidence of Malaria, though, was on the increase.

SDG 4: Education

Goal: Ensure inclusive and equitable quality education and promote lifelong learning opportunities for all.

Progress: Among all the goals, Education and Gender Equality recorded the least progress. In 2017, 262 million children and youth aged 6 to 17 were still out of school and more than half of the children and adolescents were not meeting proficiency standards in Reading and Mathematics.

SDG 5: Gender Equality

Goal: Achieve gender equality and empower all women and girls.

Progress: While some indicators like a fall in the prevalence of genital mutilation and early marriage showed improvement, the overall numbers continued to be high. Structural issues which were at the root of gender inequality such as legal discrimination, unfair social norms and attitudes and sexual partner violence of girls and women in the age group 15-49 continued to remain.

SDG 6: Clean water and Sanitation

Goal: To achieve universal and equitable access to safe and affordable drinking water for all by 2030.

Progress: Percentage of population availing of safely managed water services went up from 61% in 2000 to 71% in 2015 and remained unchanged in 2017. Basic drinking water facilities became available to another 19% of the population during 2000-2015. Safely managed sanitation services could be accessed by 43% of people in 2015 and 45% two years later as opposed to 28% in 2000. Despite these notable achievements, an estimated 785 million still lacked such minimal facilities. 700 million people were compelled to defecate in the open. One-third of countries experienced medium or high levels of water stress. As of 2019, most countries were unlikely to have full implementation of integrated water resources management even by 2030.

SDG 7: Affordable and Clean Energy

Goal: Ensure access to affordable, reliable, sustainable modern energy for all.

Progress: Access to electricity in the poorest countries had begun to accelerate, energy efficiency continued to improve and renewable energy was making gains in the electricity sector. Despite this progress, some 800 million people remained without access to electricity. Global Primary Energy Intensity Ratio improved as it fell from 5.9 in 2010 to 5.1 in 2016. The percentage of global population having access to clean cooking fuels went up from 57% in 2010 to 61% in 2017. Still, close to three billion had no access to clean fuels.

SDG 8: Decent Work and Economic Growth

Goal: Promote sustained, inclusive and sustainable economic growth, full and productive employment and decent work for all.

Progress: Global growth rate of real GDP per capita which stood at 1.9% in 2017 appeared to remain almost unchanged being about 2% in 2018-2020, a figure significantly less than the 3% rate attained in 2010. The real GDP growth rate in Least Developed Countries (LDCs) was expected to go up from 4.5% in 2017 to 5.7% in 2020 compared to the target of 7%. Globally, labour productivity had increased and unemployment was back to pre – 2008 financial crisis levels but the global economy grew at a slower rate than projected. Unemployment had fallen.

SDG 9: Industry, Innovation and Infrastructure

Goal: Promote intensive and sustainable industrialization to raise industry's share of employment and GDP significantly, and promote innovation and infrastructure.

Progress: While financing for economic infrastructure and mobile communications had made impressive progress in developing countries, many of these countries were lagging behind in doubling the manufacturing industry's share of GDP by 2030. Share of manufacturing in employment declined from 15.3% in 2000 to 14.7% in 2015 and to 14.2% in 2018. The intensity of global carbon dioxide emissions from manufacturing industries declined by more than 20% between 2000 and 2016 to 0.30 kg. of CO_2 per US$ showing a decoupling of CO_2 emissions and economic growth.

SDG 10: Reduced Inequalities

Goal: Reduce inequality within and among countries

Progress: In more than half the number of the 92 countries that reported, income of the bottom 40% of the population grew faster than the national average between 2010 and 2016. This segment received 25% of the overall income.

SDG 11: Cities and Human Settlements

Goal: Cities and human settlements should be inclusive, safe, resilient and sustainable in terms of housing, basic services, public transport, reduced mortality and protection from natural disasters.

Progress: One out of four urban residents lived in slum-like conditions in 2018. Two billion people did not enjoy waste collection facilities; nine out of ten residents breathed polluted air.

SDG 12: Sustainable Consumption and Production

Goal: Arresting the growth of global material consumption – Ensure sustainable consumption and production.

Progress: Worldwide material consumption had expanded rapidly as had material footprint per capita seriously jeopardising the achievement of this Goal as well as other goals broadly. In 2017, worldwide material consumption reached 92.1 billion tons, up from 87 billion in 2015 and a 254% increase from 27 billion in 1970 with the rate of extraction accelerating every year since 2000. Without urgent and concerted political action, it was projected that global resource extraction could grow to 190 billion tons by 2030.

SDG 13: Urgent Action to Combat Climate Change

Goal: Reduce global Greenhouse gas emissions to limit global temperature rise to not more than 1.5 degrees Celsius above pre-industrial levels. For this to be achieved, global GHG emissions need to fall to 55% of the 2010 level by 2020 and continue to fall steeply to zero by 2030.

Progress: Instead of progress, there has been regression in achieving this goal. GHG emissions reached new 'highs' with global average level of CO_2 emissions reaching 405.5 parts per million by volume (ppmv) in 2017 from 400.1 in 2015; that is, 146% of pre-industrial levels.

SDG 14: Marine Resources Conservation

Goal: Conserve and sustainably use oceans, seas and marine resources for sustainable development

Progress: Due to overfishing, fish stocks within biologically sustainable levels declined from 90% in 1974 to 66.9% in 2015. However, both protected sea area and marine biodiversity areas covered by protection went up between 2000 and 2018.

SDG 15: Terrestrial Biodiversity

Goal: Protect, restore and promote sustainable use of terrestrial ecosystems

Progress: Between 2000 and 2018, the extent of protected terrestrial biodiversity area increased from 33.1% to 46.1% of the total biodiversity area; from 30.5% to 43.2% in freshwater areas; and from 32.9% to 44.7% in mountain areas in 2019.

SDG 16: Peace and Inclusivity

Goal: Promote peaceful and inclusive societies for sustainable development, provide justice to all and promote inclusive institutions.

Progress: Progress was less than desired with the number of homicides going up, though slightly, and attacks on women and children on the increase.

SDG 17: Global Partnership

Goal: Revitalize global partnership for sustainable development

Progress: Despite calls for raising development assistance flows, net ODA flows went down to US$ 149 billion in 2018, a drop of 2.1% in real terms compared to 2017. Bilateral ODA to LDCs fell by 3% in real terms from 2017, aid to Africa shrank by 4% and humanitarian aid fell by 8% in real terms.

The message conveyed by the Report of the UN Secretary-General was, indeed, a grim one. As of 2019, the world was way behind schedule in meeting the targets under the seventeen SDGs by 2030. The global predicament was best expressed by the Secretary-General himself in these words "The natural environment is deteriorating at an alarming rate; sea levels are rising; ocean acidification is accelerating; the last four years [2015-2019] have been the warmest on record; one million plant and animal species are at risk of extinction and land degradation continues" ..... "It is abundantly clear that a much deeper, faster and more ambitious response is needed to achieve our 2030 goals." The Secretary-General called for "mainstreaming Sustainable Development Goals into national plans, policies and budgets".

SDG Transformations

One common feature that emerged after examining the Voluntary National Reports submitted to the UNCSD by member countries in 2019 on the progress they had made in achieving SDGs was that there was a lack of appreciation on the part of national policymakers of the interconnection and synergy among the Goals. This pointed to the need to adopt a coordinated approach in operationalizing the implementation of programmes under any Goal. To drive home this vital point, a report authoured jointly by the Sustainable Development Solutions Network (SDSN) (an agency promoted by the UNCSD) and a private foundation, Bertelsmann Stiftung, with the economist J. Sachs in the lead, identified six groups of interconnected SDGs and named them "Six Transformations". [Table below]

	SDG Transformations	**SDGs involved**
1.	Education, Gender and Inequality	1-5, 7-10, 12-16, 17
2.	Health, Wellbeing and Demography	1, 2, 3, 4, 5, 8, 10
3.	Energy Decarbonisation and Sustainable Industry	1-16
4.	Sustainable Food, Land, Water, Oceans	1-3, 5-6, 8, 10-15
5.	Sustainable Cities and Communities	1 – 16
6.	Digital Revolution for Sustainable Development	1-4, 7-13, 17

The rationale behind the grouping of the 17 SDGs into Six Transformations is strong as for instance good health and wellbeing are not attainable under conditions of poverty, hunger, lack of education, gender inequality or lack of economic growth. Hence, policies and actions under these goals must complement each other. Likewise, the protection of marine and terrestrial biodiversity is equally important for combating undernourishment among the poor as aquatic life provides the poor with needed proteins and mineral supplements. Similarly, to achieve energy decarbonisation and promote sustainable Industry or to develop Sustainable Cities and Communities, a sea-change in policy and action is called for interlinking all SDGs. No Goal stands alone.

To measure achievement and rank countries according to their performance in the attainment of SDGs, the SDSN Report developed a composite Index scoring system. The Index figures could be used for assessment of the performance of groups too like the OECD, EU or the G-20. For instance, the G20 countries – of which China and India are members – represent two-thirds of the world population, 85% of gross global domestic product and over 75% of global trade. The G-20 together account for 80% of global energy-related CO_2 emissions. Their achievement of SDGs or lack of it affects global performance significantly. For instance, if only China could reduce its energy-related emissions by two tons of CO_2 per capita per year (equivalent to 69.1% in China's current level of emissions) the world would be 31.4% closer to achieving the SDG target for CO_2 reduction.

Linked to the performance index is the "Spillover Score" which represents quantitatively the impact of a country's performance or lack of it in attaining its target under a SDG on the overall global result in achievement under that particular SDG. For instance, if India were to achieve its target of "Zero Hunger", as much as 23.1% of the global shortfall in performance under this SDG would have been met. Again, if India eradicates undernutrition which currently affects 14.5% of its population, the world would be 25.2% closer to achieving the SDG target on reducing undernutrition.

Despite its apparent merits, the SDG approach to addressing global economic, social and environmental problems has had its critics too. While the CSD Conference of 2015 was hailed by Mary Robinson, a former President of Ireland as the "Bretton Woods moment of our generation", the venerable journal 'The Economist' trashed the 169 SDG targets as "ambitions on a Biblical scale" that would flounder due to paucity of resources. The estimated fund requirement of US$2-3 trillion a year over a fifteen-year period (about 15% of annual global savings) or 4% of world annual GDP for achieving the targets under various SDGs was way above the current stipulated ODA level of 0.7% of GDP of the developed countries, a much lower commitment that was being honoured in the breach.

The vital issue of financing sustainable development in developing countries had been the point of consideration in two earlier UN conferences this century resulting in two international compacts, namely the Monterrey Consensus (2002) and the Addis Ababa Action Agenda (July 2015). Following the lead given by these two agreements and assuming a requirement of US $300 per capita as the requirement for realising the SDGs, Kharas and McArthur estimated the fund gap at around US $ one trillion and suggested that it could be bridged through a combination of three devices, namely, Domestic Resource Mobilization (DRM) by the developing countries (US$ 160 billion), stepped up ODA (US$ 200 billion) and lending by the Multilateral Development Banking (MDB) system (US$1.4 trillion), netting a total of US $ 1.8 trillion. Therefore, as the resources gap to implement the SDGs can be closed, the need of the hour is the will to act on the part of governments and judicious spending.

There have been reservations over the achievability of some SDG targets, particularly for poverty alleviation and ending child malnutrition. According to the World Bank, meeting the target of reducing poverty to the extent of bringing down the population of the global poor to 3% would be difficult. This goal would mean that by 2030, the entire world except Sub-Saharan Africa would be above poverty and sub-Saharan Africa will have only 200 million population, a scenario considered unrealistic as today South Asia alone has 300 million poor and eradicating poverty in this region totally by 2030 would be a major challenge (Magnus Hatlebakk).

Looking at another example, in the matter of ending all forms of malnutrition in just fifteen years (2015-2030), the target for South – Asia, where 50% of children are malnourished today "seems unrealistic". Equally doubtful is the realisation of the target of reducing child mortality in all countries to 2.5% by 2030 when the rate today in Sub-Saharan Africa is 10%. Overall, according to Hatlebakk, "the important targets of reducing poverty, mortality and malnutrition are set at a level that seems out of reach within 2030."

SDGs and Planetary Boundaries

More doubts have been raised about achieving the targets under some of the SDGs due to there being an inherent conflict between the so-called socio-economic goals (SDGs 1-12) and the environmental goals (SDGs 13-15). This leads us to look at what are called "Planetary boundaries" (Rockstrom et. al) within which human societies need to operate lest they run the risk of falling victim to an environmental catastrophe of their own making. The table below lists the planetary boundaries and the extent of space available to humanity to operate.

Planetary Boundary	Parameters	Boundary	Current status	Pre-Industrial
Climate Change	CO_2 ppm	350	398.5	280
	Radiative Forcing (watts/sq.m)	1	1.5	0
Ocean Acidification	Aragonite saturation	2.75	2.90	3.44

Stratospheric Ozone	Dobson Units	276	283	290
(i) Bio-geochemical Flows (N)	Mill.tonnes removed from atm./yr	35	121	0
(ii)Bio-geochemical Flows(P)	Mill. Tonnes entering Oceans/yr.	11	8.5-9.5	-1
Freshwater Use	K cu.m./yr per person	4	2.6	0.415
Land Use change	% global land converted to Cropland	15	11.7	Low
Biosphere Integrity	Species/mill. Extinction/ yr.	10	Less than 100	0.1-1
Aerosol Loading	Particulate matter in the Atmosphere	---- Yet to be determined ----		
Introduction of novel entities		---- Yet to be determined ----		

CO_2 = carbon dioxide; ppm = parts per million by volume; Aragonite = a crystalline form of Calcium Carbonate found in marine environment forming coral reefs; N = Nitrogen; P = Phosphorous; K = 1000

As can be seen from the Table, humanity has already crossed many planetary boundaries and is poised to remain so in the foreseeable future, thereby raising several existential questions. Global temperatures are already one degree Celsius (revised to 1.18^0 Celsius in 2022) higher than what they were 250 years ago due to the concentration of CO_2 in the atmosphere (398.5 ppm) going well above the safe limit of 350ppm. It is worth repeating that 350ppm may touch off unintended consequences like floods due to excessive rainfall in some regions and droughts in some others. An increase in the number of strong cyclones and a rise in sea levels adversely impacting coastal areas are hazards the world has been forced to grapple with. Worse still, the capacity of the atmosphere to store Greenhouse Gases without leading to a temperature rise of more than $1.5\text{-}2.0^0$ Celsius is now almost fully exploited thereby limiting the scope for further releases of such gases into the atmosphere. Since the emission of CO_2 and other GHGs is a necessary side effect of industrial and agricultural progress, the limitation of atmospheric space to store more of such gases would affect development in the major emerging industrial economies like India greatly. Equally frightening is the consequence of increasing concentrations of Nitrogen and Phosphorous in the marine environment due to fertilizer run-off from agricultural fields. This would mean restricting the production and use of known synthetic fertilizers, a step that would impact the global food situation adversely.

In addition to pointing out how perilously close we are to the Planetary Boundaries, Rockstrom et.al, in their systems model **'Earth 3',** caution that if we continue taking steps to achieve the SDGs in a business-as-usual way from 2018 to 2050, then "human societies [may] become richer, in the sense that people live in countries with higher GDP per person, but they live in more unequal societies and in an environment that is increasingly damaged by human activity." Growth without equity and without acceptable environmental quality is an unwelcome prospect!

What we need, therefore, is an optimised model of achieving SDGs that takes care of both poverty eradication and issues connected therewith and narrowing income inequality without overlooking critical environmental concerns. Poverty eradication should lead sustainable development efforts as "a world in which poverty is endemic will always be prone to ecological and other catastrophes."(Brundtland Report) We shall take up this issue for greater discussion in the next chapter where we would be dealing with "Sustainable Development and India" and later in Chapter X on "Green Economy and India". To give a foretaste of what lies ahead, it would suffice to state that the purpose of the mission of planned development India embarked upon in 1951 and which continues today in a new form has been on all fours with the concept of sustainable development.

Select References

"Our Common Future" The Brundtland Report.

"Agenda 21".

"The Millennium Development Goals Report 2015, United Nations Development Programme New York 2015".

"Report of the Secretary-General on SDG Progress 2019, Special Edition" United Nations.

"Building the SDG economy: Needs, spending and financing for Universal achievement of the Sustainable Development Goals", Homi Kharas and John McArthur, Global Economy & Development at Brookings, Working Paper 131/ October 2019.

Chapter VIII

Sustainable Development and India

Is sustainable development a totally new concept for India? A look at India's ancient culture and religions in Chapter I showed us that it was an inalienable part of the Indian way of life and long preceded its discovery by the western world. India's post-Independence economic history would show that the tradition continues.

Development Planning in India

State planning for socio-economic development has been the principal feature of the economic history of independent India for nearly three-quarters of a century. The nascent Indian republic derived its inspiration and authority to play this role from its Constitution which, in its Preamble, declared that "We, The people of India" had "solemnly resolved ....to secure to all its citizens "Justice, social, economic and political; Liberty of thought, expression, belief, faith and worship; Equality of status and of opportunity......." In interpreting its role in the economic life of its people, the Indian state was guided by the socialist example of state planning as practiced in the then Soviet Russia and adapted it to suit India's own democratic ideals. The Indian experiment was geared to usher in a 'mixed economy' involving the private sector with the state retaining its control over the "commanding heights" of the economy.

Parallels to Sustainable Development

A look at the objectives of India's Five Year Plans from their beginning in 1951 would surprise one with the similarity between them and the goals of the latter-day concept of sustainable development. The objectives of India's plans, namely economic growth with equity and social justice, full employment, self-reliance, and modernization are congruent with the principles of sustainable development which we had seen in the last Chapter. Further, a notable feature of development planning and its implementation in India was its parallel process of growth and distribution of the benefits of growth and not growth first, distribution later. Equitable and Inclusive growth has been the focal point of India's plans in much the same way it is with sustainable development. This similarity between India's development plans and the SDGs was highlighted by India's Prime Minister Narendra Modi at the UN Sustainable Development Summit in September 2015 thus: "Much of India's development agenda is mirrored in the sustainable development goals. Our national plans are ambitious and purposeful; sustainable development of one-sixth of humanity will be of great consequence to the world and our beautiful planet."

It is interesting to note what India's early planners thought of what the country needed at the time of its independence and what it would need in the years to come. This defined the objectives of planned development of an impoverished economy of 340 million people and was best summed up in the First Plan thus: "The central objective of planning in India at the present stage is to initiate a process of development which will raise living standards and open out to the people new opportunities for a richer and more varied life....Economic planning has to be viewed as an integral part of a wider process aiming not merely at the development of resources in a narrow technical sense but at the development of human faculties." Portraying planning as a serious practical mission and not an academic exercise, the planners declared that "While development planning is an all-embracing process, which cannot be compartmentalized, the accent of endeavor under present conditions in India has to be on economic development...

economic development of an underdeveloped country cannot proceed far unless the community learns how to get from its resources of men and materials a larger output of commodities and services." Resource efficiency underlined the planning and implementation effort.

Specific Objectives

It would be worthwhile to recapitulate the specific objectives of each of India's 12 Five Year Plans and the results achieved as that would help bring out the enormity of the Indian exercise and the likeness between the planned approach to prosperity in India and the goals of sustainable development. Each Plan laid emphasis on one or more than one objective in keeping with the needs of the time. Thus, mindful of the harsh reality of a vast, poor, populous land suffering from hunger and spending precious foreign exchange on importing food grains, the planners accorded high priority to agriculture, irrigation, and prevention of soil erosion in the First Plan (1951-56). As a result, the area under irrigation went up by 26.25 million hectares (MHA) and food grain production increased from 54 million tonnes to 65.80 million tonnes. The economy grew by 3.6% annually. This period also marked the beginning of the era of construction of large, multipurpose river valley projects like the Damodar and Hirakud that provided assured water for irrigation and power generation besides playing the role of a flood control mechanism. The Plan was a success and its emphasis on agriculture has since been a feature of almost all later plans, a mark of tribute to the farsightedness of the pioneers of state planning in India.

The First Plan helped create an atmosphere of economic stability encouraging the planners to turn their attention to the modernisation of the economy. Since any modernisation of a centuries-old agricultural economy in a short duration hinged on the development of basic and heavy industries, the Second Plan (1956-61) shifted gears accordingly. To encourage the participation of the country's private enterprise in this effort and to channel private investment in the right direction, the Government of India announced the Industrial Policy Resolution, 1956 and the legislature enacted the Industrial Development and Regulation Act, 1956 to give effect to the Resolution. These measures ushered in a 'mixed economy' in India and formed the bedrock of the state's efforts to establish a 'Socialistic Pattern' of society. The 4.3% growth in national income achieved during the Second Plan fell slightly short of the target of 4.5%. The result would have been better but for the foreign exchange shortage that plagued the economy during the period.

Take Off Stage -Heavy Industry

The unqualified success of the First Plan and the moderate success of the second encouraged planners to conclude that India had reached the "take-off" (a term coined by the economist W.W.Rostow) stage of growth and hence could become a self-reliant and self-generating economy. But this great expectation underlying the Third Five Year Plan (1961-66) failed to materialize with growth falling sharply to 2.8% against the expected 5.6%. A redeeming feature of the Third Plan, however, was its recognition of family welfare in the form of family planning as a core developmental concern. The following three years (1966-69) saw orderly economic planning and growth being disrupted by inimical developments on the country's borders resulting in a war in 1971. Despite these adverse conditions, the period 1966-69 saw the preparation and implementation of three annual plans and the Green 'Revolution' comprising the distribution of high-yielding varieties of seeds, extensive utilisation of the irrigation potential already created, and control of soil erosion. The experience of this long seven-year period (1966-73) was to prove beneficial later. The 'Green Revolution' turned the food grain deficit nation into a food grain surplus one. In the meanwhile, more hurdles were to arise which almost halted planning and development between 1975 and 1979.

The vicissitudes of India's politics during the years 1975 – '79 marked by the imposition of a national emergency followed by political turmoil cast their shadow on the country's economic management. These were also years of famines necessitating large-scale imports of wheat. However, this forgettable period had a silver lining in the form of the 42nd. Amendment to the Constitution which came into effect in January 1997. This Amendment made protection of the environment a part of the "Directive Principles of State Policy". A newly introduced provision, Article 48(A), read as follows: "The state shall endeavor to protect and improve the environment and to safeguard the forests and wild life of the country." Another provision included in the list of "Fundamental Duties" of the citizens of India reiterated protection of the natural environment. The relevant provision Article 51A. (g) made it a fundamental duty of the citizens "to protect and improve the natural environment including forests, lakes, rivers and wild life, and to have compassion for living creatures;".

Jurisprudential developments that followed these newly introduced provisions defined and enlarged their scope by elevating a citizen's right to a clean environment to a fundamental right under the Constitution and enforceable in law. A whole new body of green jurisprudence thus came into being, a monumental development quite unique to India. In addition, under the authority conferred upon it by Article 32 of the Constitution, the higher judiciary began entertaining plaints from interested citizens on the state's lapses in safeguarding the environment. This constitutional empowerment of the citizen known as 'Public Interest Litigation (PIL)' has been a landmark in India's environmental jurisprudence since then. The higher judiciary became the guardian of the environment.

Garibi Hatao

Despite the lull in economic planning in the years 1975-79, the quest for attaining self-reliance and eradication of poverty ('Garibi Hatao') continued. The next effort, the Sixth Plan, 1980-85 pursued the modernization of technology, particularly in the agricultural sector. The Sixth Plan saw national income go up by 5.7% compared to the target of 5.2%. Food, work and Productivity formed the foci of interest in the Seventh Plan (1985-90) during which GDP grew by a high 6%.

The year 1991 was a watershed in India's politico-economic history. The slew of economic reforms announced in July 1991 unshackled private enterprise from almost all of the restrictions constraining it till then and the state vacated much of its space on the commanding heights of the economy as an invitation to private enterprise to take over the vacated area. With the introduction of a vastly liberalized trade and investment regime, the Indian economy truly became integrated with the world economy. Foreign direct investment as well as foreign portfolio investment flowed in. The reforms of 1991 could well be called the Second Coming of independent India, a development that was soon to make India an emerging major industrial power. National income went up by 6.8% as against the target of 5.6% during the Eighth Plan period (1992-1997).

Amidst all the historic developments of 1991, the motto "Growth with Social Justice and Equity" continued to remain the goal of planning and was a special feature of the Ninth Plan (1997 – 2002). The Tenth Plan (2002 – 2007) gave special attention to social goals like gender equality, literacy, infant and maternal mortality and the provision of clean drinking water to all. The annual rate of growth of GDP remained a healthy 7.6% during the Tenth Plan. The favourable investment climate created in the country began to attract substantial direct as well as indirect investment from abroad. It was imperative that these winds of change should be harnessed to the full advantage of the economy and to enable the nation to redeem its pledge of inclusive growth. As a result, faster and more inclusive growth became the main features of the Eleventh and Twelfth Plans (2007-2012; 2012-2017). The Multidimensional Poverty Index developed by the Oxford Poverty &Human Development Initiative which ranked the performance of India and Cambodia as the best among ten selected countries during the period 2005-2006 to 2015-2016 with an added comment "they [India and Cambodia] did not leave the poorest groups behind".

To realise how well India's Five year Plan objectives and their implementation promoted its citizens' welfare and in the process met the SDGs, one only needs to look at the Voluntary National Report (VNR) submitted by the Government of India to the UN High Level Political Forum in 2017. The Report covered the country's efforts to fulfill targets under six SDGs concerned with welfare issues like Poverty (SDG1), Hunger (SDG 2), Health and Wellbeing (SDG 3), Gender Equality (SDG 5), economic and modernisation issues like Industry, Innovation and Infrastructure (SDG 9), an environmental and resource issue, namely 'Life below Water' (SDG 16) and lastly promoting partnerships to realise the goals (SDG 17). These goals were chosen for being highlighted for the reason that India's attaining the status of a major economy owed much to the collective effort of the government and the people and hence these should remain the driving forces of future development too.

On ending poverty (SDG 1), India's VNR (2017) underscored the impact of the economic reforms of 1991 which resulted in a sustained annual rate of growth of 6.2% between 1993-94 and 2003-04 and 8.3% from 2004-05 to 2011-12. This growth saw poverty "falling across all economic, social and religious groups nationally" along with the creation of gainful employment for the poor which, in turn, boosted government revenues and aided higher social spending. This experience served to highlight the synergistic impact of economic growth on overall social welfare. In a direct attack on poverty, seven large scale anti-poverty programs were launched to provide gainful employment, life insurance cover, shelter and clean cooking fuel. The massive, countrywide rural employment generation programme started under the Mahatma Gandhi Rural Employment Guarantee Act, 2005 has transformed the lives of millions in rural India.

On 'Ending Hunger' (SDG 2), the country had made outstanding progress during the decade 2005-06 to 2015-16 as revealed by the dramatic fall in the percentage of stunted children below the age of five from 48% to 38.4%. The proportion of underweight children fell from 42.5% to 35.7% during the same period. On SDG 3, ensuring healthy lives and promoting wellbeing for all at all ages, the results were quite encouraging. Rate of infant mortality declined from 57 per thousand in 2005-06 to 41 in 2015-16. Under Five mortality rate fell from 74 per thousand to 50 during this period. The government aims to immunize all unimmunized and partially immunized children against vaccine preventable diseases by the year 2030. As a form of providing guaranteed health benefits to the poor, a health insurance cover of Indian Rupees 100,000.00 (US $ 1563) has been extended to all poor families.

Since gender equality is a necessary condition for eradicating poverty in a country like India and educating the female child is an important component thereof, emphasis has been laid on promoting female literacy. As a result, female literacy went up from 55.1% in 2005-06 to 68.4% in 2015-16. Further, gender empowerment was promoted by helping women to open bank accounts of their own. This move has had a favourable response in that the percentage of women having bank accounts rose from 15.1% in 2005-06 to 53.1% in 2015-16. Since economic development is helped greatly by sound infrastructure in the form of transport and communications, electricity, and telecommunications (SDG 9), these sectors were accorded special attention.

Strange it may sound, the interlinking of the SDGs is such that the pursuit of goals seemingly as diverse as improving the health of the marine environment and ending human poverty synergise each other. India has a long coastline of almost 7500 kilometres and the sea around supports a large fisher population of four million with food and livelihood. Seafood is the principal source of protein for the poor. It is a sad fact that 61% of the fisher families are below the poverty line (Central Marine Fisheries Research Institute, 2010) Hence, protection of the health of the seas around India against land-based and marine pollution is crucial to the nation in general and to the coastal communities in particular. In India, this task is performed through rigorous monitoring and predictive systems. To conserve and sustainably harness marine resources, a movement called the Blue Revolution has been launched. This initiative brings out the relationship between SDG1 (No poverty) and SDG 16 (Life below water).

The interdependence of SDGs is also well illustrated by SDG 11,"Cities and Human Settlements" in which all SDGs barring SDG 17 (Peace) are involved. This interdependence is best described in the words of the Review submitted by India to the UN High Level Political Forum on Sustainable Development in 2018 thus: "Most of the 234 SDG indicators have a direct connection to urban policies and a clear impact on cities and human settlements. The goal on poverty is linked to access to land, slums and inadequate housing; health is often affected by 'place'; and gender equality can benefit from access to public spaces, basic infrastructure, and participation in local governance and decision-making. Urban waste management is strongly associated with safe drinking water, sanitation and hygiene; energy systems are critical for the development of safe, resilient and sustainable human settlements; and inclusive and productive cities are important for entrepreneurship and job creation..... Understanding the urban dimension of the different sustainable development goals is key to unlocking their full potential."

India's experience with socio-economic development demonstrates that there is no exclusive and everlasting path to attain any single welfare objective. No progress under any component of development is possible for long without appropriate progress in other related components. India's planned progress has always been holistic and to a good extent foresaw the strategy of sustainable development.

Has India been doing enough for its people and for the global community? The answer, expectedly, is a qualified one. Despite the fact that the results recorded under certain selected SDGs in India's VNR for the year 2017 showed up a bright picture, the finding of the SDSN Review Report (2018), to which we had alluded earlier, was not so encouraging. In the SDSN spillover scale, a score of Zero marks the best performance and a score of 100 the worst. With its score of 61.1, India ranked a low 115th among 162 nations in terms of its achievements against its targets. India, a major figure on the world stage today, needs to step up its efforts to gain internal satisfaction as well as external recognition.

NITI Aayog

The year 2015 saw a major change in India's development planning strategy. The practice of five year planning followed till then came to an end and the fountainhead of India's Five Year Plans, the Planning Commission that had been dissolved in 2014 was replaced by the

National Institution for Transforming India (NITI Aayog) in January 2015. The Aayog was conceived as a think-tank charged with the preparation of three documents, namely a 15 Year Vision, a Seven Year Strategy, and a Three Year Action Agenda. Unlike its predecessor, the Aayog does not allocate funds to the states of India for implementing the planned activities. These changes reflected the new economic situation in the country following the economic liberalization of 1991. The reform measures with their subsequent refinements and enlargements opened out a vast vista of opportunities to private investment, both national and foreign, in sectors like telecom, automobiles, mining, power generation, and oil and in services like Insurance.

Global developments, particularly in China, also had their influence in shaping the Seven Year Strategy, Three Year Agenda, and other initiatives. The times demanded a fundamental change of thinking on the productive sectors of the economy like agriculture, small, medium, and large industry, industrial productivity, self-reliance, and export promotion, and a sea change in special area development to house industry and make India a giant exporter.

Poverty reduction, which will remain the country's preoccupation for years to come, needs a multipronged approach. In this context, poverty has to be understood as "multidimensional poverty' (MPI) which means poverty accompanied by poor health, malnutrition, lack of access to clean water and electricity, little schooling and poor work quality and work environment. India's record in addressing multidimensional poverty has been quite satisfactory. The number of people below the poverty line was 640 million (55.1% of the total population) in 2005-06 and this fell to 369 million (27.9%) in 2015-16, a feat singling India out for notice internationally. Further, of all the countries only India and Cambodia shared the distinction of not leaving the "poorest groups behind" in the process.

Since employment generation has been found to be the most effective way of countering poverty, NITI Aayog has made this goal the centrepiece of its Three Year Agenda. The Agenda calls for a radical departure from the hitherto accepted norms of analysing the employment generation problem. Since agriculture is the largest employer in the country accounting for 49% of the nation's workforce but only 17% of the GDP (2011-12, National Sample Survey) the Agenda focuses on reforming this sector so as to retain the necessary number of landholders and engaging the surplus in other occupations. Through initiatives like these, the Agenda aims to double the annual per capita farm income of Rupees 120,193 (2015-16; at current market prices) by 2022-23.

In parallel with the drawing up of the Agenda, the NITI Aayog has been working on developing India – specific SDG indices for measuring progress achieved in sustainable development indicators in the states. Two national SDG Index reports (2018 and 2019) have been released.

Sustainable Development and Resource Use Efficiency – Circular Economy

Even as discussions were in progress globally on sustainable development, another powerful idea had been engaging the attention of economists, planners, and policymakers. 'Circular economy', as it is known, carries a simple message, that is, resource use efficiency is at the heart of all sustainable development. Excessive resource use leads to all that goes against sustainable development like rapid exhaustion of resources, greater waste management problems, environmental pollution, and poor business economics. The idea has had a good reception from industry the world over. Hence, to weave the principles of 'Circular economy' into its sustainable development strategy, the NITI Aayog conceived of a National Resource Efficiency Policy, the draft of which was published in 2019. The aim of the

Policy is not to shun resource-intensive industries but to promote resource efficiency in industry through regulatory and consultative mechanisms. We shall take up resource use efficiency for detailed treatment in the next Chapter.

Financing Sustainable Development in India

India's admittedly modest ranking among other nations in human development shows that it has a long way to go in meeting most of the SDGs. In addition, as we saw earlier, India's share of global shortfalls (the "spillover") is so pronounced that India's performance would determine, to a large measure, the realization or otherwise of "The Future We Want" at the global level too. To fulfill its onerous role, India would need, besides the best of will and commitment, steady availability of ample finances. According to the Standard Charted SDG Investment Map (2020), India would need an Investment of USD 2.64 trillion to meet its SDG targets by 2030. While half of this Investment may be made by the government, the rest may have to be shouldered by the private sector.

Of the total Investment, the major component would be Clean Energy (1.6 trillion), Transport Infrastructure (0.5 trillion), Digital Access (0.38 trillion) and Clean Water and Sanitization (0.019 trillion). A massive fundraising effort with full support from private enterprise both from within the country and abroad, international financial institutions and bilateral assistance is called for. Despite all the efforts the country may make, there would be a sizeable population of 330 million living below the poverty line (INR 10,000 per household per month) even in 2050. The aspirational middle class (currently in the Rs. 10,000 – 40,000 monthly income bracket) would grow from its prevailing strength of 280 million to 900 million in 2050 creating a massive demand for education, jobs and gainful self-employment.

Population and Income Distribution

Household Monthly Income (INR)	Population (millions) Year	
	2016	2050
Below 10,000	890	330
Between 10,000 and 40,000	280	900
Above 40,000	70	200

Despite the odds it faces, India must succeed in meeting the SDGs for the welfare of its teeming millions and the rest of the world. As a UN spokesperson put it "The success of Agenda 2030 globally will depend, in a decisive way, on the progress India makes on the Sustainable Development Goals in the next decade. It is not just the size of India's population or the scale of its interventions that makes it so critical to the SDGs, but its unique convergence and economic growth, commitment to sustainability, and social and technological innovations."(Yuri Agnasiev).

Given the reality that sustainable development embraces both human welfare and care for the planet and is the best possible solution arrived at therefor after years of negotiations between the rich and the poor, it is surprising that the old, divisive, enervating environment versus development debate should still survive, particularly in India.

Select References

Government of India – Cabinet Secretariat –Resolution – 15 March 1950 – The Planning Commission (Yojana Ayog)

India's Five Year Plans, Planning Commission

Government of India Resolution on the NITI Aayog – no. 511/21/2015 – Cabinet Secretariat, Government of India.

"SDG India Index Baseline Report, 2018" NITI Aayog, Government of India.

"Yuri Agnasiev, UN Resident Coordinator, New Delhi, 14 December 2018, quoted in NITI Aayog's SDG India Index Baseline Report 2018]

Chapter IX

Green Economy

Historical Background

A marked feature of the global environment movement since the 1960s has been its progressive transformation in defining the man-environment relationship. In the movement's history, first came the strident call for total environmental protection in the 1960s and '70s which questioned the vigorous pursuit of economic growth everywhere. Developing countries were apprehensive of the true purpose of the new movement for the reason that since many of them were rich in floral and faunal resources, the message of man-nature harmony and care for the interests of future generations would be applied to them more than to the developed countries and would stall their development. This, they feared, would lead to the perpetuation of their backwardness and to the continued industrial and economic hegemony of the developed world over the rest. Next to this phase of apprehension came reconciliation and assurance in the form of sustainable development made possible by the Brundtland Report and the deliberations of the Rio Conference (1992). Agenda 21 adopted at the Conference struck a balance between development and safeguarding natural resources and changed the course of the debate by according as much relevance to economic growth as to green concerns and to the welfare of the present generation vis-a-vis that of its successors. This led to the framing of the Millennium Development Goals in 2000 and Sustainable Development Goals in 2012 which provided a workable compromise promising environmental, economic, and social well-being to all, the world's poor in particular.

Green Growth and Green Economy

"Green growth", "Green Economy" and their later versions "Inclusive Green Growth" and "Resilient Green Growth" are some additions to the green lexicon in the last three decades. The term "Green Economy" was first used in a report titled "Blueprint for a Green Economy" commissioned by the UK Government and authored by three environmental economists of repute, Pearce, Markandeya and Barbier. Released in 1989, the purpose of the exercise was "to advise the UK Government if there was a consensus definition of the term "sustainable development" and the implications of sustainable development for the measurement of economic progress and the appraisal of projects and policies". The Report argued that "most environmental problems have their origins in the misworkings of the economic system, and that their solution, therefore, lies in the correction of those misworkings." The Report set out to relate what the authors called "a coherent story" about "how to assess priorities, how to identify the fundamental causative factors [of the existing state of the human environment] and how to design environmental policy based on economic incentives."

The 'Blueprint' made a forceful argument for making investment decisions guided by cost-benefit analysis placing a monetary value on goods and services provided by the environment. That is, the environment is not to be treated as a free good but its utility in monetary terms must be factored in while working out the costs and benefits of any project that may have a depleting or deleterious effect on the environment now or in the foreseeable future. Based on the principles of Environmental Economics, the Blueprint argued for a combination of the command and control approach, incentives and market-based instruments like tradeable permits to guide decision-making on matters involving interference with nature and their implementation. The authors extended the application of such an approach to address global problems like Ozone Layer depletion and global warming as well as regional and local issues like tropical deforestation and resilience loss in natural ecosystems in the developing world. The message of the Report could be taken as having identified decision-making based on green considerations as the defining characteristic of sustainable development. The end result of adopting this practice would be a 'Green Economy' and the decision-making and development process that marks the economy would be 'Green Growth.' It is worth noting that the adjective 'green' used in this context is not restricted to flora and fauna but extends to all that occurs in nature, animate or inanimate. Green came to signify all that was a part of the environment, natural or man-made and all human activity that was environment – friendly.

Seoul Declaration, 2005

The thread of **The Blueprint** was picked up in 2005 by the Seoul Declaration of the Fifth Ministerial Conference on Environment and Development in Asia and Pacific organized by the Economic and Social Commission for Asia and Pacific (ESCAP) from 23rd to 29th. March 2005. The 'Seoul Initiative', as it was called, presented three targets to mark the idea of 'Green Growth'. Green Growth was defined as growth governed by the environment's capacity to sustain growth. Capacity, in turn, was understood to be related to resource availability and planetary boundaries limiting the planet's capacity to assimilate waste generated by the growth process. This meant that the environment should be looked upon as the prime determinant of growth instead of being treated as a passive, massive, unguarded warehouse that could be sacked at will and as a limitless receptacle of waste. Public and private policies should be so framed as to promote environment-friendly investment, technology and research. In addition, market regulations should be introduced to create conditions favourable to generating and promoting demand for green goods. The environment was highlighted as "the driver and opportunity for economic growth and development" and not an afterthought in the development process or to be looked upon as a hurdle.

The Seoul Initiative went on to claim that Green Growth "seems to create a win-win synergy between the environment and the economy and to present the environment as an opportunity for economic growth and private sector business". To take advantage of this potential latent in the environment, investments needed to be made in environmental technology and related research, and a "positive synergy" to be created between the environment and the economy and involving the private sector. The private sector was recognized to have a substantial role to play in green growth. In essence, the Seoul Initiative impressed upon governments and people, in general, that green growth did not come through state fiat alone; it required private sector involvement and above all, active and willing public participation.

Stern Review (2006) and the IPCC Report (2007)

Two other events of importance that occurred at this juncture and influenced later developments need to be noted. One was the Stern Review (2006) commissioned by the Government of the UK to assess the possible economic cost of runaway climate change vis-à – vis the cost of mitigation action taken now. The other was the Fourth Report of the Intergovernmental Panel on Climate Change (IPCC, 2007) set up under the UNFCCC with experts drawn from the world over to review periodically the developments on the climate front and report its findings to the Conference of Parties to the Climate Change Convention.

Stern Review (2006)

The Stern Review, authoured by two British economists, Nicholas Stern and Michael Jacobs, put the overall costs of damage due to climate change resulting from a 1° Celsius rise as being equivalent to losing about 5% of global GDP each year, now and forever. Since these damage costs could go up to as much as 20% of GDP in the future, the Review recommended early action to bring down emissions. A more alarming projection of the Review was the "real possibility" of a 5 degree Celsius rise and its cataclysmic aftermath. The authors estimated the costs of action to be taken now to limit temperature rise to one – degree Celsius at 1% of global GDP and at 2% to a two-degree rise. Calculating the values of damage arising out of inaction and the benefits of early action in monetary terms, the Review's finding was that each tonne of CO_2 emitted would cause damage to the tune of at least USD 85 compared to the cost of mitigation of USD 25 incurred now to avoid the damage and hence mitigation should be the chosen course of action for the world now. The Review advised early action to be taken by governments to limit warming to what had occurred already and help humanity to adapt itself to the physical and economic challenges that the warming already caused would bring about.

IPCC Fourth Assessment Report (2007)

IPCC's Fourth Report released in 2007 came out with alarming findings on the impact of global warming and climate change foreseeable in the 21st Century. Noting the substantial increases in the concentrations of Greenhouse Gases in the atmosphere over their pre-industrial levels and the temperature rise of 0.74° Celsius that had occurred over the same period, the Report forecast a possible temperature rise of almost 1.8° Celsius in the 21st century over pre-industrial levels. This temperature rise, among other things, would result in excessive melting of glaciers, rise in sea levels, heavier than normal rainfall in some regions and droughts in others, increase in the incidence of floods and hurricanes of high intensity inflicting great damage on life and the economy. Melting of polar ice caps leading to sea-level rise may pose a threat to people and property in coastal areas and may worsen the global climate further by causing changes in the circulation of ocean currents which determine weather and climate patterns.

The Fate of the Stern Review

The Stern Review was met with reservations that it was based on projecting the costs of reducing GHG emissions at a low level and the value of benefits that would accrue at high levels by adopting a low equilibrium discount rate of 1.3 % per annum for all-time. Critics questioned the adoption of such a low rate which deflated the costs which had to be incurred today and inflated the benefits of remedial measures that would flow not so much today but in the distant future. By adopting such an approach, the Review justified early action in taking up mitigation of Greenhouse Gas emissions and in adapting to the consequences of climate change that would result as a consequence of warming occurring already. Reservations over the validity of the application of low discount rates in cost-benefit analyses of investments in environmental protection were expressed by leading economists like Nordhaus who in his critique on the Stern Review remarked that the choice of a 'near-zero' discount rate of 1.3 percent per annum could be justified only under dire conditions of the possibility of extinction of the human race in the foreseeable future. Others were even more dismissive of the Review as "an exercise in advocacy as it is on economic analysis of climate change" and as a "political document". Thus, despite the urgent ring of the Stern Review and the IPCC Report, the world had to wait a little longer for being goaded into giving a meaningful response to the climate challenge.

Latin American Crises

Like the oil shocks of the 1970s, something as drastic had to happen to shake humanity out of its torpor to act against the enveloping environmental crisis. Three such causes presented themselves of which the effects of one – a balance of payments crisis – were already manifesting themselves in Latin America. Of the other two causes, one came in the form of a debt repayment problem that hit the countries of the same region following the sub-prime lending crisis in the US in 2008 and the last owed itself to the revival of the long-feared threat of exhaustion of oil resources and a consequent fall in earnings through oil exports. It is worth looking into these crises in some detail as the fears they held out stoked developments leading to the birth of the concept of 'Green Economy'.

The first crisis had its origin in the twin policies of "extractivism" and "redistribution" followed in Latin America since the 1970s. The global oil crises of 1973 and 1979 which resulted in crude prices ruling high throughout the 1970s and 1980s led to windfall gains to oil producers almost everywhere, including those in Latin America, and these funds found their way to the 'money-center' banks in the US which, in return, made funds available to the depositors at low rates of interest. Many countries in Latin America availed of this opportunity generously. With the funds borrowed, infrastructure projects were taken up on a large scale generating mass employment. The extent of Latin American borrowings can be gauged from the fact that, collectively, their debt burden rose from USD 29 billion in end 1970 to USD 159 billion in end 1978 and scaled USD 327 billion in 1982. Oil exporters like Venezuela, Mexico and Brazil expected world oil prices to continue to rule high and lighten their loan repayment burden. Instead, this worsened further in 1979 when interest rates went up in the US to control inflation, a measure that had its impact on Latin American borrowers too. This set the stage for the policy of "Extractivism" to be adopted by them to raise state revenues to pay back the loans. Extractivism advocated stepped up export of primary metals and minerals over value-added manufactures in addition to augmenting traditional exports of farm and agricultural products. The so-called "Washington Consensus" espoused since 1987 by the Bretton Woods twins – the International Monetary Fund and the World Bank – favoured such primary exports by poor but natural resource-rich countries to tide over their external debt and balance of payments problems.

The second financial crisis to visit Latin America was in 2008 following the prolonged depression in oil markets. Crude prices fell from a prevailing high of USD 144.7 per barrel in July 2008 to a low of USD 33.8 in just five months. Even after 42 weeks, the price level could crawl back to USD 50 only. The greatly depressed export earnings made external debt repayment difficult. To meet this situation, Latin American countries, almost all of which were endowed with ample natural resources, resorted to the policy of "Reprimarization" which amounted to greater "commodification" of exports necessitating the clearance of vast areas of forests and grasslands to set up cattle farms and to bring more land under cultivation. In Brazil, huge tracts of forests and "Cerrado" (treeless meadows rich in wildlife) were cleared either for mining metals and minerals or raising cattle for meat to be exported or cultivating corn and sugarcane. The US meat industry was a big importer of corn to feed its meat livestock. As for sugarcane, its increased production could boost sugar exports and also enable the manufacture of ethanol for blending with gasoline for use as automobile fuel.

The consequences of stepped-up exports were mixed. Between 2005 and 2011, the proportion of industrialized products in Latin American exports fell from 80% to 59% of their total exports and the share of minerals and agricultural products rose to 40%. Brazil's exports of primary products went up from 48.5% of its total exports in 2003 to 60.9% in 2009. The experience of other Latin American countries was no different. In the Andean Community, primary product exports went up from an already high 81% in 2008 to 82.3% in one year and in MERCOSUR countries from 59.8% in 2003 to 63.15 in 2009. These developments took a heavy toll on South American tropical forests and meadows rich in biodiversity and robbed the planet of a part of its green lungs. [MERCOSUR, an acronym in Spanish meaning 'A Southern Common Market' was formed in 1991 with Argentina, Brazil, Paraguay, Uruguay and Venezuela as its members along with seven other countries as Associate Members; Venezuela's membership was suspended in December, 2016].

Yet another development of 2008 was the financial crisis that shook the US following the sub-prime lending debacle touched off by the liberal lending policies of US banks. Thanks to the liberal credit policies followed in the US since the year 2000, disbursal of housing loans was strong even to those whose repaying capacity was weak and this led to a wave of defaults in repayment. As instances of default rose and the mortgaged properties were put on sale by the lenders to recover their loans and interest, property prices fell due to a surfeit of availability of mortgaged assets. This fall in prices affected repayments even further and the loans turned sour landing the lenders in a crisis. The response of the US government to the situation was to extend massive financial assistance to the tune of USD 3 trillion to their banking system. This sparked off a fear in environmental circles that the assistance would only lead to more resources being made available for lending to projects as usual and help rejuvenate the ecologically destructive "fossil capitalism".

Peak Oil

The threats were far from over. Lurking in the background was one having its origin in the high volatility of oil prices. During the period 2004-08, oil prices, as we saw earlier, had displayed an increasing trend. Though they fell substantially by end 2008, the impact of the four-year spurt was reflected in a steep fall in the demand for oil and consequent fall in global economic output, all resulting in high rates of unemployment. The annual growth rate of global economic output fell from 5.2% in 2007 to a pitifully low 0.6% in 2009. The subsequent fall in oil prices could not assuage the fears of investors over the future growth of the oil industry as reports of "peak oil" had come to gain currency. "Peak oil" referred to a prediction made as early as in 1956 by a Petroleum Geologist, King Hubbard that world oil resources were getting exhausted and oil production would start to peak in the third quarter of the 20th. Century in the US and in early 21st Century elsewhere and fall thereafter. As if to prove this prediction right, US oil production from its traditional oilfields reached its zenith in the 1990s and started declining since then causing consternation in oil markets. It must, of course, be noted that production from other sources like oil shale formations more than made up for the US shortfall.

The above string of adverse developments and governmental intervention in the years following the release of the Stern Review caused UNEP to express concerns like "Are these reforms going to create a post-recession economy that is sustainable in the medium to longer term? And would it not be efficient and wise to invest now to build that future sustainability, while stimulating the economy for growth, jobs and tackling poverty?." Fear grew that the massive financial response may translate itself on the ground in the form of investments that would take a heavy toll on natural resources. An added concern was that this step might crowd out fund availability to efforts to achieve sustainable development goals. Already, signs of environmental hazards that would follow global warming were becoming visible in the form of natural disasters varying from hurricanes of high intensities to accelerated species extinction. This challenging world situation in 2008-2009 was dubbed a 'triple crisis' as it saw growth, employment and the environment all being threatened at the same time.

Global Green New Deal

To counter the possibility of the continuance of the fossil fuel age primed by easy availability of funds to revive the global economy – a trend adverse to the environment – and to pave the way for "a green economy", UNEP came out with the suggestion of "green stimulus" packages. In October 2008, UNEP launched its "Green Economy Initiative" to provide "policy analysis and policy support for investment in the green sector and for greening environment – unfriendly sectors. This was followed by the release of UNEP's "Global Green New Deal" (GGND) in 2009. The GGND emphasized priority to be accorded to the promotion of four thematic objectives, namely poverty eradication, economic recovery, reduction of carbon emissions and forest degradation and providing a framework for green stimulus policies. Towards this end, the Deal identified the following thrust areas for priority lending under the USD 3.1 trillion of assistance made available to the financial institutions by governments:

Energy efficiency in old buildings;

- Renewable energy technologies, such as wind, solar, geothermal and biomass technologies;

- Sustainable transport technologies, such as hybrid vehicles, high speed rail and bus rapid transit systems;

- The planet's ecological infrastructure, including freshwaters, forests, seas and coral reefs; and

- Sustainable agriculture, including agricultural productivity."

Carrying the proposal of GGND further, UNEP desired that "financial assistance should give priority to energy efficient buildings and investment in sustainable transport and renewable energy. Developing countries should prioritize investment in agricultural productivity measures, freshwater management, and sanitation as these have demonstrable and exceptional social returns". Abolition of subsidies that encouraged wasteful consumption, and encouragement of sound land-use and urban policies also found mention in the Green New Deal.

The Green Deal was followed up by the UNEP coming out with a definition of its own of the term "Green Economy" in 2011. According to the UNEP definition, a "Green Economy is one that results in improved human wellbeing and social equity, while significantly reducing environmental risks and ecological scarcities". A Green Economy is essentially "low carbon, resource efficient and socially inclusive".

Green Economy and Green Growth

The terms 'Green Economy' and 'Green Growth' are often used as synonyms for strategies to achieve the same end. The former is said to be a 'top-down' approach and the latter a 'bottom-up' one. This view may explain that intrinsically there is no difference between the two terms. The position is perhaps best stated in the words of the Organisation for Economic Cooperation and Development (OECD) thus: "Green growth is a policy perspective aimed at operationalizing the normative concepts of green economy and sustainable development." Simply put, Green Economy is an ideal state and green growth is both the process to realize this ideal as well as the depiction of the process in a quantified form. As we observed earlier with definitions of terms used in environmental discourse, slight changes in emphasis laid on certain words highlighting certain concerns or goals are held out as the basis of differentiation, though the end result sought to be achieved by all definitions might be the same. As a result, we have eight definitions of "Green Economy" contributed by different UN agencies and international trade bodies. "Green Growth" can boast of as many as thirteen. To add to the babel, more terms like "Inclusive Green Economy" and "Resilient green Economy" have made their debut in green literature to emphasize accelerated reduction of income-inequality as the goal of green efforts and to avoid the pursuit of business-as-usual policies which lead to entrenchment of inequality.

In a country like India, a macrocosm of economic, social and environmental concerns of a basic nature, subtle, semantic distinctions sought to be made between terms like Green Economy and Green Growth matter little. What is of essence is their message of promoting an economy that is inclusive and capable of arresting the perpetuation of the present 'mindless' exploitation of nature. What needs to be emphasized here is that Green Economy is to be understood as an economy that takes into account the imperatives of the environment and 'Planetary Boundaries' that we had looked into earlier and not just promotion of green interests at the expense of the economy. This position is brought out forcefully by the OECD thus "Two broad sets of policies are essential elements in any green growth strategy: The first set consists of a broad framework of policies that mutually reinforce economic growth and the conservation of natural capital. These include core fiscal and regulatory settings such as tax and competition policy which, if well designed and executed, maximize the allocation of resources. This is the familiar agenda of economic policy with the added realisation that it can be as good for the environment as for the economy." (OECD, 2011).

With the introduction of the concept of 'Green Economy' in environmental discourse, doubts have been expressed over the sufficiency of SDGs in ushering in such an economy. The SDGs were considered by the proponents of the Green Economy as being mundane as they addressed issues that should in any way be addressed by humanity in the interests of social and economic justice and hence were nothing different from the usual approaches to development. Further, the SDGs were perceived to fall well short of the larger ambition of creating a society run totally on the principles of a circular economy in which all decisions were dictated more by the requirements of the natural environment than simply by human needs.

The criticism of SDGs by Green Economy advocates evoked a strong riposte that drew attention to the inadequacy of a green economy in addressing inequality and inclusivity issues which SDGs did specifically. Further, it was pointed out that green economy as practiced in some countries fell short of "fairness". The Green Economy Coalition observed that "evidence is emerging that green policies are not inherently fair ones, and that tackling inequality and promoting inclusion are needed from the outset." OECD, a proponent of green economy, agreed that many growth policies based on low carbon technologies did not "obviously tackle equality or factor in distributional impact, particularly for excluded groups." Research done by IIED (International Institute for Environment and Development) and CAFOD (Catholic Agency for Economic Development) found that if green policymaking did not explicitly take account of social issues, it could result in significant costs for people living in poverty… "If GE [Green Economy] plans are going to be green and fair, if they are going to power the SDGs in any transformational way, they need to respond to the new agenda. This is particularly relevant as many plans were developed before the SDGs and Paris Agreement [the Paris Climate Agreement, December 2015] were agreed upon and urgently needed updating."

The interesting round of exchanges between the proponents of SDGs and the Green Economy came to an end in favour of the former, a result that found acceptance with the UN High Level Forum on Sustainable Development. Taking note of the views expressed on the inadequacy of the principles of a Green Economy in promoting the SDGs, the Forum came out in 2019 with its declaration of the principles that underlay the vision of such an economy. According to this Declaration, the following five "key principles" guide a Green Economy:-

(i)   the 'Wellbeing Principle' which laid down that "A green economy must create genuine, sustained, shared wellbeing beyond monetary wealth to prioritize human development, health, happiness and prosperity";

(ii) Justice meaning emphasis on equity, equality, community cohesion, social justice and promoting human rights";

(iii) Planetary priorities, that is the limits of the earth's ecosystems that support life;

(iv) Efficiency and Sufficiency meaning a low carbon, diverse and secular society; and finally

(v)   Good governance, that is, "building dynamic, democratic" and accountable institutions that "combine science and local knowledge."

A look at the above requirements of a Green Economy would show that such an economy, despite its appealing relevance to the times and conditions, is more of an ideal to aspire for than a physical and economic reality that could emerge in the foreseeable future. Nor are the SDGs, as identified for achievement in the period 2010-2030, sufficient in themselves to usher in such an economy or solve all of humanity's problems by the terminal year or soon thereafter. The SDGs need to be revised both qualitatively and quantitatively and augmented from time to time depending on the state of the global and national economies and political developments, internal and external, peculiar to each country. SDGs are real, palpable, and capable of being experienced. Green Economy, on the other hand, would remain an ideal state of social, economic, and ecological order to aspire for.

Select References

"Alternative Pathways to Sustainable Development", Part 1/ Development Alternatives in Latin America, "Commodity-Led Development in Latin America", Jose' Antonio Campos, p.51-76, https:// doi.org/10.4000/ poldev 2354

"Blueprint for a Green Economy", David Pearce, Anil Markandeya, Edward Barbier, September 1, Routledge.

"The 5 Ps of SDGs: People, Planet, Prosperity, Peace and Partnership" – UN Sustainable Development Group, 11 March 2022.

"Climate Change 2007 – Impacts, Adaptation and Vulnerability" Report of Working Group II: Contribution to the Fourth Assessment Report of the Intergovernmental Panel on Climate Change, 2007.

"Economics of Climate Change: The Stern Review" Nicholas Stern, Cambridge University Press.

"UNEP (United Nations Environment Programme): Global Green New Deal, Policy Brief, March 2009.

"Towards Green Growth: Monitoring Progress" OECD indicators, OECD (2011), OECD Publishing http://dx.doi.org/10.1787/9789264111356-en.

Federal Reserve History: "Latin American Debt Crisis of the 1980s" (1982-89) by Jocelyn Sims, Federal Reserve Bank of Chicago and Jesse Romiero, Federal Reserve Bank of Richmond.

Chapter X

Green Economy and India

We saw in Chapter VIII how well India's development plans and performance were in sync with the spirit of the latter-day concept of sustainable development. Their areas of concern as well as their goals and those of the SDGs that arrived on the scene almost six decades later were, as we found them to be, quite similar. A further extension of our inquiry into how adequately India's socioeconomic development plans and performance till 2017 and their continuance in a modified form thereafter had addressed the country's basic requirements would show that the Indian exercise had been in broad agreement with the steps to usher in a Green Economy. This inquiry would also bring out the nature and magnitude of India's problems and the unfinished agenda.

In 2011, UNEP came out with a definitive statement that "Ecological scarcity and social inequity are definitional signatures of an economy which is very far from being green." Ecological scarcities, according to UNEP, were "threats to human food supply systems like fisheries, agriculture (in the form of overuse of water and chemicals), freshwater and forestry." Therefore, "Ecological security" and a Green Economy can be achieved only by warding off these scarcities. For this to happen, an economy needs to strengthen what UNEP calls the "Mutually reinforcing Six Pillars" identified below:

- Climate change action;

- Resource saving;

- Environmental protection;

- Ecosystem protection and recovery;

- Water conservation; and

- Natural disaster management.

To investigate how far India's economic development efforts have been guided by the concerns of today's Green Economy, we may examine the course of events and achievements in the above six areas in India with our examination extending back in some sectors to the years under colonial rule. This exercise would also bring out, as committed in Chapter VII, how India had grappled with its task of development by substituting a part of its natural capital with manmade capital for promoting both present and future welfare.

Climate Change Action

Global warming and resultant climate change have been at the centre stage of global environmental parleys ever since the Rio Summit (1992). The debate between developed and developing countries over the implementation aspects of the UNFCCC had come up for our repeated notice earlier, particularly in Chapter V. While agreeing that global warming and climate change had to be addressed urgently by the rich as well as the poor, India had always taken the firm stand of differentiating their respective responsibilities as provided for in the Convention. This differentiation was based on the need for equity in dispensing climate justice. India's stand was upheld after long years of intense discussion at the Conference of Parties to the Convention and found acceptance in the Paris Agreement (December 2015) which reiterated the principle of "common but differentiated responsibilities and capabilities and respective national capacities" in taking climate action. Under the dispensation of Nationally

Determined Contribution (NDC), Parties to the Agreement could choose the path and milestones of their choice and could fix their voluntary national targets for emissions reduction and adaptation and the modes of achieving them. Lest the Parties peg their aims and targets at a minimum, the Agreement implored them to display an element of ambition in their commitments.

Climate Action - Three-pronged Strategy

India ratified the Paris Agreement on the 2nd October 2016 and submitted the written text of its NDC to the UNFCCC a year later. India's NDC outlined a three-pronged strategy to decarbonize its economy, one, by reducing the GHG emission intensity of its economic growth; two, by stepping up the share of the country's installed renewable power generation capacity to a level of 40 percent of its overall capacity; and three, creating an additional carbon sink through afforestation and raising tree cover to sequester 2.5 to 3.0 Giga tons of carbon dioxide, all to be achieved by 2030.

Further quantifying the commitment given in its NDC to decarbonize the economy, India undertook to reduce the GHG emission intensity of its GDP by 33 – 35 percent below 2005 levels by the year 2030. Despite this, the country's economic growth in the years up to 2030 would result in a massive annual increase of emissions by 177-185% over the country's 2005 levels. But this increase must be seen in the light of figures of annual per capita emissions of India and other industrial economies and the global average. Among major economies, India's annual (2019) per capita emissions of 2.48 t CO_2e (tons per unit of carbon dioxide equivalent) are way below that of others like China (9.06t), EU (7.56t), Canada and the US (15.74t) and the global average of 6.27 t (Statista). Even in 2030, the relative positions would not vary. It is also worth keeping in mind that the Indian economy has been growing at a much faster rate than almost all other large economies, except that of China. The salient point to be noted is that, despite the growth in overall emissions, India's carbon intensity of economic growth would go down over the years.

Renewable Energy

As noted earlier, the strategy being adopted by India to green its energy scene is to make energy generation increasingly carbon-free. An encouraging start towards decarbonisation of energy has been given by taking steps to raise the share of renewable energy generating capacity to 40 percent of the country's total capacity by 2030. In its march towards this goal, India had recorded an addition of 38 per cent by 2019. As further proof of its determination to step-up renewable power generation, an interim target of 175 GW (Giga watts) of installed renewable capacity has been committed to be attained by 2022. This would mean a quantum leap of 125 percent from the renewable energy installed generating capacity of 64.4 GW in 2010 and a 370 percent leap from the capacity in 1990. By the end of November 2020, the country had attained an installed capacity of 90.4 GW of renewable energy generation (The Hindu Business Line, December 15, 2020) and a grid-connected capacity of 92.5 MW by February 2021 (Union Budget, 2021). As of November 2021, the renewables capacity stood at 150.54 GW and nuclear capacity reached 6.78 GW making a total of 157.32 GW which accounts for 40.1 percent of the total installed capacity. Thus, the target of 40 percent of the total capacity being green and to be attained by 2030 had already been achieved by November 2021.

It must be admitted that solar energy capacity addition efforts had somewhat slowed down in recent years despite the falling prices of solar panels. The reason lies in the pricing formula being adopted for power purchases which factors in this fall and fixes prices accordingly. The introduction of competitive bidding also contributes to the driving–down of prices. In addition, in 2019 and 2020, demand for energy, in general, remained muted, initially due to sluggish economic conditions in the country and later due to the outbreak of the COVID – 19 pandemic. These factors may result in the target of 175 GW set for the end of 2022 being missed. The reason for this cautionary observation is that by mid – 2022, only 114 GW of capacity had been added (The Economic Times, July 19, 2022.)

Lastly, to tap the carbon dioxide sequestration potential of forest growth, an additional forest sink capable of absorbing 2.5 to 3.0 Million tons (MT) of the gas per annum is planned to be created through afforestation measures by 2030.

Progress in Climate Action

India has been walking its climate talk. India's NDC and its follow-up on the ground would testify to this claim. As a mark of recognition of this achievement, Climate Action Tracker (CAT), an international non-governmental body, noted that of the pledges made by major economies, only India's proposals as contained in its NDC (2017) were compatible with the action required of it to limit the global temperature rise to 2° Celsius by 2050. The PBL Netherlands Environmental Assessment Agency, in its report released in 2018, observed that whereas India's GDP growth was only about 1% point lower than the average in the years before, emission growth rate nearly halved, from 4.8% before 2015 to 2.3% in 2015 and 2.9% in 2016 and 2017. Actual progress made till the end of 2019 supports these findings. Climate Transparency (2019) reported that among all countries, significant action already being taken or under consideration was to be found only in Brazil, China, the EU, India, and South Africa.

Though India's efforts may not be sufficient to promote progress towards the target of containing global temperature rise to a desirable level of 1.5° Celsius, they are nonetheless commendable. In response to a call to all nations to display greater ambition than shown in their NDCs to combat climate change, India made a bold promise at COP 24 (December 2018) of the UNFCCC that "If there is a need and if the whole world is acting on it, India will be leading in this also", an undertaking repeated by India's Prime Minister at other international fora. This bold assurance was reiterated at COP 26 in Glasgow, UK (November 2021) where India made the following commitments referred to by its Prime Minister as the "five nectar elements, Panchamrit":-

"First – India will take its non-fossil fuel energy capacity to 500 GW by 2030.

Second – India will meet 50 percent of its energy requirements from renewable energy by 2030.

Third – India will reduce the total projected carbon emissions by one billion tons from now till 2030.

Fourth – By 2030, India will reduce the carbon intensity of its economy by less than 45 percent.

And fifth – by the year 2070, India will achieve the target of Net-Zero."

Spearheading climate action among developing countries, India initiated the move to establish the International Solar Alliance at the India – Africa Summit held a little ahead of the Paris Climate Conference (2015). The Alliance would help countries called the 'sunshine' or 'sunbelt 'countries – countries lying fully or partly in the region between the Tropic of Cancer and the Tropic of Capricorn – to expand their solar power generation capacities. These countries already account for 135 GW of the 531 GW of installed global solar power capacity. As of July 2020, as many as 87 countries had affixed their signatures to the Framework Agreement of the Alliance and 67 had submitted their Instruments of Ratification. The Alliance has its official headquarters in India.

India's bid to bring down its net GHG emissions through greening its energy sources has resulted in considerable success on the public health front too. Replacement of traditional smoke-emitting domestic fuels like coal, Kerosene, or biomass with electricity and gas has brought down drastically the morbidity rates and deaths due to indoor air pollution. Between 2014 and 2018, about 100 million cooking gas connections were given under the state-sponsored Ujjwala Yojana of which 40 million benefitted poor households. Another 750 million people gained access to electricity. Despite these efforts, about 300 million households are still without such access, a gap that would hopefully be bridged under the national government's goal of providing "Universal and affordable energy access 24/7" to all by 2030. It is gratifying to note that due to the efforts made since 1990 to combat air pollution (both indoor and outdoor), Disability Adjusted Life Years (DALYs, a measure of economic loss) fell steeply from 68 million to 5.58 million.

Energy and Resource Conservation – Energy

Heartwarming though the above results are, India's energy problem is so huge that greening the energy scene substantially is indeed a vastly challenging task. To start with, for a major emerging economic power with more than a billion population, energy security is a priority. Despite the progress achieved in promoting renewable energy so far, India is still highly dependent on fossil fuels for which it finds itself heavily reliant on imports. Currently, India imports more than 80% of its oil requirements, 90% of gas and 85% of coking coal. With the ambitious growth targets envisaged for the economy, the demand for these inputs would reach such proportions as to account for two-thirds of all internationally traded fossil fuels by 2030 (NITI Aayog, 2017). In the process, according to the International Energy Agency (IEA, 2020) India would be surpassing China in its oil imports and its total energy consumption would exceed that of Organization for Economic Cooperation and Development and Europe combined.

The growing dependence on oil and gas imports places the country in a dilemma; either it remains dependent on imports with all the vagaries of international trade and politics surrounding oil and gas while maintaining growth at the desired, ambitious rate or scale down ambition, reduce demand for energy and live with stunted development. The latter option, needless to say, is unacceptable. Hence, the only way out of this fossil fuel induced impasse is to wean the economy away from fossil fuels and enable its transition to one using renewable energy predominantly. This, as we shall see below, is easier said than done.

Given the economic growth estimates made in 2018, International Energy Agency (IEA), had made projections of primary energy consumption in 2050 (Table below) keeping in mind climate implications. The present economy which is heavily reliant on fossil fuels would need to lessen its dependence on fossil fuels and substitute them with clean energy from renewable sources and at the same time take steps to promote energy use efficiency; in short to reduce the energy intensity of growth.

India's approach to primary energy consumption to boost economic growth can take any of the three courses, namely, the Business-as-Usual (BAU) but climatically unacceptable approach resulting in substantially increased carbon emissions or the climate-friendly Rapid Growth and Net Zero Growth models in which the share of sustainables in the energy-mix goes up resulting in lesser carbon emissions than now. The Net Zero Growth model has the added attraction of absorbing as much carbon dioxide as would be emitted. The table below shows the projected fuel mix under each strategy and the resultant impact on emissions.

India's Primary Energy Consumption (EJ = Exa Joules; 1 EJ =10^{18} Joules)

	2018	2050		
		BAU	Rapid	Net Zero
Total	34	86	75	77
Composition				
Oil/gas	12	36.2	21.9	11.5
Coal	19	35.0	9.2	3.9
Nuclear	0.3	2.7	4.6	5.3
Hydro	1.2	2.3	2.7	3.0
Renewables (Incl: biofuels)	1.2	19.0	37	54
Emissions (Net CO_2 GT)	2.5	4.7	1.2	0.0

GT = Giga Tonnes; 1GT= 10^9 tonnes

Source: [BP Energy Outlook 2020 – Insights from the Rapid, Net Zero and Business – Usual scenarios-India]

Even a casual look at the above figures would show that the economy would continue to place significant reliance on oil, gas and coal in the foreseeable future too. This makes the country highly dependent on oil and gas imports for meeting its energy requirements. The BAU approach is clearly unacceptable as it needs high energy imports and would drive up Carbon emissions by a high 90% over today's levels in violation of the undertaking given to the world community under the Paris Climate Change Agreement.

Under the "Rapid Growth" approach, the share of renewables in the energy supply goes up phenomenally from the current 1.2 EJ to 37 EJ by 2050 at the expense of coal, oil and gas with carbon emissions falling to half of the present level of 2.5 Giga Tonnes (GT). This approach involves creating a market for emissions avoided by a firm by enabling the savings to be sold to other firms who fail to conform to the emission limits. The price determined by the market acts as an incentive to efficient firms and as a disincentive or penalty to inefficient ones. Under this system of regulation – cum – incentive called PAT (Perform, Achieve and Trade), introduced in India in 2012 and lasting till 2015, 478 plants spread over eight sectors were covered effecting a saving of 8.6 Mtoe (Milliion tonnes of oil Equivalent) of energy corresponding to a reduction of 31 million tonnes of carbon dioxide. This was followed by Cycles II, III and IV covering 848 designated plants. Lastly, the ambitious "Net-Zero" path would involve all the features of the Rapid Growth model and in addition call for marked societal adjustments to reflect public awareness of the challenges posed by both fossil fuel exhaustion and global warming and profligate energy consumption.

India is thus in an unenviable position so far as its energy future is concerned. Its forced reliance on coal is already under close scrutiny as India is poised to displace the US in its contribution to global carbon emissions. Those who wish to hasten the arrival of the post-coal, near nuclear-free and limited hydropower age would recommend increased reliance on gas for meeting both base and peak demands of power which, in turn, would enhance the country's reliance on gas imports. In addition, it must be remembered that though gas is much cleaner than coal or oil in terms of its GHG emissions, it is neither renewable nor totally clean. In recent times, Hydrogen has come to be looked upon as a promising source of clean energy but how soon commercial use of the technologies now being talked about for its introduction would materialise is uncertain.

Methane Emissions

Methane, known in earlier times as marsh gas, though having a vastly less residence time of 9.8 years in the atmosphere compared to the 100 years of carbon dioxide, has a global warming effect twenty-five times more that of the latter. Being a major producer of rice and having a large cattle population of 500 million heads, India's methane emissions of 22.5 terra grams (2010-2015) account for about 16% of the country's total emissions of GHGs and 14% of global emissions of the gas (MOEF: II BUR submitted to the Climate Secretariat In December 2018). This makes India's methane emissions a cause for concern on the climate front. The sources of methane emissions in India are many, ranging from enteric fermentation in ruminants that accounts for 44% of the country's total methane emissions, solid waste dumps and wastewater (20%), fossil fuel use (19%), and rice-paddy cultivation (12%) [Anita Ganesan *et al*;] Decay of algal matter in large reservoirs is yet another source of the gas which, though insignificant, is cited as an argument against construction of large dams in the country.

On the farm front, several initiatives have been started to reduce methane emissions. Mention may be made of diversification of crop cultivation from the water-intensive rice paddy to pulses, oilseeds and cotton; the Rainfed Area Development Programme under the National Mission on Sustainable Agriculture; National Innovations on Climate Resilient Agriculture, promotion of traditional methods of agriculture like the 'Paramaparagat Krishi Vikas Yojana' ; and the National Policy on Management of Crop Residues, a truly impressive array of meaningful interventions to combat climate change.

Energy and Resource Efficiency

Since 1981, despite the increase in per capita energy consumption, the energy efficiency of India's GDP growth has been rising. This trend has continued well into this century. Whereas per capita energy consumption went up from 20790 meta joules in 2012-13 to 24453 meta joules in 2018-19, GDP intensity of energy use fell from 0.465 mega joules (mJ) per rupee in 1981 to 0.2747 mJ in 2011-12 and to 0.2321 mJ in 2018-19 (the two latter figures are at 2011-12 prices). This efficiency gain can be attributed to both the less energy-intensive Service sector's increasing contribution to the economy and genuine energy efficiency improvements undertaken by industry in general.

With all the compulsions of energy demand, availability, and carbon emission reduction in mind, the Draft National Resource Efficiency Policy strives to make India's sustainable development effort truly resource-efficient. The strategy chosen to achieve this goal is the application of the "6 R's", a set of optimising principles to guide all manufacturing and service activities and after-use of goods beyond their useful service life. The 6 R's are "Reduce, reuse, recycle, refurbish, redesign and remanufacture" which cover a product's life from the stage of extraction of raw materials and manufacture of inputs to be fed into the production process to the delivery of the final output and its use at the consumers' end, that is, throughout the product's useful life and its final disposal. This line of resource use, manufacture, and consumption of products is also known by other names like the 'Life cycle Analysis Approach' (LCA) and the 'Cradle to grave' approach.

The 6 Rs have been put into practice successfully abroad, particularly in the EU. In India, they are being followed with a fair degree of success in household and industrial energy use. The enactment of the Energy Efficiency Act, 2001 and the establishment of the Bureau of Energy Efficiency (BEE) under the Act in 2002 to lay down standards for energy consumption in appliances and machinery have yielded much-desired results. The comprehensive National Resource Efficiency Policy on the anvil (2021) may, hopefully, elevate the message of resource use efficiency to a national motto.

Mineral Resources Conservation

India's growth to a US $2.6 trillion (2015) annual GDP economy had been secured at a substantial consumption of natural resources from 1.8 billion tonnes (bt.) in 1970 to 7 bt. in 2015. Already, India's extraction of materials, metallic and non-metallic, is high, being of the order of 1580 tonnes per acre compared to the world average of 450 tonnes. In addition, material recycling rates are low in India, being only 20-25% of its total metal production compared to 70% in Europe. Projections show that an annual growth of 8% of the economy till 2030 and 5% thereafter would mean material consumption of 14.2 bt. composed of biomass (2.7 bt.), minerals (6.5bt.), fossil fuels (4.2 t.), and metals (0.8 bt.). Being deficient in deposits of coking coal required by the metallurgical industry and being endowed with only poor grades of metal deposits other than iron ore, India has to remain highly dependent on imports of coking coal and a wide variety of metals for its needs. The demand for strategic metals like Molybdenum, Nickel and Cobalt, is met entirely through imports. As for Copper, the dependence on imports is to the tune of 95% and for oil it is 70%. It is amply clear from these facts that resource use efficiency is imperative.

Saving Biotic and Abiotic Resources

Though the ecosphere we live in is a strong, resilient and dynamic entity, it is also sensitive to major perturbations caused by human activity and natural causes. Its processes, apparent and not-so-apparent, that provide goods and services essential for human survival have varying levels and degrees of tolerance to interference, human or natural. For example, as we saw in Chapter VI, bees play a critical role in crop pollination and a fall in their numbers brought about by indiscriminate use of insecticides may bring down crop yields alarmingly. As Liebig's Law of the Minimum states "If one of the essential plant nutrients is deficient, plant growth will be poor even when all other essential nutrients are abundant." This weakness of the ecosphere makes it imperative for man to safeguard the health of all its constituents, namely, the living segment of plant and animal life called biotic resources and the non-living inert segment of abiotic resources comprising air, water, land and minerals. In the Indian context, both categories of resources are under threat thanks to population pressures, poverty, and economic development at times insufficiently inspired by environmental awareness.

Abiotic Resources – Air

Poor ambient air quality is a feature of metropolitan India almost round the year. Indoor air pollution, more prevalent in the much larger rural part, complements the former in its contribution to the estimated 1.24 million deaths (2017) attributed to air pollution in the country, a figure that is only second to mortality caused by malnutrition (2016) [Source: Factors Study (Global Burden of Diseases Study) 2016]. In economic terms, outdoor air pollution accounted for 6.4 per cent of the total DALYs (Disability Adjusted Life Years) in 2016 compared to 4.5 per cent in 1990. The contribution of indoor air pollution stood a little higher at 4.8%. In terms of absolute numbers, both led to 2750 cases of severe illnesses per hundred thousand population annually.

The adverse health effects of polluted air are attributed to the presence of 'Particulate Matter' of 2.5-micron size (referred to as PM 2.5; a micron is one-tenth of a millimeter) above a threshold level.

India's population is exposed to a population-weighted PM 2.5 level of 89.9 micrograms per cubic metre, one of the highest in the world (ICMR/Gates Foundation) and far exceeding the permissible level of 40 micrograms per cubic metre. Other important contributors to air pollution in urban areas, in general, are PM10, Sulphur dioxide, and Nitrogen oxides. It is of interest to note that the main contributors of Particulate Matter in urban areas, as revealed by studies on air pollution conducted in Delhi and the National Capital Region (NCR), are road dust and automobile exhausts. Dust arising at construction sites, smoke generated by burning of crop residues in the agricultural areas nearby, and fireworks displays during the festival season are significant contributors to the seasonal rise of particulate matter levels in the atmosphere in both rural and urban areas in the Indo-Gangetic Plain. These factors account for the autumn and winter seasonal air pollution crises in Delhi and the NCR. Further, local and regional meteorological factors like atmospheric inversions also play a part in worsening the quality of ambient air.

A number of initiatives have been launched to combat air pollution in India, starting with the enactment of the Control of Air Pollution Act (1976) which enabled air quality standards, ambient and source specific, to be prescribed and to designate special geographical regions for being bestowed special attention like Delhi and the surrounding National Capital Region. Other initiatives like the ban on the use of leaded gasoline and prescription of automobile fuel standards had been taken since the 1990s, the most recent one being the introduction of BS VI (Bharat Standard VI) for automobiles akin to European Standards. Still, due to a lack of adequate mass transit facilities and last-mile connectivity and failure to enforce a scrappage policy to rid the roads of decrepit, polluting old vehicles, the country's urban areas present a picture of high levels of air pollution earning the nation the dubious distinction of being the one having many of the most polluted cities in the world.

Realising the inadequacy of measures taken to combat air pollution in Indian cities so far, a number of initiatives have been announced in recent times to deal with the problem in a comprehensive and effective manner. Of these mention may be made of development of Air Quality Indices for cities, extensive monitoring of pollution levels and identifying 122 polluted urban areas as 'non-attainment centres'. An ambitious project is the umbrella initiative of National Clean Air Programme (NCAP, 2019) which aims to reduce air pollution levels in the country by 20%-30% from the levels in 2017 by 2024. The principal tasks to be undertaken under the NCAP are: (i) Monitoring of PM2.5; (ii) Establishment of a Ten City Super Network; (iii) Air Quality Management Plans for 100 non-attainment cities; and (iv) an 'Extensive Plantation Drive'.

In the matter of air pollution and its health effects in India, an interesting observation thrown up by surveys is that sustainable development helps in keeping down the adverse impacts of air pollution, in general. States with a higher Sustainable Development Index (SDI) have a lower number of deaths attributable to air pollution (Risk Factors Study, GBD 2016). This underscores the thesis that any step towards socioeconomic development confers on the people other benefits in addition to the merely intended ones.

Water Conservation

Nothing illustrates better the existential crisis faced by India than the inadequate availability of water to its citizens and to its vast agricultural and industrial economy. India has 18 per cent of the world's population but only 4 per cent of world's freshwater resources almost all of which being dependent on precipitation for their annual replenishment. Statistics of precipitation reveal that during the period 1817-2017, India's mean annual rainfall was 1136 mms. According to a projection of India's hydrological balance for the year

2030 made by the National Commission on Agriculture (Nag and Kathpalia, 1974), of the 400 million hectare metres (mham) of water replenishment received annually, the two monsoons, Southwest and Northeast, account for 300 mham and precipitation during non-monsoon periods accounts for the remaining 100 mham. Of this total replenishment, about 70 mham are lost due to immediate evaporation, 115 mham find their way into surface water bodies, and 215 mham percolate into the soil. After negotiating the avenues of the hydrological cycle, impoundment in reservoirs, and catering to flows in rivers and streams, about 35 mham would be available for extraction as groundwater and 70 mham as surface flows. That is, of the total 400 mham received, only about 105 mham (70+35) would be potentially available for utilization. In 2008, utilization stood at 69.5 mham. Later estimates differ only marginally from these figures. As a matter of passing interest, we may note that since snowmelt accounts for hardly 2% of the water flow in Indian rivers, prognostications of global warming and melting of glaciers resulting in floods are in the realm of fantasy.

India's water problem is four-fold, uncertainty, regional variation, less than optimal utilization of available water, and pollution attributable to the discharge of wastewater into water bodies by municipal, industrial and commercial sources. This quartet of problems has been in the spotlight for decades now highlighted by its impact on people's psyche, public health, and the nation's economy. The fatalism that marks the lives of the agriculture-dependent section of the population induced by the errant Indian monsoon is proverbial.

Monsoon Vagaries

Let's begin with precipitation. The Indian monsoon is a meteorological phenomenon peculiar to South Asia. Received annually in two installments, the major one called the South-west, active from July to September accounts for 70% of the total precipitation benefiting the western, northern, eastern, and central parts of the country. The minor one, the northeast, lasting from October to December, covers the southern and north-eastern regions. Both are prone to delays in arrival, duration and contribution. These uncertainties cast such a determining influence on the economy that even after emerging as a major industrial power with the manufacturing and services sector contributing to almost 80% of the national income, India's economic health remains captive to monsoon vagaries. Years of drought and resulting famines alternating with years of excessive precipitation and devastating floods make it difficult to forecast agricultural production and supply of wage goods and even supply of raw materials like cotton to industry. Worse still, 50% of the country's annual precipitation is received in mere 15 days, that too within a few hours, and 90% of river flows occur in just four months (World Bank). This uneven spacing of precipitation leads to difficulties in its storage in reservoirs and in regulated releases of water for agriculture. This, in turn, results in the wasteful run-off of a substantial part of the precipitation into the sea.

How erratic the behavior of the monsoons had been in over the last one hundred and fifty years can be gauged from the distribution of droughts and deluges during the period 1871-2015. In this long span, there were, in all, 19 years of major floods and 26 years of major droughts. The unevenness of the occurrences of plenty and paucity of precipitation can be seen from the fact that whereas in the space of about 40 years from 1921 and 1964 there were only three years of drought, in the next 23 years (1965-1987) the country experienced as many as ten. [D.R.Kothawale, Dr .Jayahree Revadekar, "Interannual Variations of Indian Summer Monsoon"] This uncertainty and unpredictability are attributable to the influence exerted on the Indian monsoons by oceanographic phenomena called El Nino and La Nina originating in tropical eastern Pacific. El Nino, it is said, arises under conditions where the temperature of ocean waters goes up and as the circulating, warm ocean currents reach the Indian Ocean region, they impact adversely the generation of monsoons and rainfall. La Nina, in contrast, results from lower ocean temperatures than usual and the circulating currents cool the waters in the Indian Ocean enabling the building up of strong monsoons and copious precipitation. Recent work (2020) has it that factors that have their origin in the North Atlantic determine the behavior of India's monsoons more than El Nino or La Nina.

The present estimated potential availability of 105mham would fall short of the requirements in the future unless it is augmented substantially and in addition, utilized optimally. The situation is expected to become more critical by 2050 with the requirement estimated at 118 mham. Another way of looking at the water availability situation is from the angle of per capita annual water availability. Over a period of a little over half a century, from 1951 to 2015, the availability of water per capita per annum fell from 5178 m^3 to 1508 m^3 and may fall further to 1228 m^3 in 2051 (CWC: Annual Reports). The current per capita availability of 1100 m^3 per annum (2018) is well below the 'water stress' level of 1700 m^3 per capita and is only a shade above the 'water scarce' mark of 1000 m^3 per capita (World Bank).

Since agricultural water needs are met mostly by groundwater sources, excessive withdrawals accelerate groundwater depletion leading to water salinity and loss of valuable agricultural land irrigated by such saline water. The intrusion of seawater into freshwater aquifers and subsoil water structures due to their over-exploitation is a common feature of coastal hydrology in India. The factors that encourage the wasteful consumption of water in agriculture are many, notably the lack of legislation on groundwater management and use in some states, tardy enforcement of legislation where it exists, and the facility of low or zero tariffs enjoyed by agricultural consumers using low capacity water pump-sets. It is not uncommon to see pumps in rural areas and even in industry to be powered by electricity drawn unauthorisedly from the grid. Such unlawful access to electricity along with delays and lapses in billing such consumed power is classified as transmission and distribution losses and accounts for a high 22% revenue loss to the power distribution utilities. At the bottom of it all lies the harsh truth that water carries a price, whether it is paid or not, a reality often overlooked and providing yet another example what Garret Hardin called the "Tragedy of the Commons"!

Climate change predictions point to an aggravation of the temporal and spatial disparities in precipitation over India. Analysis of data gathered since 2000 shows that spells of drought had become more in number compared to the period 1970-2000 affecting close to 300 districts in the country. As for floods, while three occurred per year between 1970 and 2004 impacting 19 districts, the frequency rose to eleven per year between 2005 and 2019 spread over 55 districts. Another noticeable impact of climate change is the transformation of regions earlier visited by frequent droughts (the North-west) to flood-prone areas and the flood-prone regions of Peninsular India (the South) becoming drought-hit. (Water: Mohanty Abhinash, 2020).

Besides the uncertainty surrounding water availability, there exist in India the problems of lack of adequate storage capacity of water and wasteful consumption of available water. India is one of the largest consumers of water per unit of GDP. Its annual consumption of 760 million cubic metres per unit of GDP is more than that of China (600 million cu.m) and the US (480-490 million cu. m; Hannah Ritchie and Max Roser). Nearly 80% of available water is consumed by the agriculture and farm sector at highly inefficient rates of utilization and accounting for a mere 21% of value-added. For instance, Indian agriculture consumes 560 litres of water to yield one kilogram of paddy compared to China's 330-340 litres and 480-490 litres in the US. The high consumption in India is due to lack of adoption of known and well-practised precision agronomic and watering techniques followed in countries like China and Japan and due to other reasons which we shall encounter a little later.

A factor generally ignored in water resources utilization is the ecological demand of the water source itself. This demand is the minimum flow or storage required to sustain aquatic life in the source and also to preserve the wholesomeness of water in the water body. This is true of any aquatic environment, whether it be an ocean, a river or a large reservoir, or a seemingly insignificant body like a village pond. The compulsion to preserve the ecological character of the waterbody, big or small, marine, estuarine, riverine, lacustrine or marshy, or be it a wetland, requires satisfaction of parameters like sufficiency of flow, the volume of dead storage and permissible levels of storage (minimum or maximum) and of water quality indicators like Dissolved Oxygen (DO), Biological Oxygen Demand (BOD) and Chemical Oxygen Demand (COD), bacterial (coliform) and metal content. Ignoring these characteristics would result in the biological demise of the water source itself and end its utility totally.

Following precedents set in some developed countries to give up construction of water impoundments of any significant size or dismantle those existing already in the name of ecology, there is a clamour in developing countries too to follow such a policy. In the developed world, people accord priority to the leisure and amenity values of rivers and streams and this has led to movements to dismantle structures to impound waters. The advisability of adopting such an action in a populous land like India which is home to 18% of the world's population and which is becoming increasingly water scarce and which, according to its official think-tank (NITI Aayog, 2018) has yet to provide water at the doorsteps to as much as 75% of its population, is debatable.

Water Quality

India's water woes are further compounded by the poor quality of its surface and ground waters resulting from biological and chemical contamination. With 70% of the available water being affected by pollution, India ranks a low 120 out of 122 countries evaluated for their water Quality (MPI – Oxford Poverty and Human Development Initiative and UNDP). The economic impact of consumption of polluted water has been the subject of many a study. According to one of them – a study conducted by the World Bank – the annual cost of pollution, overall, to the nation's economy was 4.5% of GDP of which 60% was attributable to drinking water rendered unsafe for consumption by discharges of untreated industrial and domestic effluents and disposal of waste into freshwater sources (Brandon and Hommann, 1998).

The Age of Dams and Tube Wells

Accessing groundwater by sinking open wells, usually shallow, has been a time-honoured practice in India. This elementary strategy to satisfy the water needs of small habitations supplemented by impounding a part, however small, of the seasonal precipitation and runoff in manmade tanks, lakes, or weirs built across local rivers and streams, and its regulated releases reveals the longstanding engineering capabilities of Indian society. The British brought with them modern science and technology that enabled the construction of massive structures to impound the seasonal surface flows and manage their regulated releases in sync with the demands of the cropping seasons and provide a degree of protection to the downstream communities from disastrous floods. By the late 19th. century, the strategy of intercepting the flows of even major rivers like the Indus and its tributaries, and diverting their waters through canal systems to 'command areas' had established itself as the prime mover of food production and rural prosperity. The extensive barrage and canal systems with their irrigation potential of 2 million hectares that came into being in the province of Punjab in the North served by the Indus and its tributaries and 0.9 million acres in the northern areas of the then Madras Presidency in the South drained by Godavari and Krishna rivers brought copious and assured irrigation making these regions the granaries of modern India. The wisdom to conserve water in times of plenty to tide over dry spells brings to one's mind the words of Arthur Cotton, the British Engineer who was the planner and architect of the Godavari irrigation system. Cotton wrote "Why blame Almighty God for the famines that they occur because he does not send rain when, as a matter of fact, He does send enough for all our needs, but we are too careless to store it against the day of need".

The first task before India's development planners was to make the country self sufficient in food. The sine qua non for achieving this goal was a big leap in agricultural production which, in turn, hinged on bringing more land under cultivation, adequate and timely water availability, improved seeds, application of synthetic fertilizers to provide plant nutrients, and adoption of other modern agronomic practices. It followed logically that construction of water impoundment systems with extensive canal networks should be taken up to make available the volumes of water demanded by modern agriculture. In addition, dams had multiple uses like hydropower generation, flood control, providing drinking water, and meeting industrial demands. Promoting inland navigation to transport goods was another inviting prospect. These considerations and the availability of knowledge and experience gained during the British days ushered in the age of big, medium, and small reservoirs and management of water on a river basin basis in India.

In 1950-51, India had an irrigated cropped area of 20.9 mha of which nearly 40 percent was served by canal systems and close to 29 percent by groundwater sources which included open wells and diesel-run shallow tube wells. Later, since groundwater-based irrigation was found to be more efficient (70-80 per cent) compared to canal-fed irrigation (24-25 per cent; Vibha Dhavan) and access to electricity was extended to rural areas on a nationwide scale, electric powered tube-wells came into common use along with diesel driven ones. During the period 1950-51 to 2002-03, area under tube-well irrigation went up remarkably to 62.4 percent of the total cropped area (Vibha Dhawan). The impact of these developments as well as that of policies that promoted easy access to electricity for irrigation purposes was that the country's food-grains production rose from around 200 thousand tonnes in 1950-51 to a little over 1600 thousand tonnes in 2014-17 (NITI Aayog, National Water Policy, 2012). A nation that depended on imports of food grains to feed itself in the 1960s and 1970s, freed itself totally of such compulsions by the 1980s thanks to its adoption of a package of policy measures to promote the conservation of precipitation in large storage structures and its distribution through widespread canal networks, and tapping groundwater through traditional shallow dug wells and deep bore wells. However, over the years, the exploitation of groundwater with scant regard to the recharging capacity of the aquifers had a negative effect in the form of falling groundwater tables and saline intrusion into groundwater structures in coastal areas rendering fertile croplands increasingly unsuitable for cultivation. Also, uncontrolled supply of groundwater to agricultural operations resulted in waterlogging in the lands irrigated, spread of soil salinity and fall in the cropped area, and finally in reduced output. As early as 2005, the World Bank cautioned India that 15% of the country's food production was the result of over-extraction of groundwater. It may not be out of context to suggest here that the recent move to promote ethanol-blended gasoline in India by sourcing ethanol from sugarcane, a highly water-intensive crop, should be evaluated carefully.

One other reason for the slowdown in the construction of large storages was the coming into prominence of a vocal body of public opinion which held that India's food security had been achieved at a high human and environmental cost. These critics pointed to the displacement of large populations and social discontent generated by the acquisition of large tracts of land, mostly agricultural, on a compulsory basis to construct reservoirs and canals. They point to the huge delays in payment of adequate compensation to the population deprived of its land holdings and in resettlement and rehabilitation of the project-affected communities. Also, other real concerns like clearance of forest land for construction of projects, destruction of wildlife habitats, and interference with traditional rights of forest dwellers and in villages nearby to collect minor forest produce were highlighted and portrayed as being anti-poor. Despite the fact that these felt shortcomings were addressed in later years through prior, detailed environmental impact assessment of projects and building in adequate safeguards, raising compensation rates for the acquired lands, and ensuring rehabilitation and resettlement of the affected population, the opposition has continued.

The construction of irrigation projects of large storages with an extensive network of canal distribution systems has been a contentious issue between traditional water managers and green activists on other grounds too, one of them being the progressive decline in the storage capacity of reservoirs over time due to excessive siltation. Excessive siltation of reservoirs and canals resulting from the inflow of top soil eroded from catchment areas reduces significantly their storage and carriage capacity and impacts project economics. The annual loss of storage capacity due to siltation is not insignificant, being about one percent (1.95 billion cu. metres) of total storage and has been valued at Rs. 20.17 billion at replacement cost. (H. Thakkar and Swarup Bhattacharya). This well-substantiated demerit of large water storages highlighted by critics can be addressed through extensive soil conservation in the catchments of rivers and control of land use, supplemented by periodic dredging of the reservoirs. But abandoning the practice of creating more than minor storages and allowing water to flow wastefully into the sea would be drastic self-denial on man's part of nature's generous offer. Similarly, other frequently voiced objections like the redundancy of hydropower projects in an age where solar and wind power have emerged as the energy sources of choice overlook many proven and multiple advantages of the former.

The anti-dam sentiments need to be viewed in the background of the water storage capacities created in India and in some high and middle – income countries. The Table below shows India has the least storage.

Water Storage Capacity per Capita

Country	Storage capacity (Cu.m per capita)
US	6,000
Australia	5,000
China	2.200
Spain	1,500
Morocco	500
India	304

[Source: Asad Sarvar Qureshi, "Managing Surface Water for Irrigation" International Centre for Biosaline Agriculture, July 2018, Research Gate]

An added statistic of interest is that India can store only about thirty days of rainfall compared to 900 days in major river basins in arid areas of developed countries. India has harnessed only 20% of its economic hydropower potential as against 80% achieved by many developed countries. These facts indicate the need for augmenting existing storage and creating new storage and not less. The human problems that result from land acquisition and displacement of populations that necessarily accompany such projects and their mitigation are dealt with later in Chapter XII.

National Water Policy 1987

India's national water policy has been a subject of periodic revision addressing issues historic as well as evolving. Conservation through impoundment of monsoon surpluses and their controlled releases, promoting conjunctive use of surface and groundwater, management of catchment areas of large river systems and river basins, and prevention of pollution of water sources have been some of its principal features. The National Water Policy of 1987, while recounting the progress notched up in creating additional irrigation potential since 1947, noted that irrigation potential went up from 19.5 million hectares to 95 million hectares and with this increased availability of assured irrigation along with the application of improved inputs in adequate doses led to the increase in production of food grains from irrigated areas from 50 million tonnes to 208 million tonnes, thereby ensuring food security to the nation. The 1987 Policy established an order of priority in water conservation and management according primacy to "Drinking water" followed by "Irrigation, Hydropower, Ecology, Agro-Industries and non – agro-industries, Navigation and other uses." Reiterating the philosophy accepted by water managers all along in India, the Policy was categorical that "Water resource development should as for as possible be planned as multipurpose projects" and that "The drainage system should form an integral [part] of any irrigation project right from the start." The Policy also advocated the need for conjunctive use of surface and groundwater resources and the adoption of appropriate land-use practices in the areas brought under irrigation.

The 1987 Policy has been revisited three times, in 2002, 2012 and 2019 with the latter two taking note of the requirements under the National Action Plan for Climate Change (NAPCC, 2008). The Policy Revision of 2002 acknowledged the impressive progress that had been achieved in creating a large irrigation potential and the increase in food production in the period 1947-2000 which had made the country self-sufficient in meeting its food requirements. Policymakers, however, felt that the strategy pursued till then should undergo a "paradigm shift" from the "creation and expansion of water resources infrastructure for diverse uses" to "improvement of the performance of the existing water resources facilities". The Policy established an order of priority in water conservation and management according primacy to "Drinking water" followed by "Irrigation, Hydropower, Ecology, Agro-Industries and non – agro industries, Navigation and other uses." Reiterating the philosophy followed by water managers all along in India, the Policy was categorical that "Water resource development should as for as possible be planned as "multipurpose projects" sector "... to ensure that "the needs for development as well as operation and maintenance of the facilities are met." An interesting point made in the Policy was to encourage private sector participation in assessing the impact of climate change on water resources and in "planning, development and management of water resources sector, wherever feasible".

The NAPCC (2008), a comprehensive data base in public domain, focused attention on overexploited areas, increasing water use efficiency by 20%, promotion of basin level integrated water resources management and foster state-citizen cooperation in water resources augmentation and preservation. According highest priority to satisfying the water needs of the population, the National Water Policy, 2012 laid down that "Safe Water for drinking and sanitation should be considered as pre-emptive need" followed by high priority allocation for other basic needs (including needs of animals), achieving food security, supporting sustenance agriculture, and minimum ecosystem needs. Available water, after meeting these needs, should be allocated in a manner to promote its conservation and efficient use". The Policy clearly recognized the importance of demand management of water through rationalization in its consumption in all sectors, agricultural, industrial, commercial and residential, and through fair pricing. A new Water Policy (NWP 2020) is on the anvil.

In 2018, NITI Aayog developed a "Composite Water Management Index" (CPMI) to "Establish a clear baseline and benchmark for state level performance of key water indicators" as this "would promote competitive and cooperative federalism". Nine broad sectors with 18 indicators were identified to constitute the Index like "Source Augmentation, Watershed development and Sustainable on-farm water use practices". Ranking of states' performances was also a part of the CPMI exercise. Based on the encouraging participation of the states, the CPMI is undergoing a revision.

Interlinking of Rivers

A proposal much discussed and currently being worked upon is the interlinking of rivers to transfer surplus waters from one river basin to another through link canals. This proposal is claimed to serve the interests of drought-prone areas, act as a flood control measure in basins prone to heavy precipitation, and in general as a measure to conserve wasteful run-off. As many as thirty such links have been identified. Though an attractive proposition, interlinking has met with environmental objections like its possible adverse impact on ecologically sensitive areas through which the link canals will pass and on the newly irrigated tracts that had remained unirrigated hitherto. Further, since many water surplus river basins fall entirely within one state and the new beneficiary areas fall in another, political hurdles like lack of agreement between the concerned states on land submergence and displacement in the participant states and sharing of benefits of irrigation have also affected the progress of river linking.

Private Enterprise and Water

Before we end this account of the steps taken in India over the last 150 years to conserve its water resources and their management, we may note the initial outcome of one of its recent experiments, namely the participation of private enterprise in this effort. As we noted above, promoting private enterprise participation in the water sector which had become popular in many developing countries since the 1990s made a beginning in India with its mention in the National Water Policy of 2002. In the beginning, private involvement was limited to the augmentation of supply projects or operation and maintenance of the assets already created. However, foreign entrepreneurs did not find the ground promising enough in India. Participation had been forthcoming only from local interests. A study conducted by WSP (a multi-donor partnership administered by the World Bank) and released in 2011, observed that such projects were affected by tariff concerns and commercial viability in the absence of support from public funds. Whatever be the shortcomings hitherto in the policy framework governing water projects and involvement of private enterprise, a variety of approaches like pure public investment not restricted to central and state governments but involving local authorities as well, public-private partnerships and fully privatized ventures and other initiatives like the peoples' cooperatives in Gujarat with a regulatory regime in place need to be tried. Precedents in the form of joint ventures functioning successfully are available in the field of industrial promotion.

Ecosystem Protection and Recovery and Protection of Biodiversity

India's biological diversity is vast and legendary. In terms of numbers, India is home to two major biogeographical realms (the Paleoarctic and the Indo-Malayan), ten biogeographical regions, and three biomes, namely the tropical humid forests, the tropical deciduous forests and the warm desert and semi-desert areas. The country's colourful mosaic of physical and climatic variations supporting 1,35,000 species of flora and fauna makes it the home of about 8% of the world's recorded species. Further, it is the place of origin of 167 crop species and 320 species of wild crop relatives earning it the distinction of being one of the eight Vavilovian Centres of the world. India, along with five other countries, accounts for over 60% of the world's forest area. The asset value of India's forests alone may be said to be the richest subset of the nation's wealth.

Quite understandably, few subjects arouse as much passion amongst the laity and intelligentsia in India as the nature and content of management of its green wealth. This extends to the point of questioning the very need for management on the premise that such acts would amount to interfering with God's grand design and scheme of working of the universe and of all that it contains. Consequently, nothing illustrates the environment and development conflict in India better than the debate on its efforts to promote economic growth with due regard to its rich biodiversity. As we saw in Chapter I, ever since the dawn of civilization, flora, fauna and their abode the land, the forests and the rivers were treated with veneration and worthy of man's protection with minimum utilization for his needs. Hence, biodiversity conservation is not new to India. Scientific management of these resources was a late 18th and early 19th Century development preceding scientific intervention in agriculture in India by almost half-a-century. Considering the importance of the subject, it has been taken up for detailed attention later in this Chapter.

Forest Management

Any enquiry into management of forests in India on a scientific basis should begin with the second half of the 19th Century, a period by which the British had extended their rule over most of the sub-continent. Forests, then, accounted for 33% of the country's total land area and like the rest of the land belonged to the state. The dense forests were under the direct control and management of the government, forests of a poorer quality bordering these were leased to intermediaries called Zamindars and Jagirdars and the rest were managed mostly as village commons by local communities in accordance with prevailing social and cultural traditions and practices.

As the consolidation of colonial rule over a land that was of the size of a sub-continent threw up the need for an extensive service infrastructure like a rail network, a huge demand arose for timber to make sleepers to be laid on the rail tracks. These demands could be met only through extraction of timber from forest lands. It was estimated that about 860 sleepers were required for laying a kilometer of rail track and the annual requirement of sleepers was projected at around a million a year with a sleeper's life span being 12-14 years. There were other major expectations from forests in the form of fulfilling the requirements of the Royal Navy for timber wood, satisfying the fuel needs of both rural and urban communities, earning revenue to the exchequer through sale of major forest produce like timber and bamboo and minor ones like kendu leaves, gum and honey and exporting highly valued spices like pepper, cloves and cardamom.

A Commission appointed by the British government in 1860 observed that India's forests were being destroyed by poor management. Forest management as was practiced at the time was considered inadequate and "a melancholy failure" (Dalhousie) in meeting the heavy demands and expectations placed on forests. A Commission appointed in 1860 observed that India's forests were being destroyed by local peoples' mismanagement thus paving the way for increased governmental intervention. Further, according to the Commission, to improve forest productivity, scientific management had to be introduced. These recommendations led to the appointment of Dr. Brandeis, a German Forester of renown, as India's First Inspector General of Forests in 1860 followed by the enactment of the first piece of forest legislation in India, the Indian Forest Act, 1865. The Indian Forest Service was created in 1870. In passing, it may be recalled that in Chapter III, we had noted that German forestry principles greatly influenced forest management practices elsewhere, particularly in newly colonised North America. They were to be introduced in India too.

The Forest Act of 1865, though silent on scientific principles of forest management vested the state with the authority to declare any land, whether having tree cover or not, as 'government forest" and barred the participation of local communities in its management. The legislation that followed the 1865 Act, namely the Indian Forest Act, 1878 was more draconian in vesting the state with absolute property rights over forest lands. The new law categorized forest lands as "reserved", "protected" and "village" forests; vested full authority in the government to manage the 'reserved forests and give directions on the management of other forests.

Since agriculture was considered to be a form of land use having priority over forestry – a view that prevailed even in the 1970s – the work of framing a national policy on forests was entrusted to an agricultural scientist, Dr. Volker who had been commissioned to chalk out a policy on Indian agriculture. The Volker Report (1893) on forest management formed the basis of India's First Forest Policy announced in 1894. The objectives of the First Forest Policy Statement were comprehensive and were as follows:-

(i)   Management of forests for the well-being of the country;

(ii)   Maintenance of adequate forest cover for preservation of physical and climatic conditions and fulfillment of the needs of the people;

(iii)   In matters of landuse, primacy to be given to permanent cultivation over forests;

(iv)   Satisfaction of the local needs of forest produce at non-competitive rates;

(v)   after fulfilling the above conditions, revenue maximization should be the guiding factor."

Today, it is not unusual to hear strong criticism of the 1894 Policy not only for its objectives but also for the inspiration it gave to policies on forest management adopted later both during and after British rule. It is denounced as being responsible for the substantial loss of forest cover in India. However, in fairness to the Policy, one can find a strong defence for it keeping in focus the demands of the time and canons of scientific forestry. First, it relegated revenue maximization to a low order of priority. Social and local needs to be met by forests were addressed forthrightly. The modernisation of the country in the form of endowing it with an extensive mass movement service infrastructure like railways was given the highest consideration. The Policy recognized the role of forests in influencing local climate and local conditions at a time when climate change concerns had not emerged as a global threat. The critique that it sought to supplant age-old "institutional structures" (Gadgil and Guha, 1992) and "cultural traditions" (Gadgil et.al 1993) with the practices of scientific forestry seems to be an overkill. Above all, one cannot afford to overlook the fact that in the years to follow and well after Independence, the availability of forest timber wood for railway sleepers enabled a prodigious expansion of India's railway network as the accompanying table would show. For record, one may note that though use of cast iron sleepers was experimented with in India as early as in 1870s they came into common use only much later. They took another 140 years to account for 50% of the sleepers in use. Concrete sleepers saw their widespread application only as late as in 1958.

Table

Year	India's Rail Network (kms.)
1860	1,349
1870	7,678
1890	25,000
1910	51,658
1946	76,500
2019	1,14,500

Today, India has the fourth longest rail network in the world after US, Russia and China. This rapid growth in service infrastructure played a big role in the modernization of India and in its economic growth and in strengthening its social, cultural and political integration. Perhaps, the only criticism that could be made of the 1894 Policy was that it accorded precedence to agriculture over forests in matters of land use overlooking the environmental utility of forests but it must be conceded that the ecological role of forests had not come into prominence at the time. One may also note that loss of forests during colonial rule was not an experience unique to the developing world.

The fate of US was not dissimilar; it lost nearly 48% of its forest area between 1620 and 1872 thanks to each settler usurping two acres of forest land for cultivation. Deforestation was a continuing phenomenon in the US till 1910.

The next milestone in the history of forest management in India was the enactment of the Indian Forest Act, 1927. This piece of forest legislation was cast in the same mould as the one of 1875 and adhered to the principles of the 1894 Policy with further strengthening of the provisions relating to restrictions on rights enjoyed by traditional forest dwellers and those living on the periphery over cultivation of treeless forest patches, collection of timber and fuel wood for their domestic needs and collection of minor non-timber forest produce for sale. Traditional dwellers were, more often than not, evicted from their forest dwellings. Though these stern measures were successful in enabling scientific forest management and extraction of increased quantities of timber to serve the War effort, expansion of the rail network and netting revenue to the state, they led to the alienation of local communities from the government in predominantly forest rich regions and stoked their disaffection towards the government at a time when the movement for India's freedom was in full cry.

The approach to forest management in the early years of independent India followed closely the guidelines laid down in the 1894 Policy. The Forest Policy of 1952 upheld that "National interests overrode all other interests" and reaffirmed the role of management of forests through 'Working Plans to ensure enhanced and sustained timber extraction, to maximise revenue generation to the government [and] also to arrest soil erosion. The Policy called for enlarging forest cover from the then existing level of 21% of the country's total land area to 33%.

Two of the prescriptions of the 1952 Policy, however, raised a debate in later years. These were, putting best land to best use and maximizing annual revenue from forests to ensure meeting the costs of providing forest management services then and in the future. These guidelines were not taken to kindly by the post – 1960 green movement which viewed them as having sowed the seeds of forest destruction in the country. However, to be fair to the Policy, it must be said that from sustainable development point of view, it was right in recognizing forest resources as natural capital of weak substitutability and strong sustainability and hence in that capacity to undergo liberal conversion to man-made capital. Though a natural forest ecosystem is different from a manmade one and hence has to be treated differently from other renewable natural capital, from utility point of view there is little difference between a natural forest and a plantation.

The increasing awareness of the ecological importance of forest ecosystems and the interconnectedness between their floral and faunal populations and the urgent need to make a departure from existing principles of forest management based largely on sylvicultural practices and economic gain, led the Union Parliament to introduce a new provision (Article 48A; 42nd.Amendment; January, 1977) in the Constitution of India elevating protection of forests to the pedestal of a Directive Principle of State Policy. Article 51A. (g) made forest and wildlife protection a Fundamental Duty of every citizen of the country. Following this major development in the area of environmental protection, the Union legislature enacted the Forest Conservation Act of 1980 restricting the power of state governments to deserve reserved forests and prohibited use of forest land for non-forest purposes. Nor could forest lands be assigned to anyone other than a government controlled company. The Act permitted reforestation of existing denuded forest land but disallowed raising nurseries on such lands even for the purpose of raising plants for afforestation elsewhere.

Strict enforcement of the Forest (Conservation) Act, 1980 proved successful in arresting further loss of forest land thereby stabilizing the country's forest cover (Table).

Year	1880	1930	1975	1985	1995	2005	2013
Forest Cover (Mha)	104	86.9	65.3	63.8	63.0	62.7	62.5

[Table based on data available in Reddy *et. al*;]

Figures released by NITI Aayog (2019) show fair agreement with the figures in the above Table. According to the Aayog, diversion of forest land per annum fell from around 1.65 lakh acres during the period 1951-52 to 1975-76 to about 35,000 acres in the years following the coming into force of the Forest (Conservation) Act, 1980.

The next stage in India's history of forest management was the announcement of Forest Policy, 1988 which was a marked departure from earlier policies in its emphasis on forest protection as opposed to forest utilization and economic gain. Expressing concern over "serious depletion of forests attributable to ever increasing demand for fuelwood, fodder and timber...," the new Policy disapproved of "diversion of forest lands to non-forest uses without ensuring compensatory afforestation and essential environmental safeguards; and the tendency to look upon forests as revenue earning resource." The Policy goal was to raise the country's forest cover to a third of the total land area and to promote 'Social Forestry" – a term that referred to forests raised on wastelands outside reserved forest area by local authority – as the answer to meet the demands of fuelwood, timber and industrial raw materials like bamboo and other softwoods. These provisions in the 1988 Policy led to the introduction of initiatives like Joint Forest Management (JFM) which encouraged the participation of local populations in raising and managing community forests. Finally, while staunchly safeguarding forest interests, the Policy gave due recognition to the rights of Scheduled Tribes and other traditional forest dwellers over cultivation on forest lands and collection of non-timber forest produce. This led to the enactment of the Forest Dwellers Act, 2006, a step that elicited mixed response, welcomed by civil society groups as vindication of people friendly environmental protection and criticized by others as being harmful to forest conservation.

The Forest Policy of 1988 is now sought to be replaced by a new one, a draft of which has been under circulation since 2019 to elicit public opinion. The objectives of the draft new policy are:-

   (i)   Maintenance of environmental sustainability through preservation and conservation of natural forests;

  (ii)   Rehabilitation of degraded forests without compromising their natural profile;

 (iii)   Soil and water conservation; and

 (iv)   To increase forest and tree cover in the country to one-third of the total land area through afforestation and reforestation.

At present, Forest and Tree cover of India accounts for 24.56% of the country's total geographic area (Table below).

Table

Forest and Tree cover of India in 2019
(Forest Survey of India 2019)

Class	Forest Cover Area (sq.km.)	Percentage of Geographical Area
Very Dense Forest	99,278	3.02
Moderately Dense Forest	3,08,472	9.38
Open Forest	3,04,499	9.26
Total Forest Cover*	**7,12,249**	**21.67**
Tree Cover	95,027	2.89
Total Forest and Tree Cover	**8,07,276**	**24.56**
Scrub	46,297	1.41
Non-Forest#	25,28,923	76.92
Total Geographic Area	**32,87,469**	**100.00**

* Includes 4,975 sq.km under Mangrove Cover

'Non-forest' includes Tree Cover; 'Very dense' canopy means canopy density equal to or more than 70%; 'Moderately dense' means canopy density equal to or more than 40% but below 70%; 'Open Forest' means canopy density equal to or more than10% but less than 40%; Scrub has less than 10% canopy density. FSI, 2019.

It is all too clear from the above figures that India's forests are badly degraded and need restoration through both reforestation and afforestation measures and intensified scientific management. Reversing their further degradation and increasing their canopy density is a task that needs to be attended to more urgently than bringing more area under forest cover. This view had been expressed earlier too in the Mid-term Appraisal of India's 11th Five Year Plan wherein the progress of enhancement of area under Forest and Tree Cover during the ten-year period, 1997 – 2007, was reviewed and found to be an increase of less than one percent of the country's geographic area. The Appraisal went on to record that "Given this historical track record, and the ever-increasing pressures on land due to the needs of development, getting large amounts [of] additional land under forest and tree over the next few years seems difficult and unrealistic. There is a need to change our mindset away from a 'quantity' focus towards a 'quality focus. .....This would mean greater emphasis on increasing the density of our forests, regenerating our degraded forest land, and eco-restoration of our scrub and grassland...."

Increasing the density of forest and tree cover would also enrich the Soil Carbon Stock (SOC) trapped in the forest floor which is highly essential in the interests of combating climate change. As we saw earlier, India's climate strategy envisages carbon sequestration through the creation of an additional carbon sink capable of absorbing 2.5 to 3 million tonnes of carbon dioxide per year by 2030. This target looks stupendous given the fact that the increase in carbon stock has been slow so far, as the figures below would show:-

Carbon Stock (million tonnes; FSI, India State of Forest Report, 2019)

Year	1994	2004	2011	2015	2017	2019
Carbon Stock	6071	6663	6941	7044	7082	7124

In addition to the fixation on area expansion, the forest policies adopted ever since 1980 have also come in for criticism for their reluctance to release forest land not only for meeting the needs of private enterprise but also for public purposes like the construction of highways, airports and tourist resorts. Further, they have been charged with overlooking the wide gap between the country's demand for timber and other varieties of commercial wood necessitating resort to substantial imports as can be seen in the table below.

India's Wood Statistics by Volume (in 1,000 cu.m.), 2018

Wood Type	Production Qty.	Imports	Domestic Consumption	Exports
Logs (Indl. Roundwood)	49,517	4,480	53,989	8
Sawnwood	6,889	863	7,742	10
Veneer	295	402	692	4
Plywood	2,537	151	2,657	32

Wood Imports (Rs.billions)

2011	168.95
2019	428.41
2020 (upto Sept.)	396.99

[Source: Statista, 2021]

The Draft National Forest Policy, 2019 addresses the above demand and indigenous availability mismatch and the growing dependence on imports through promotion of agro-forestry, farm forestry and production forestry on land outside forests and improving productivity of forest plantations by introducing scientific management practices and introducing genetically engineered varieties of plant material. To attract private capital to nature conservation, avenues like public-private partnership in undertaking afforestation and reforestation activities on land outside forests and on lands held by Forest Development Corporations in the states has found mention in the Policy. Public limited companies may also be entrusted with the responsibility of improving forest and tree other raw materials is to raise commercial plantations on sparsely wooded Open Forest area (canopy density of over 10% and less than 40%) and on Scrub Jungle (canopy density of less than 10%) which are now part of the area declared as Reserved or Protected Forest.

A final version of the Draft Forest Policy, 2019 is awaited (April, 2021).

While on the subject of India's forests and their conservation, it may be useful to have a look at a few figures that would enable us to evaluate better the charge of state sponsored landuse leading to the shrinkage of forest area since 1880. Table below shows the changes in landuse cover during the period 1880-2010.

Table

Changes in Landuse Cover (area in mha)

Year	Cropland	Forest	Builtup
1880	92.6	89.7	0.46
1950	110.1	71.1	0.74
1970	120.4	64.7	1.02
2005	135.0	65.1	1.7
2010	140.1	63.4	2.04

(Source: Richards and Flint)

The decrease in forest cover during the years 1880 to 1950 was mostly attributable to the practice of clear felling to extract timber and to extend agriculture. The fall during 1950 to 1970 was almost wholly accounted for by peoples' efforts to bring in more and more land under cultivation following the incentives and improvements introduced during the Green Revolution and increased availability of means to tap groundwater for irrigation. The historical increase in cropland area at the expense of forests has now clearly decelerated. As for urbanization leading to increase in built-up area carved out of forests, the areas involved are small indeed. Reason would demand that all these developments be looked at in the backdrop of a rise in the country's population from 200 million in 1880 to 1200 million in

2010 and to a projected 1300 million in 2021 living in a state of food security. Urbanization driven by economic opportunities is on the rise and by the middle of the century urban population may account for a high 50% of the total population.

We may conclude this account of India's forests and their management by recounting the Rio Forest Principles (1992) and SDG 15. According to the first, "Forest resources and forest lands should be sustainably managed to meet the cover. A suggestion that may be offered here to meet the internal demand for timber, bamboo and social, economic, ecological, cultural and spiritual needs of present and future generations"; and "Natural Forests also constitute a source of goods and services, and their conservation, sustainable management and use should be promoted." SDG 15 reiterates this message. Forests need management to sustain their health and serve as a source of goods and services on a sustained basis, not shuttered isolation.

Biodiversity Conservation

Biodiversity, a term in common use ever since the adoption of the UN Convention on Biodiversity in 1992, refers, in simple terms, to the variety of living organisms – flora, fauna, and microbes – that inhabit any particular area be it land (a terrestrial ecosystem), sea (a marine ecosystem) or any water body like a river or a lake or a pond (an aquatic ecosystem). Some of these ecosystems are endowed either with unique species or subspecies of flora or fauna or with such an abundance of these that they serve as natural germ pools of many food crops or plants of medicinal, chemical, or other commercial value. This is particularly true of India which is one of the eight Vavilovian Centres of the world housing 8% of the world's flora, fauna, and microbes. Vavilovian Centres are regions where a high diversity of natural relatives of domesticated crops are found. The protection of such ecosystems is a key element of the sustainable development agenda of India and in greening its economy. We had seen earlier that growth with equity and concern for nature are integral parts of the Indian nation's fundamental law, the Constitution of India which has enshrined these concerns in the 'Directive principles of state policy" (Article 48 (A). Further, to press home the need for care for nature and wildlife, Article 51(G) of the Constitution makes such care one of the "Fundamental Duties" of the citizens.

It was not that nature conservation gained prominence in the country only after Independence. On the contrary, it has an almost a 120 – year-old modern history not to speak of its sanctification in the country's pre-historic, ancient and mediaeval past as dealt with in Chapter I. The British with their fetish for nature conservation introduced not only modern science but also, through their choice of German foresters as Heads of forest management, mirrored the Continental yen for earning revenue out of natural resources. On the ground, these objectives were pursued by adopting different standards, one towards flora and another towards fauna. Spread over 11 phytogeographic zones, India's flora received a favourable treatment quite unlike that handed over to fauna which, at best, were treated as 'game' or 'wildlife' and at worst as 'vermin'.

Buoyed up by the prospect of discovering and cultivating plants of medicinal or commercial value, the East India Company set up Botanical gardens at Sibpur (near Kolkata), Pune, Saharanpur, and Madras (now Chennai) to serve as centres of research and experimentation. Exploration, survey, and cataloguing of plant resources on a countrywide scale and on modern lines was the next logical step. This led to the establishment of the Botanical Survey of India (BSI) in 1890 to explore and document the country's floral taxa and their regional distribution. In 1954, the Institution received a fresh mandate to intensify this work and also study the ecology of the taxa described and their commercial potential. Under its new mandate, BSI is "to act as the custodian of authentic collections" of the country's plant material.

The surveys conducted by the BSI over the years have brought to light the occurrence of about 47,000 species of flowering and non-flowering plants in the country accounting for 11% of such flora found globally. Another unique feature of India's floral wealth is that 28% of it is endemic. Further, of its 17-18 thousand flowering plants, about 7,000 are known to be of medicinal value as well (CSIR-CIMAP). The National Bureau of Plant Genetic Resources (NBPGR) set up in 1976 maintains a gene bank of the orthodox seed of 1584 species of plants, including cereals, agro-forestry species, and medicinal and aromatic plants.

India's plant wealth is in danger of being lost if left unprotected. According to the International Union for Conservation of Nature's (IUCN) Red List (2020-2), there are 414 "threatened Species" of plants in India of which 85 are "critically endangered", 182 are "endangered" and 147 are "vulnerable" to becoming endangered. Plants of medicinal and commercial value and the genetic material of indigenous varieties of food crops, in particular, are prone to piracy. With the changed international legal regime ushered in by the Marrakesh Agreement of 1994 governing grant of intellectual property rights (IPRs) in respect of newly found plant species, plant products and processes for manufacturing such products, the magnitude of this threat has heightened. Traditional knowledge of local plant wealth and its food and medicinal values is easily prised out unwary local communities. India has sought to protect its plant wealth from such threats through enactment of appropriate legislation like The Protection of Plant Varieties and Farmers' Rights Act 2001, the National Biodiversity Conservation Act, 2002 and the Wildlife Protection Act, 1972.

In contrast to the treatment given to flora, animals were treated casually during the colonial rule for they were perceived to be of use for limited, lowly purposes, either as load haulers or game for sport. Elephants thus became "friends whose capabilities are [were] known and trusted both at work and play."(Burton: Quoted in Vijaya Mandala). In short, animals that could be domesticated were given some consideration while others were treated as quarry that could be hunted down. While this imperious scorn was shared by most Britishers in authority, there were some notable exceptions among them who had a genuine love for India's fauna and were interested in its scientific and systematic study. One of them, Sir William Pearce founded the Asiatic Society of Bengal in 1784 which in turn set up a museum of its collections in 1814. Such overtures and the active role played by some British officers like Burton and the legendary Col. Jim Corbett led to a change in the government's attitude to fauna in general.

The changed attitude towards animal life was reflected in the establishment of the Zoological Survey of India in 1916 with the mandate "to promote survey, exploration, research leading to advancement in our knowledge of various aspects of exceptionally rich wildlife" found in the country. Over the years, ZSI has described – that is explored, surveyed and catalogued – 96,000 species of fauna ranging from the single-celled amoeba to the elephant. The Survey has been designated as the 'National Repository' for this varied and large collection of zoological specimens under the National Biodiversity Act, 2002. Wildlife protection in India took a major step in 1972 with the enactment of the Wildlife Protection Act under which, over the years, 104 National Parks covering 1.33% of the country's land area and 566 Sanctuaries spread over 3.72% of the land area have been established. In addition, conservation of keystone animal species like the Tiger and the Elephant through the creation of protected areas called 'reserves' has led to a substantial increase in their populations. The Tiger Reserves, in particular, are a major destination for tourists, Indian and foreign. The newly created home of Kuno –Palpur in Madhya Pradesh for Cheetas brought from Rhodesia is the site of a bold experiment in wildlife conservation.

Life Below Water

Concern for land and all that is found above it has always overshadowed life in the aquatic and marine environment. So it has been in India too till recent years. The importance of life in the terrestrial aquatic and marine environment of India and its economic and social relevance cannot be overstated. With a long 8100 km. coastline, an Exclusive Economic Zone (EEZ) of 2.02 million sq.kms., an inland waterspread area of 3.52 million hectares (in small and big reservoirs) and a riverine length of 200 thousand kilometres, India's fisheries potential is vast indeed. Its annual fish catch of 13.76 million tones is the third highest in the world following China and Indonesia. Between 2014-2015 and 2018-2019, the fisheries sector recorded a higher annual growth rate of 10.87% compared to the 7.16% growth of the national economy (at 2011-2012 prices). Marine fisheries alone contribute Rs. 65,000 crores annually to the economy. A good 24 million strong inland and 3.8 million coastal population is dependent on marine fishing for its livelihood.

Considering the importance of fisheries in the nation's economy, the Government of India came out with the National Marine Fisheries Policy in 2017. This Policy anchored in the Doctrine of Public Trust had, as its objectives, the principles of "sustainable development, socio-economic upliftment of fishers, principle of subsidiarity [delegation of powers among several layers of authority from the local to the national], partnership, inter-generational equity, gender justice and the precautionary approach." To harness the estimated harvestable annual potential of 4.4 million metric tonnes of marine fish, the Policy aimed to put in place an 'ecosystem [based] approach' giving due consideration to the "wellbeing of all living and non-living constituents of the marine ecosystem and the social attributes of all stakeholders". In other words, a "blue economy" realized through this approach is what a 'green economy' is all about!

Realising that India's fishery resources, set in diverse ecosystems – from montane to mangrove, riverine and estuarine – needed a "mountain to sea-scape approach" for their conservation and management, a draft comprehensive policy framework was published in 2020 inviting national discussion on it. This Policy, yet to be finalized as of 2021, seeks to modernize existing fishing vessels, fishing gear, regulate fishing activity with due regard to the number of vessels in operation and conserve 'Ecologically and Biologically Safe Areas (EBSAs)' and 'Vulnerable Marine Ecosystems (VMEs)' like coral reef formations, mangroves and estuarine belts.

Natural Disaster Management

Natural disasters like floods, droughts, cyclones, and earthquakes have forever been a threat to development the world over, more so in a vast country like India. 68% of India's land area is drought-prone, 40 million hectares are vulnerable to floods and 8% of the area is visited by cyclones every year. In addition, 60% of the land mass is said to be quake-prone Adding to the disasters brought about by the fickleness of nature are pest attacks on crops and outbreaks of epidemics, endemic and exotic to the country. For statistics, in modern times, famines had visited the Deccan region regularly since the late 17th century and became frequent all over the country from the late 18th century onwards with 24 major famines occurring between 1850 and 1899. The Bengal Famine of 1870 claimed ten million lives wiping out a good one-third of the state's population. Given this proneness of the land to natural and other disasters, it is little wonder that its people are inclined to be fatalistic as reflected in their helpless, resigned attitude to calamities. On the other hand, Governments, both during the British rule and later had been quite alive to the problem.

Though economic historians differ over the reasons for the occurrence of frequent famines in India's pre-Independence days – ranging from failure to transport surplus food grains from surplus regions to the deficient parts and failure to create purchasing power in the hands of the affected people to buy grain to government's steps to divert grain for export – there was no lack of earnestness on the part of the colonial government to deal with famines through the issue of detailed instructions called Famine Codes to the government machinery on starting relief works to provide employment to the affected population, fix wages in cash or kind and open fair price grain centres. The drive to insulate agriculture from the vagaries of the monsoons and promote agricultural productivity through small, medium, and large irrigation works was the outcome of the government's anxiety to deal with drought induced famines at national level, it was felt by the British rulers that development of scientific methods of prediction of natural disasters and well defined contemporary disaster management techniques were an urgent necessity. The devastating earthquake in Kutch in 1819 led to the formation of the Geological Survey of India in 1851. The frequent occurrence of cyclones affecting shipping in the Bay of Bengal saw the establishment of the India Meteorological Department in 1875 tasked with the preparation of reliable weather forecasts based on science. To control the outbreak of epidemics, of which there were many since 1817, a healthy body of legislation in the form of the Epidemics Act, 1887 was brought into force empowering central and state governments to take appropriate measures beyond what was permitted under other laws like the Indian Penal Code, 1860.

To check pest attacks on crops, the Destruction of Insects and Pests Act came into effect in 1897. With this welter of laws and experience in handling events, it can be said with the assertion that India had acquired adequate expertise in dealing with natural disasters even prior to its independence. For the record, the almost 125 – year – old Epidemics Act was invoked to deal with the COVID-19 crisis of 2020-2021.

The second half of the 20th century brought with it a chain of calamities ranging from the prolonged droughts in the 1960s to the Smallpox Outbreak in 1974 and the cyclonic destruction in Orissa in 1999. The 21st century began no better. The Bhuj Earthquake in western India in 2001 and the tsunami that struck India's eastern seaboard in 2004 served as grim reminders of the heavy human and economic toll extracted by natural disasters. An estimate put India's GDP to have gone down by 2% because of the 431 major and minor natural disasters that struck the country between 1991 and 2005. Given these occurrences and the increasing international attention being bestowed on the need to mitigate the growing adverse influence of natural disasters induced by global warming, India took several steps to institutionalize its disaster mitigation efforts and mechanisms. The coming into force of the Disaster Management Act, 2005 (DMA) was the first step in this direction followed by India becoming a Party to both Hyogo and Sendai Frameworks administered by the United Nations Disaster Relief Organization (UNDRO).

The Hyogo compact was operative over the period 2005-2015 and its successor the Sendai Framework would guide the activities over the next 15 years. Hyogo's objective was to reduce loss of human lives and protect social, economic and environmental assets of communities and countries. However, a stocktaking of the achievements of the Hyogo Framework brought out that there was no reduction in physical losses and economic impacts following its introduction and hence a paradigm shift in approach to the problem of natural disaster risk mitigation was considered necessary. The result was the Sendai Framework of 2015 that shifted the "focus of national and international attention ...from protecting social and economic development against external shocks, to transferring growth and development to manage risks, in a holistic manner."[UN: Sustainable Development Goals: Knowledge Platform]. In short, disaster mitigation became an integral part of the development planning and implementation process instead of being a graft to a plan developed without it.

India's DMA, 2005 addresses both natural and manmade disasters. Under its aegis, a "National Disaster Management Authority" has been set up with the Prime Minister of India as the Chairman. The National Authority directs the formulation of a National Disaster Management Plan for the whole country that integrates disaster mitigation measures with the normal development plans and among other things lays down minimum standards of relief to be offered to the affected populations. To execute the National Plan, an Executive Committee has been formed consisting of senior officials of the central government. The first Disaster Management Plan was released in 2016 following India becoming a member of the Sendai Framework. The Plan covers all four phases of Disaster Management, namely prevention, mitigation, response and recovery. Similar plans are prepared at the state and district levels.

The DMA and the work being done under its authority have been supplemented by the Prime Minister's Ten Point Agenda on Disaster Risk Reduction (2016) which lays emphasis on the following ten aspects of disaster relief governance:-

(1)   "Mainstreaming Disaster Risk Reduction in Public Expenditure";

(2)   "Risk coverage for all";

(3)   "Greater role for women in Disaster Relief Management";

(4)   "Mapping Disaster Risk";

(5)   "Leverage Technology";

(6)   "Develop a network of universities to engage in disaster prediction, risk assessment and related work";

(7)   "Involvement of Social Media and Mobile Technologies";

(8)   "Invest in Local Capacity";

(9)   "Post-disaster Recovery"; and

(10) "Bring about greater cohesion in international response to disaster".

Under the DMA, as many as thirty guidelines have been issued relating to various types of disasters including the one on biological disasters issued in 2008. These kinds of adverse events have also come in for special attention in the revised version of the National Disaster Management Plan, 2016 that was released in 2019. It is a matter of interest that the Central and State governments impose "lockdowns" on almost all public activity under the authority vested in them by the DMA. To finance disaster relief operations, a National Disaster Relief Fund has been created with similar funds functioning at state levels. Thus, a robust institutional system has been put in place in India to deal with natural disasters of various descriptions.

A Green India

India's long history, traditions and mosaic of cultures had guided its growth along a green path long before the rest of the world even became aware of the need for such a growth paradigm. The foregoing inquiry into the socio-economic development of India in the light of the tenets of a green economy and ensuring social justice in the process would, in all expectation, convince one of the correctness of the claim that India, given its size, complexity and commitment to remain and grow as a participative democracy, is treading the path to a Green Economy with quite assurance.

As a matter of comparative statistical interest, one may note that out of 130 countries, India was ranked 35th from the top for its achievements as a Green Growth Economy during the period 2010-2018. The ranking follows a composite score called the Green Growth Economy Index (GGEI) constructed on the basis of the performance of a country towards erecting each of the "six pillars" of a green economy referred to in this Chapter.

Select References

"Planetary Boundaries: Exploring the Safe Operating Space for Humanity"; Stockholm Resilience Centre, 2015; Ecology and Society E&S Home>Vol 14, No.2>Art 32

"Report on the improvement of Indian Agriculture", John Augustus Voelcker, Cornell University Library. https://www.archive.org/details/cu319240010 39324

"Assessment and Monitoring of Deforestation and Forest Fragmentation in South Asia since the 1930s", Reddy et.al; Global and Planetary Change, February 2018.

"For a Breath of Fresh Air" (Two Years of Progress and Challenges in Urban Air Quality Management in India 1993-2002)", Environment and Social Development Unit, South Asia Region, The World Bank.

"Freshwater withdrawals by country: Water Use and Stress", "Our World in Data" Hannah Ritchie and Max Roser].

"Water and Agriculture in India" Vibha Dhavan, The Energy Resources Institute (TERI)

"Siltation of Reservoirs in India Together" H.Thakkar and Swarup Bhattacharya, 26 Oct. 2020.

"MOEF, Draft National Resource Efficiency Policy 2019.

"The Lancet: "Planetary Health" Vol.3, Issue 1, E-26-E-, January 1, 2019; Risk

"Number of disability adjusted life years (DALYs) attributed to air pollution across India from 1990 to 2019", Ian Tiseo, June 17, 2022, Statista.

"Anita Ganesan et.al. Nature Communications, Nat. Commn, 8, 836 Oct 2017"

"Preparing India for Extreme Climate Events; Managing Hotspots and Response Mechanisms 2021", Council on Energy, Environment and Water; Quoted in "Data Point, The Hindu, 3, January 2021).

"Towards a Green Economy: Pathways to Sustainable Development and Poverty Eradication: A Synthesis for Policymakers, UNEP."

"A Guide to the Green Economy" UN Division for Sustainable Development, 2011, Appendix (1).

"Statista: Climate Watch, World Resources Institute, February 6, 2020".

"Railways in Colonial India: An Economic Achievement?" 1853-1938" Dan Bogart, Latika Chaudhary, August 2011, SSRN Library May 2012.

"Understanding the history of the Development of Railways in Colonial India" Jyotosana, Sabarmati University, Ahmedabad University, in "International Journal of Creative Research Thoughts (IJCRT)" 2021, Vol.9, Issue 12 December 2021.

"Shooting a Tiger: Big-game Hunting and Conservation in Colonial India", Vijaya Ramadas Mandala, Oxford University Press, December 2018;

https://doi.org/10.1093/309780199489381.00 /.0001

"Trends in Global CO_2 and Total Greenhouse Gas Emissions", PBL Netherlands Environmental Assessment Agency, 2018, a compilation done by Dual Citizen LLC, a US-based private consultancy supported by subscriptions.

Chapter XI

Greening the Corporates

"There is actually just one Bottom Line"

The story of private enterprise is as old as recorded history. Whether it was ancient Greece or Rome or China, the state contracted out most of society's economic activity to private enterprise and in return recognised the enterprise's right to hold property, freedom to choose its lines of activity, make profits and of course to remain ever wary of competitors to stay alive. Though the governing bodies of business groups did impose rules of conduct on their constituents, the state allowed the enterprises such a degree of freedom that the arrangement was called "laissez-faire-nous" or "leave me alone" which meant in effect, as in Taoism, "do nothing." A corollary of the principle, as it developed over time, was that the "pursuit of self-interest by individuals was "not always or necessarily antisocial" (Bowen). Though this freedom to indulge in freewheeling was reined in to a good extent by law since the days of the Industrial Revolution, the free enterprise ethos has for long remained one of a not – too-well defined relationship with the state and of aloofness from societal concerns.

Corporate Social Responsibility

Free enterprise's preoccupation with its bottom line has had its critics as well as its ardent supporters. The earliest among the critics was Howard Bowen who is regarded as the founding father of the concept of Corporate Social Responsibility (CSR). In 1953, Bowen came out with a messianic statement that "Corporate leaders had an ethical responsibility to consider the needs of society." Bowen's thesis was built on the argument that this responsibility to society, in turn, rested on four philosophical pillars, namely Social Contract theory, Social Justice, Rights theory and Corporate Accountability. Briefly put, according to the Social Contract theory, there exists a series of "explicit and implicit contracts between individuals, organizations and institutions" to ensure that the exchanges between the three take place "in an environment of trust and harmony."(Mel Wilson). This relationship requires corporates to display "good behaviour" in their dealings with society. The second pillar of CSR, which is Social Justice, requires an equitable sharing of wealth, power and intangibles among the members of society and requires corporates to be conscious of this requirement in the distribution of their goods and services. As an aside, one may say that, though laudable, this requirement is more for the state to fulfil than for a corporate house. The third pillar of CSR, 'Rights theory' may be taken to mean that "property rights should not override human rights." All too often, this third issue comes into prominence in the form of conflicts between development and the environment ending in a permanently uneasy relationship between the developer and the people. The fourth and last pillar of CSR, Corporate Accountability, has been, traditionally, a fiduciary relationship between the shareholders of a corporation and its management body. The shareholders are looked upon as "Principals" who have entrusted their capital to an agent, the management, to run the business profitably. This traditional fiduciary model can be understood to include managing the firm's business by the agent in full compliance with the law thereby making the management accountable for its actions or failures to abide by the law. This responsibility could be extended to the conduct of the firm's business by the management in an environmentally sustainable manner too.

As the slogan of CSR was gaining currency, defenders of the faith of unbridled free enterprise shot back with statements such as "The only corporate social responsibility of a company is to maximise its profits" or in Milton Friedman's forceful words "[the] business of business is business". Friedman, the high priest of the faith of free enterprise, went on to say "The doctrine of 'social responsibility was a 'fundamentally subversive doctrine' in a free society" and in such a society "there is only one social responsibility of Business – to use its resources and engage in activities designed to increase its profits so long as it stays within the rules of the game that is engagement in open and free competition without deception or fraud." Decrying Corporate Social Responsibility totally, Friedman added a warning that the doctrine would only "lead towards totalitarianism".

Social Contract – Giving Back

Whatever the theological discussion on the applicability of the principle of social responsibility to free enterprise was, the well-publicised protests against industrial pollution in the 1960s and the '70s and fears of exhaustion of natural resources in the foreseeable future could not be ignored either by the industry or the governments of the 'free world'. It was not that the entire corporate world was so grossly inward-looking that it needed to be reminded of its poor public image and its duty to society. There were notable exceptions. Some of the bigger ones among them in the US had made philanthropy one of their cherished activities and this led to hefty contributions being made to promote the cause of higher education. However, such acts of munificence were more often the outcome of individual initiative than of innate institutional philosophy expressed through corporate policy. Sensing the urgency to remind US private enterprise of its social milieu, the Committee for Economic Development set up by the US Congress introduced the concept of "social contract" to be recognized formally in 1971. The contract laid emphasis on the then little realised fact that the corporate sector owed its existence and functioning to tacit and explicit public consent and therefore owed an obligation to respond to the needs of the public, a viewpoint that came to be known as 'giving back'. Thanks to the Congressional initiative, CSR attained widespread approval in the US in the 1990s.

CSR Pyramid

As in the early years of the environmental movement when scholarly publications set the course of developments, further elaboration of the place of the firm in society and the formalization of that relationship also came from the academia. In 1991, Archie Carroll of the University of Georgia posited four areas of a company's functioning as forming its 'CSR Pyramid'. These consisted of the firm's economic, legal, ethical and philanthropic functions and activities. The economic area which means profitable working is clearly the raison d'etre for a firm's existence; the legal criterion refers to the functioning of the firm in full compliance with the laws of the land; the ethical aspect goes beyond the requirements of the law, and philanthropy begins once the first three requirements are met. Of the first of the four areas, that is profit, it may be said that a company that does not function profitably is actually destroying wealth instead of creating it. Continued lossmaking erodes a company's net worth ultimately leading to its failure to discharge its liabilities and ending in its bankruptcy and winding up. For a firm, making a profit is a virtue, not a vice; a must, not an option.

Profit-making, however, needs to be distinguished from profiteering. Whereas profit is determined by production efficiencies and the play of market forces, profiteering owes much to the manipulation of markets by some elements, often in violation of the law. Profit also results from costless or less than full-cost use of the "commons" (land, water or air) leading to environmental degradation. This points to the need for society's intervention making it obligatory for enterprises to report the record of their functioning in compliance with the laws of the land and also require them to make public their belief in business ethics and morals. In addition, a successful, law-abiding and ethically strong company should make public its gratitude to society by 'giving back', that is making a generous contribution to society's welfare, in cash or in kind. This interpretation of the place of a firm in the society marked the arrival of CSR and altered corporate thinking and governance in a profound way. More changes were to follow.

Brundtland Report and CSR – Eco-footprint

As the corporate world was getting initiated into the concept of CSR, another undercurrent was building up actuated by the realisation of the limitation of natural resources and its impact on economies. This led the Brundtland Report (1987) to add a new dimension to CSR vastly enlarging the scope of the concept and introducing in the process, a new and revolutionary idea called "Corporate Sustainable Development (CSD)". Highlighting the responsibility of a firm to society, the Report declared that this responsibility was not confined to mere adherence to business ethics and law and 'giving back' but to discharge a larger and more important duty in the form of effecting economy and efficiency in resource management, that is, minimising the firm's 'eco-footprint'. A firm could look upon CSD as a screen that flashed scenarios of the future of the firm given varying backgrounds of resource consumption and operational behaviour. Also, it gave a peep into the future state of the planet's health with and without appropriate corrections that may be made to the current practices of the firm and of others of like description. To illustrate, all firms engaged in manufacturing cement need to bring down their emissions of carbon dioxide since the cement industry is a big emitter of this global warming gas per tonne of output. In the present climate-conscious world, the continued functioning of this industry would depend on its ability to bring down its carbon dioxide emissions to desired levels, that is, for its survival, it has to internalise an environmental externality at least cost. CSD reminds the firms of this onerous responsibility and drives home the point that corporate governance should go beyond the conventional approach to business economics, ethics and philanthropy by accommodating nature's compulsions.

Bhopal and Alaska – Valdez Principles

It is a matter of morbid interest that the course of corporate governance has often been scripted by disasters. So it was with CSD too. The need for introducing concepts like CSD and CSR, into corporate governance became a matter of urgent public concern, thanks to two major accidents, one claiming thousands of human lives in Bhopal (India) in 1984 and the other devastating the marine environment in Alaska (USA) in 1989. The first was an industrial accident in a chemical manufacturing facility belonging to a multinational company that resulted in the release of a highly toxic gas (methyl isocyanate) into the atmosphere over a nearby densely populated area and the second was a shipping accident involving an oil tanker, the Exxon Valdez, in the Alaskan coastal waters causing spillage of huge quantities of oil into the marine environment and death of fish and bird life. The Alaskan situation was rendered all the worse due to the vehement, longstanding opposition to oil exploration and drilling in this eco-sensitive region, an opposition that survives to the present day.

Following the Bhopal and Alaskan incidents, the Coalition for Environmentally Responsible Economies (CERES), a public body, joined by UNEP, started work on developing a disclosure framework for corporates on sustainability information and came out with the 'Valdez Principles' (also called CERES Principles) and the Global

Reporting Initiative (GRI) in the year 2000. The Valdez Principles, ten in number, were as follows:-

(1) Protection of the biosphere;

(2) Sustainable Use of Natural Resources;

(3) Reduction and disposal of waste;

(4) Wise use of energy;

(5) Risk reduction (for employees and communities);

(6) Marketing of Safe Products and Services;

(7) Damage Compensation (for damage caused to the environment);

(8) Disclosures;

(9) Environmental Directors and Managers (appointment); and

(10) Assessment and Annual Audit.

The Valdez Principles sought to highlight, besides other things, the responsibility of the management to ensure due observance of environmental precautions and its accountability to restore the damaged environment to its original state. Environmental issues thus became a business risk to be taken into account and environmental safety record became an important determinant of a firm's market value. The Global Reporting Initiative provided standard formats for companies to disclose their performance in a number of operational and governance areas and also made available industry benchmarks under each operational area to enable firms to evaluate their performance against the benchmarks. The GRI format has been revised over the years, the last revision being in 2020. GRI has emerged as the global standard for sustainability reporting.

The Triple Bottom Line

In the meanwhile, in 1988, John Elkington, a business consultant, had put forward an interesting concept called 'The Triple Bottom Line'. Whereas the prevalent principal reporting format on the performance of a firm released to its shareholders and the public was a single-pronged one showing excess or deficit of income vis-a-vis expenditure, the new one, appropriately named 'The Triple Bottom Line (TBL)', was an enhanced three-pronged format reflecting the firm's financial performance, its concern for maintaining environmental quality and commitment to social justice. The latter two entities, basically qualitative, were assigned quantitative expression by adopting the simple method of booking the expenditures incurred on them by the firm and not by the more exacting exercise of quantifying monetarily the actual impacts made.

The Triple Bottom Line method of assessing and reporting on corporate governance and performance was to prove popular with big corporate houses, notably the oil giants and others having a multinational presence on one hand and investors, both public and institutional, on the other. Shell was the first to adopt and publish its Annual Report in 1997 in the TBL format. Pilkington had rightly predicted that "Future market success will often depend upon a company's ability to satisfy the three-pronged fork of profitability, environmental quality, and social justice." Firms stood to gain by adopting TBL as it projected their green credentials and the shareholders and investors felt secure that the growth in their wealth and wellbeing would remain sustained by investments in the firm. As proof of this expectation, companies that integrated climate concerns into their business philosophy and action saw an 18% jump in their returns on equity. Further, CSR and CSD have proved popular with the young, especially the millennials. Surveys have brought out that the young are disinclined to serve in firms with poor CSR practices and would rather join those that have, even at a lesser pay (Cone Communications). The young showed a pronounced desire to serve in corporates that gave them an opportunity to grapple with social and environmental problems.

Despite the favourable response it received from corporates and the markets, TBL was also to prove a target for criticism. It was depicted as nothing as revolutionary as it was claimed to be. McDonald and Norman downplayed the concept as being "...a good old–fashioned Single Bottom Line plus vague commitments to Social and Environmental concerns." Their criticism went further by questioning the motive behind corporates welcoming the TBL. To quote "Why should advocates of responsible business be worried about perpetuating the 3 BL rhetoric? Because, it allows just about any business to claim to believe in the Triple Bottom Line, and even the best forensic accountant will not be able to prove that they are morally bankrupt." This was prejudice against the corporate world going too far!

Sustainability Indexes

The concepts of CSR and CSD inspired the arrival of many popular formulations for corporate reporting like the GRI referred to earlier, the S&P (Standard & Poor) Dow Jones Sustainability Index (DJSI) and the UN Global Compact enshrining the six "Principles of Responsible Investment (PRI)". While both GRI and DJSI enable a company and its stakeholders to benchmark a company's CSR and CSD performance against industry standards, the scope of DJSI extends further. The DJSI groups the participating firms regionally and after assessing their performance in the light of their sustainability practices, picks the results of the top ten among them for being forwarded to investment firms. The investment firms in turn assess the movement of the stocks of the firms referred to them on the Morgan Stanley Capital

International Index. On the basis of this exercise called 'Corporate Sustainability Assessment' (CSA), the top ten performers are identified and the results are announced as industry benchmarks for investment purposes. Other popular reporting systems are the S&P Environmental and Social Responsibility Index which covers 500 companies listed by S&P, the Bloomberg Environmental, Social and Governance Disclosure (ESGD Index) and the CSR-CSD based reporting system for disclosure of a firm's financially-material sustainability information to investors developed jointly by the Sustainability Accounting Standards Board (SASB) and the Value Reporting Foundation.

Governance Disclosure is no longer anathema to firms. In 2011, when trust in corporates was at a low following the failures of the housing mortgage market in the US, Michael Porter and Mark Kramer came out with the finding that companies that believed in the principle of 'Creating Shared Values" (CSV) that is "creating economic value in a way that also creates value for society by addressing its needs and challenges" were successful in their business too. Such firms believed that their success and social progress were interdependent. Based on this finding, Porter and Kramer advocated that firms "should focus on the right kind of profits that create social benefits rather than diminish them." They concluded that such a broader, collegial business outlook rather than a moral or ethical compulsion like CSR or philanthropy was more conducive to success as the latter two portrayed the task of satisfying societal needs as a burdensome responsibility to be discharged. Just as the cost of abating a negative externality has to be internalised in the conduct of business, so should be the expenditure on societal needs.

Governments and CSR

As the public and shareholders' demand for CSR and CSD has become strong, governments have been grappling with the advisability of making the two practices mandatory and reportable under the law. Opinion has differed on this matter with the US and the UK preferring not to have any 'hard' law and a number of others like India, China, France, Denmark and South Africa preferring legislation for the purpose. The British view is that making CSR a legal requirement would "not necessarily raise the standards of CSR expenditure and instead, would put an extra burden on small and medium enterprises." Regulation through directive instead of law is considered desirable in the UK as that may encourage companies to define their CSR expenditure as per their "core competency." Hence, short of prescribing a legal mandate, the UK Accounts Modernisation Directive requires large public companies to report publicly on environmentally significant matters.

Corporate India's tryst with CSR and CSD began with the issue of what was called "National Voluntary Guidelines on Social, Environmental & Economic Responsibilities of Business" (NVGs) by the Ministry of Company Affairs, Government of India in July 2011. These Guidelines rested on Nine Principles of which the following three were of direct and immediate relevance to corporate social and environmental concerns:-

"Principle 2. Businesses should provide goods that are safe and contribute to sustainability throughout their lifecycle;

"Principle 6. Businesses should respect, protect and make efforts to restore the environment; and

"Principle 8. Businesses should support inclusive growth and equitable development."

The NVGs were followed up in 2012 by a reporting format called "Annual Business Responsibility Report (ABRR) to be furnished to the stakeholders laying out the performance of the company in observing the NVGs and explaining any shortcomings in performance and remedial action proposed. A notable feature of the ABRR is its "Apply or Explain" provision requiring company management to inform the stakeholders of the action taken to implement the NVGs or explain why they failed to do so. These efforts of the government were strengthened by the watchdog of India's capital markets, the Securities and Exchange Board of India (SEBI) in May 2021 prescribing an annual Business Responsibility and Sustainability Report (BRSR) to be made available to investors by the top 1000 listed entities (by market capitalization) to enable investors to "have access to relevant and comparable information to "identify and assess sustainability-related risks and opportunities of companies and make better investment decisions". The release of such reports would also enable companies to showcase their sustainability credentials. The submission of annual BRSR Reports is mandatory with effect from the financial year 2021-22 (1ˢᵗ April '21 – 31ˢᵗ March '22). This measure, inspired by the Paris Agreement on Climate Change (2015) and the relevance of the COVID pandemic to the ESG (Environment, Social and Governance) performance of companies, is intended to encourage sustainable investing.

Issuing executive instructions to corporates apart, India leads the world in according legal recognition of CSR through an amendment to its extant law governing companies. In 2013, a new provision – Section 135 – was added to The Companies Act, 2013 requiring companies having a net worth or turnover or net profit above certain prescribed limits to spend annually at least two percent of their average net profits on CSR activities in their local areas in pursuance of their CSR Policy. To oversee the implementation of this requirement, the Board of Directors of a company is required to constitute a committee of not less than three Directors of whom at least one shall be an independent Director. The law includes an illustrative list of activities expenditures that shall qualify for recognition as CSR expenditures. This list being illustrative only does not prohibit companies from taking up other activities of a similar nature under their CSR policy. An amendment made in 2021 to the Rules framed under the Act makes it obligatory on the part of the companies to display their CSR activities on the company's website, conduct an impact assessment study of the projects funded under CSR and most importantly transfer the unspent balance of CSR funds at the end of a prescribed period to certain specified Funds administered by the government. The new Rules have also enlarged the scope of CSR activities by including "Eradication of poverty, hunger and malnutrition, health and sanitation, drinking water. Education, gender equity, environmental sustainability, rural and urban development projects [and] disaster relief" in Schedule VII to The Companies Act, 2013. The scope of assistance under CSR to serve public purpose has been enlarged further by declaring the COVID-19 pandemic a natural disaster under the Natural Disaster Relief Act.

Sustainability Reporting

Sustainability reporting by the Industries and Services sectors is being promoted actively by Industry Associations in India. Three of the more popular efforts are those organized by the CII-ITC Centre for Sustainable Development (a body promoted jointly by the Confederation of Indian Industry and the agro-products major ITC), the Federation of the Indian Chambers of Commerce and Industry (FICCI) and the Indian Chamber of Commerce (ICC). The CII-ITC exercise is an elaborate one based on the methodology developed by the European Foundation for Quality Management (EFQM), a body founded in 1988 to promote the competitiveness of the European industry. This methodology, in turn, is based on Deming's Principles of Total Quality Management (TQM) and rests on assessing the CSR and CSD credentials of an organization by looking into the purpose which guides the organization's functions, how the functions are intended to be guided and the results achieved. The CII-ITC awards are given in four areas, Environmental Management, Corporate Excellence, CSR and Biodiversity. Industries are divided into categories on the basis of capital invested in them to provide a level playing field for large, medium and small industries. The assessment process involves two stages; in the first, the commitment of a firm to CSR and CSD is assessed on a desk evaluation based on the replies furnished in response to a questionnaire and the second stage consists in verifying the information provided by paying a visit to the site of the organizations shortlisted in the first stage. Authentic information thus becomes available of the purpose that drives a firm's functioning, the existence of 'enablers' that help in achieving the purpose and the 'results' achieved. 'Enablers' include the factors of leadership, its relations with internal and external stakeholders, availability of key resources to translate policy into practice and appropriate processes to guide the practice into yielding results. 'Results' consist of 'Learning and 'Innovation', satisfaction of internal and external stakeholders and finally the performance in key result areas. This regimen of rigorous efforts followed in evaluating a contestant's observance of CSD precepts in practice has helped to spread sustainable development and social responsibility consciousness in the Indian industry.

CSR and the Market

Has compliance with practices like CSR and CSD become common in the industry? Yes, it appears to be so. The reports available are encouraging. For the record, in 2019, out of the 800 companies in emerging markets that were assessed under the DJSI procedure, 98 (including 12 from India) found a place in the DJ Emerging Markets 2019 Index. Results of a survey of firms drawn from all over the globe revealed that 80% of the top 250 in the Forbes 500 Ranking reported regularly on their sustainability performance. Japanese companies take the lead in furnishing such reports with Indian firms taking fourth place ahead of those in the US and Sweden (KPMG Survey of Sustainability Reporting 2020).

The fact that a large number of corporates think it fit to practice ESG (Environmental Social Governance) through CSR and CSD and make public their record raises the irrepressible question of whether they perceive any gains in doing so. Available evidence has it that they do see gains, both tangible and intangible. The Credit Rating Information Services of India (CRISIL), a subsidiary of the American Company S&P Global, has analysed data provided by 225 Indian companies falling into 18 categories for three annual data reporting cycles starting 2017-18. The analysis was done under a proprietary analytical framework and scores were awarded from zero to one – hundred. According to CRISIL, companies with high ESG scores within a sector outperformed the sector average by nearly nine points. It was also reported that "over 80% of issuers and institutional investors intend to integrate ESG in their decision making." It is claimed that ESG will "redefine corporate India's approach to risk management for sustainable value creation." Assuring words indeed!

COVID-19 provided corporate India an opportunity to walk its talk of abiding by CSR. CRISIL estimated that in fiscal 2020, overall CSR spending of Indian companies, liable under the statute, stood at a shade over Rs.21, 000 crores and rose to Rs.22, 000 crores up to June in fiscal 2021. It is estimated that a good part of the expenditure was on COVID-19-related relief work demonstrating corporate India's sense of social responsibility. This goes to prove the point that for India's corporate sector "Sustainability is not a departure from the traditional business imperative to promote profit – it is rather a refinement."

Select References

Howard Rothman Bowen, "Social Responsibilities of the Businessman"; 1953, Harper & Brothers, University of Iowa Press. Harold Bowen "Social Responsibilities of the Businessman"; 1953, Harper & Brothers; University of Iowa Press.

Mel Wilson, March 2003; "Corporate Sustainability: What is it and where does it come from?" Ivey Business School; https://iveybusinessjoural.com/author/mwilson/).

Milton Friedman "Capitalism and Freedom", 1962; New York Times, September 4, 1970.

KPMG: Survey of Sustainability Reporting, 2020.

Michael Porter and Mark Kramer "CSR – Creating Shared Value: How to reinvent Capitalism – and unleash a wave of growth", Harvard Business Review, The Magazine, September 2011; "The Ecosystem of Shared Value" The Magazine, October 2016.

John Elkington "Cannibals with Forks: The Triple Bottom Line of 21st Century Business", New Society Publishers, 1998.

Chapter XII

Growth, Equity and the Environment

In the preceding chapters of this book, we traced the evolution of the concept of Sustainable Development in the second half of the last century and of environment-friendly growth paradigms like the Green New Deal in the early years of the present. We also looked at some length the socioeconomic development model adopted and pursued by India over the last 75 years and observed its similarity with the latter-day environment-oriented pathways to progress like sustainable development. India, a deindustrialised colony till 1947, sought to reconstruct its shattered economy by laying emphasis on industrialisation without overlooking the claims of its people's basic occupation of agriculture implying all along that a nation of its size and population needed both agriculture and modern industry for its socio-economic progress. Less explicit but more implicit in this process was the country's regard for the environment expressed through the conservation of natural resources like soil, water, forests, wildlife, and biodiversity and tapping renewable sources of energy like hydropower. The gains made in natural resource conservation have been truly impressive.

Environment versus Development

Given this background, one would expect an atmosphere congenial to development to prevail in India and the development process to proceed smoothly and speedily. The economic reforms of 1991 opened up new opportunities for private enterprise, both local and foreign, to participate in India's nation-building never seen before. Despite such tailwinds, one witnesses delays in approving investments of a large capital nature and in project execution due, among other reasons, to public agitations and litigation, leading at times to unfortunate law and order situations and abandoned plans and assets. Such an atmosphere is hardly conducive to accelerated economic growth, job creation, and welfare.

Causes of Unrest

A look at the causes behind some of the well-known agitations against development projects brings out that they could be grouped into the following major categories:-

(a)   Land acquisition and related issues;

(b)   Denial or curtailment of traditional rights over the "commons" especially forests;

(c)   Apprehension of threat to environment and ecology; and

(d)   With nuclear power generation, a special reservation against such plants.

It is not unusual to find a combination of these causes being advanced in support of the opposition in many cases. Of these causes, (a) and (b) are real, specific, and immediate and impact individuals and communities, mostly the poor. Cause (c) could be real or merely possible or mostly imagined and may materialise in the short, medium, or long term or not at all. The ambit of apprehension is also quite large and vague in most cases, stretching the scope of the 'Precautionary Principle' to its utmost or impossible lengths. Cause (d) is a heightened version of (c) inspired by stray cases of accidents that occurred abroad and the spread of disinformation about atomic power projects. Given this experience, one may wonder whether some issue of a more fundamental nature is responsible for the opposition in general. This may well be the common man's perception that development favours the already better-off and would simply pass him by. We shall examine, in some detail, the nature of opposition to development projects in India in the light of these groups of causes and seek possible remedies to overcome them.

In a country where people were used to living in poverty and with poor health, societal discrimination, and official apathy, the arrival of freedom and planned development with their promise of socio-economic prosperity was greeted with a sense of awe, relief, and expectation. The awe and expectation were generated by the size of the engines of growth that were coming up like river valley projects with their massive reservoirs and canal systems, power plants and transmission networks crisscrossing the countryside, wide highways, steel mills, and other large manufacturing facilities, and higher institutions of scientific and industrial education and research unseen in the country till then. These "temples of modern India", as India's first Prime Minister Jawaharlal Nehru referred to them, induced a feeling of relief bordering on euphoria among the masses and raised visions of prosperity for all. However, deep down among the poor and the marginalised this euphoria was tinged with an apprehension that ultimately the fruits of development may not be theirs but would accrue to the already better-off. This simmering fear was reflected in opposition to large-scale land acquisition for projects or to curtailment of longstanding traditional rights over the 'commons' like the collection of minor forest produce. Over the years, fear turned into militancy due to the political empowerment of the rural masses and the rise of civil society to champion their cause. The growth of social media and its coverage of demonstrations of public protest played no small part in this transformation. The availability of information on green protests abroad also served to inspire opposition to large projects in India.

Land Acquisition

If planning, an essentially intellectual exercise, marked the first step in the march towards development, the second, in most cases, was clearly a physical down-to-earth one in the form of land acquisition for project development. Whether a plan laid emphasis on water resources development or heavy industry or transport infrastructure, land acquisition followed by dispossession of the holders of their lands was unavoidable. Statistics has it that, during the period 1950 – 1980, out of the 61 million people dispossessed of their land following land acquisition by the state for all purposes, development projects accounted for about 21 million of which the share of dams was 16.4 million, mining 2.55 million, Industrial Development 1.25 million and creation of new wildlife preserves 0.60 million (NITI Aayog, Indian Social Institute). Of the total population displaced, 40% belonged to tribal communities and an equal number was accounted for by socially backward classes.

Land acquisition affected the small, marginal, and sub-marginal landholders more than the bigger ones as the three groups constituted 80% of the agricultural community. (NITI Aayog, Eleventh Five Year Plan 2007-2012, February 2007: Report of the Working Group on Natural Resources Management). Under the archaic piece of legislation governing land acquisition for public purposes, namely the Land Acquisition Act, 1894, in force till 2013, neither the decision of the authority to acquire land nor the fairness of compensation paid for the acquired lands was justiciable. The impact of such compulsory acquisition under the "Doctrine of Eminent Domain" embedded in the law followed by dispossession was felt not only by the landholders whose lands were acquired but also by others like landless labour and rural artisans dependent on the landholders for their livelihood. In many cases, entire villages and large parts of districts had to be evacuated of their residents. At times, the displaced who relocated themselves at a new site were to face dislocation from the new site too as it was acquired for construction of another project. The plight of those displaced by the Ban Sagar project on the river Son in Madhya Pradesh is a case in point. They were displaced thrice before they found a permanent home.

A leading example of an agitation against land acquisition and dislocation of large populations was the Narmada Bachao Andolan (Save Narmada Movement) to protest the construction of a series of dams across the river Narmada in two states, namely, Madhya Pradesh and Gujarat to generate power and to provide regulated releases of water for irrigation in these two states with some incidental benefits to the nearby states of Rajasthan and Maharashtra. Of the more ambitious among the slew of 30 major, 130 medium, and 3,000 minor projects identified in the states of Madhya Pradesh and Gujarat, two, namely the Sardar Sarovar Project (SSP, Gujarat) and the Narmada Sagar Project (NSP, MP), together involved submergence of around 50,000 hectares of forest and agricultural land in over 450 villages displacing thousands of people, mostly of tribal communities. Almost all of the affected forest area and a majority of the displaced people belonged to Madhya Pradesh. Though the quantum of power to be generated by the two projects was substantial (1,000 Mw from SSP and 600 Mw from NSP) and their combined irrigation potential was high – a little over 2 million hectares – the human misery involved was heavy with over 250 villages to be evacuated of their population totally. The specially tailored relief packages providing alternate land for resuming agricultural operations and allotment of developed residential sites for resettlement could not enthuse the displaced populations with the result prolonged demonstrations and litigation dogged the construction of the projects. Their construction to their full designed capacities could be accomplished only with the intervention of the Supreme Court of India and the provision of an acceptable rehabilitation and resettlement package to the displaced population.

Prior to 2013, the misery of project-affected communities could not be alleviated due to a lack of provision in the land acquisition law to provide palliatives like allotment of alternative sites for cultivation or other relief and rehabilitation measures like fresh skilling and livelihood development. Relief from the pains of acquisition came only as late as in 2013 when the Land Acquisition Act, 1894 was repealed and a new law addressing the shortcomings of the repealed Act came into effect. Even the new legislation, evocatively titled "The right to fair compensation and transparency in land acquisition, rehabilitation and resettlement Act, 2013" which enhanced the rates of compensation considerably and provided welfare benefits to the affected populations has not had an unqualified welcome from the civil society.

Exclusion from "Commons"

Displacement manifested itself in other forms too like extinguishing or curtailing traditional rights of access to the 'commons'. For example, under the laws governing forests from time to time, traditional rights enjoyed by local communities to graze cattle within forests or collect minor forest produce like honey and gum, or timber for making agricultural implements stood extinguished or curtailed. Even national parks created to protect wildlife under the Indian Wildlife Act, 1972 led to community exclusion in the form of eviction of forest dwellers from their traditional habitats or depriving those living on the periphery of the protected areas of their customary easy access to collect minor forest produce. Such exclusion resulted in demonstrations like the celebrated 'Chipko movement' (1973) in Uttarakhand by local communities to protest against the denial of their traditional right to collect wood from forests at concessional rates for making implements of domestic use. The people's anger was all the more as the state government permitted a private firm to extract willow from the forests for manufacturing sports goods. This proximate cause of the Chipko movement acquired a green shade when people began offering resistance to the commercial exploitation of forests in the area on grounds of soil erosion and landslides giving rise to flash floods. It may be recalled that the year 1970 witnessed such floods causing extensive damage.

The exclusion of local populations from the commons aimed at the protection of wildlife has also proved to be a source of discontent. The law, namely The Wildlife Act, 1972 under which national parks or nature conservation areas are established, specifically extinguishes traditional rights like fishing in lakes or streams inside such areas. The list of such instances would be incomplete without reference to the debate generated by the enactment of legislation to settle forest dwellers in their traditional habitats inside forest limits. Ardent nature and wildlife lovers were furious at the thought of regularising human habitations in the forests through the law, whether they be habitations of traditional forest dwellers or of encroachers of recent times. Many civil society groups, however, favoured the legislation.

Threat to Environment and Ecology - Ecosystem Protection - Silent Valley

It was only in the second half of the 1970s that one witnessed a genuine nature conservation versus development conflict. At the centre of the dispute was a proposal to construct a hydropower-cum-irrigation project in **Silent Valley**, a tropical ecosystem in Kerala consisting of evergreen, moist forest. The uniqueness of the area is that it is a climax community of plants and home to some endangered species of fauna like the Lion-tailed Macaque. It may be helpful to note that climax vegetation denotes a community of plants in the final stage of succession and it remains relatively unchanged until destroyed by an event like a fire or human interference. Opposition to the project arose out of the certain prospect of submergence of a large part of the forest area under the reservoir that would come up as an essential part of the project. Thus, a site of rare botanical and zoological interest that would serve as a valuable reference point for future studies would have been lost forever. The movement against the project spearheaded by a state-level science promotion body drew support from the country's leading environmentalists of the time and international agencies engaged in promoting nature conservation like the World WildLife Fund (WWF, now Worldwide Fund for Nature, WWN). After a detailed investigation into the ecological uniqueness of the site, the proposal was given up making the 'Save the Silent Valley' movement a milestone in the history of nature conservation in India.

It may be noted that the Silent Valley project hardly involved any displacement of populations or acquisition of private land but only diversion of forest land to a non-forest use. Opposition arose from the certain prospect of losing an unique forest area, an irreparable blow to biodiversity. Rightly, such an instance of apprehension of serious injury to biodiversity backed by expert opinion was viewed seriously and the project proposal was shelved. However, in later years, the Silent Valley decision and the Precautionary Principle enunciated in Agenda 21 were to be invoked in a cavalier fashion to oppose the construction of projects anywhere in general and in forest areas in particular.

Environmental Impact Assessment and Forest Conservation

The impact of the Silent Valley movement on the procedures to be adopted for according approval of projects was significant and highly constructive from both development and nature conservation points of view as well as local peace and harmony. Since the requirement of forest land for projects was on the increase, the procedure governing the diversion of forest land to non-forest uses was tightened up greatly through the enactment of the Forest Conservation Act, 1980. Close examination of proposals to divert forest lands to non-forest use and making compensatory afforestation compulsory on an area twice that of the acquired forest land were the main features of the new Act. The strict enforcement of the new law along with the incorporation of mitigating measures like compensatory afforestation and realising the Net Present Value (NPV) of the forest wealth that may be lost and the costs of wildlife protection resulted in bringing down the area of diverted forest land from 4.135 mha (million hectares) during 1951 – 1975 to 1.2 mha in 1986-2010.

With the coming into force of the Forest Conservation Act, 1980, proponents of any project of a significant size had to consider and document its possible adverse impact on the environment and incorporate precautionary measures in the planning, execution, and operation of the project. Later, rules were prescribed under the Environment Protection Act, 1986 for submission of an Environmental Impact Assessment and an Environmental Management Plan for approval by the Ministry of Environment and Forests (as it was known then) before any project could be taken up by the Central or state governments for execution. A special feature of the assessment procedure was the "Public hearing', an opportunity given to local communities and civil society representatives to put forth their grievances, if any, over the proposed project and help incorporate relevant protective and remedial measures in the management plans. The requirement of conducting a study into the possible adverse impact of the proposed venture on the lives and economies of neighbouring communities, called Social Impact Assessment, has also helped to relieve opposition to projects. Lastly, the validity of an approval given to a project overriding objections could be challenged before the National Green Tribunal and its regional benches.

A matter of interest here is that of the 14,000 sq. km. of forest land diverted over the period 1986-2016 for other uses, mining projects accounted for 4,947 sq. km. followed by defence needs (1549 sq. km) and hydroelectric plants (1357 sq. km). Mining activities, hydroelectric projects, and defence infrastructure are all site-specific. Mining coal for power generation, as we saw in Chapter X, is unavoidable as a good part of the country's primary energy demand is met by coal. The Indian steel industry survives on Indian iron ore deposits for its raw material requirements and the nation earns valuable foreign exchange through the export of the rich indigenous ore. The growing demand for Aluminium both within the country and abroad calls for mining the bauxite deposits found in the hilly tracts of East-Central India. Since the country is not well endowed with rich non-ferrous metal deposits, recycling of imported scrap or metal wastes for winning the primary metal is a much-needed industry to be promoted.

'Go, No Go'

The site-specific nature of hydropower power projects, mining projects, seaports, airports, and major road and rail infrastructure cannot be overemphasized. Hence, such needs of a major emerging industrial economy like India and its national security should inform decision-making in matters of granting environmental and forest clearances to projects sought to be located even in supposedly eco-sensitive locations. A trade-off that restricts damage to the environment to the minimum and not outright rejection is desirable. The principle of designating areas as "Go" or "No Go" on the basis of their ecological sensitivity, as was done with the Western Ghats by two expert groups, one headed by Madhav Gadgil and the other by Kasturirangan would, to a good extent, help in investigating possible alternative locations.

Pollution of the Environment

Pollution of air and water arising out of urbanisation and the operation of industries is often a cause of public agitations of a local nature against projects proposed to be set up or operating already. Pollution by industries goes unchecked due to poor enforcement of pollution control legislation. At a fundamental level, however, the cause of damage is a lack of proper land-use planning leading to the location of industries on inappropriate sites or allowing incompatible land use in adjoining areas. The Bhopal Gas Tragedy (1984) was one such instance of a major mishap in a densely populated settlement of poor people that had sprung up in the 1970s close to an existing chemical plant in the city of Bhopal. The enactment of the Environment Protection (Control of Pollution) Act, 1986 was a direct outcome of the Bhopal incident. Strict enforcement of the "Polluter Pays" Principle for ensuring recovery of loss caused to the environment due to any polluting activity of an industry has also acted as an effective instrument in curbing pollution.

The labour-intensive ship-breaking industry at Alang on the Gulf of Cambay in Gujarat offers a good example of operating an undertaking involving hazards to both the environment and human life. India is the biggest shipbreaking centre in the world because of its relatively cheap labour and favourable ocean bed conditions to berth large ships. Discarded vessels, declared as scrap, are imported to be taken apart mostly for their steel and non-ferrous metal content and the recovered material is sold to the metal recycling industry. The economics of shipbreaking is favourable to India as the recovered non-ferrous metal is cheaper compared to imported primary metal. The ship-breaking industry is, however, hazardous in nature as some of the materials like Asbestos and Poly Chloro – Biphenyls discarded in the process are harmful to both human health and the marine environment. Workers' safety was of immediate concern as they were exposed to several risks to life and limb like falling from heights and build-up of Asbestos fibre in their lungs leading to a condition of lung impairment called "Asbestosis". It was noticed that the industry had failed to pay much attention to these dire needs of occupational safety.

The seriousness of the working conditions in Alang was brought to the notice of the Supreme Court of India by a Non-governmental Organisation through a Public Interest Litigation petition. Thanks to this initiative and the directions given by the Court in a case of refusal of permission to the berthing of a large naval vessel, **Clemenceau** in 2006 for dismantling, the operations were rendered safe so much so that Alang has emerged as the largest shipbreaking yard in the world. It is a matter of interest that the world's largest ship ever built, the **"Seawise Giant"**, was dismantled in an environmentally acceptable manner in 2007 in Alang. The notorious **"Exxon Valdez"** – encountered in Chapter IV and Chapter XI – was dismantled here in 2009.

Fear of Nuclear Power

Opposition to nuclear power generation projects is not uncommon in India. On the contrary, it can be said to command a cult following. Instances of accidents in nuclear power plants abroad like the Three Mile Island (US 1979), Chornobyl (Ukraine 1986), and Fukushima Daiichi (Japan 2011) are often quoted in support of the opposition. Admittedly, although such incidents have been very few, extreme caution has to be exercised in locating and operating the plants and management of nuclear wastes. But this argument cannot be pushed too far to abandon nuclear-based electricity generation altogether.

Three facts are often overlooked in antinuclear protests. One is that nuclear energy can play a definitive role in phasing out fossil-fuel-based power and contribute to fulfilling India's pledge to reduce its emissions of global warming carbon dioxide by 2030. On a global level, of the 89 mitigation scenarios considered by the Intergovernmental Scientific Panel on Climate Change (IPCC) to keep global temperature rise below 2 degrees Celsius by 2050, nuclear power is seen to hold the greatest promise (IEA).

According to the World Nuclear Energy Association, nuclear energy met 10% of the world's electricity needs and emerged as the second biggest carbon-free source of energy in 2018. At present, out of the 32 countries having nuclear power generation facilities, as many as 11 have a fair share of their electricity requirements met by nuclear sources. India and China enjoy a modest 10 percent and 5 percent respectively.

The second fact is that India's nuclear power plants have an excellent safety record both in operations and in the management of nuclear wastes generated. In six decades of operation since Independence and 18,500 cumulative reactor years, there have been only five incidents in all resulting in zero direct casualties and only six indirect ones. Thirdly, critics of nuclear energy are unaware of the fact that nuclear power plants contribute a minuscule 0.42 to 39.6 millisieverts of radiation per year to the surrounding atmosphere whose natural level of radiation is as high as 2,400 millisieverts. Hence, shedding reservations, India must pursue a vigorous nuclear power expansion programme. By encouraging nuclear power, India's contribution to arresting global warming would be appreciable.

Share of Nuclear Power (% of country's total generation)

France	69
Slovakia, Ukraine	50
Belgium	50
Republic of Korea	28
USA	19.6
India	3.2
China	5

The reliability of nuclear-powered electricity generation in India can be gauged from the fact that although the share of installed nuclear power capacity is only 1.7 percent of the total capacity, its contribution to overall power generation has been 3.2 percent. It is possible to step up the installed nuclear capacity to over 20,000 MW by 2030 leading to substantial augmentation of fossil-fuel-free power generation.

Electricity Generation in India

Fuel Category	Installed Generation Capacity (Mw)	% share (Mw)
Nuclear	6,780	1.70
Total Fossil Fuel	1,53,876	39.60
Total Installed Capacity (Fossil + Non fossil + others)	3,88,134	100.00

[Source: Ministry of Power, GOI, "Power Sector at a Glance, 31 Aug. 2021, updated on 20 Sep. 2021]

It is gratifying to note that India's Report on Nationally Determined Contributions (NDC) for the year 2022 has expressed faith in nuclear energy's role in decarbonising Indian economy.

Wealth and Income Inequality in India

Extending further the search for causes that may explain the common man's disinclination towards massive projects, one may look into the trend of income and wealth distribution among different cross-sections of society over the years. It is seen that India's fairly impressive economic performance over the years, particularly after the reforms of 1991, has been accompanied by a skewed income and wealth distribution among the different cross sections of the society.

Income Inequality in India

(Share of population in total income, in % (1961-2020)

Year	Top 1%	Top 10%	Middle 40%	Bottom 50%
1961	13.0	37.2	42.6	21.2
1971	11.7	34.4	44.0	22.8
1981	6.9	30.7	47.1	23.5
1991	10.4	34.1	44.9	22.2
2002	17.1	42.1	39.2	19.7
2012	21.7	55.0	30.5	15.1
2019	21.7	56.1	29.7	14.7

[Govt. of India: Economic Survey Report 2020-21, Vol.1, Chapter 4]

Wealth inequality in India

(Share of the population in total wealth, in % (1961 – 2021)

Year	Top 1%	Top 10%	Middle 40%	Bottom 50%
1961	11.90	43.20	44.50	12.3
1971	11.20	42.30	46.00	11.8
1981	12.50	45.00	44.10	10.90
1991	16.10	50.50	40.70	8.80
2002	24.40	55.60	36.30	8.20
2012	30.70	62.80	30.80	6.40
2020	42.50	74.30	22.90	2.80

[Govt. of India: Economic Survey Report 2020-21, Vol.1, Chapter 4]

The above figures speak for themselves. Antagonists may argue that high growth brings with it income and wealth inequalities which lie at the root of the poor's opposition to development projects. That is, rapid economic development in a country like India sets off class resistance against development that seems to pass the poor by. This leads to the suggestion that economic growth should necessarily be accompanied by narrowing the inequality gap. In this context, the experience of developed countries is cited where targeting income inequality for reduction is an economic policy objective.

Contesting such suggestions, GOI's Annual Report of the Economic Survey 2020-21 hastens to point out that the Indian situation is qualitatively different from that of the advanced economies. In the latter, economic growth rates are low, income inequality is high, absolute poverty is non-existent and the socio-economic indicators of the poor are low. In the Indian situation, growth rates are by no means low, income inequality is high but socio-economic indicators have consistently displayed a rise. The Survey relied on the state-level indices on health and education which in themselves were aggregated figures of a large number of indicators. Some of the impressive achievements of India in the public health sector since 2005 are:-

- Average Life Expectancy went up from 64 years to 68 years by 2015;

- Marked downtrend in communicable diseases since 2014; India became Polio-free in 2014;

- Defecating in the open went down from 65% of the population in 2014 to 20% in 2020;

- Neo-natal mortality came down from 57 per thousand in 2005 to 37 in 2015; and

- 70% of the population gained access to subsidized food.

On the basis of the above figures, the Economic Survey Report, 2020-21 concluded that, under Indian conditions, income inequality seems to have little impact on overall socio-economic improvement. On the other hand, an increase in per capita income, an indicator of rising national income, displays a strong correlation with rising social indicators. The Survey claimed that "given India's stage of development India must continue to focus on economic growth to lift the poor out of poverty by expanding the overall economic pie". Redistribution of wealth or income is possible in a developing economy only if the size of the economic pie grows.

For a developing country like India with its huge population, low average per capita income, and high absolute poverty, a high rate of economic growth is not merely desirable but essential. Despite the fact that the state and central level social sector indices show encouraging growth, India ranked a low 62 out of 109 countries in its achievements under the Multi-Poverty Index system of the UNDP for the year 2021 clearly indicating the need to accelerate its efforts to eradicate poverty in all its forms. This would be possible only if the economic growth rates are high.

The COVID-19 Pandemic

No discussion on economic growth and sustainable development in India would be complete without making a reference to the viral curse that swept the country from the closing months of 2019 to the end of April 2022. The COVID-19 virus and its successor variants took a heavy toll on human lives and caused significant damage to both global and national economies. What began as a public health issue soon ballooned into an economic emergency. Official estimates (4 December 2021) put the loss of lives in India since the outbreak at 4,80,000. [Govt. of India: my GOV]. 100 million jobs were lost between April 2019 and May 2020. While most of the affected could return to work, around 15 million of them could not. They were rendered jobless.

Indian economy contracted by 7.3 percent in 2020-21 compared to 2019-20, its worst performance since Independence. Household incomes dropped by as much as 12 percent (Centre for Monitoring Indian Economy, CMIE). A fall of 12 percent in household incomes would translate itself into a fall of 12 percent in household consumption which, in turn, would lead to an additional 218 million people (168 million rural and 50 million urban) being pushed below the poverty line, a supremely tragic scene in the pandemic play.

The year 2021 – 22 turned out to be no better. With poverty rates expected to have gone up by 15-20 percent, around 150-199 million more of the population would have slipped below the poverty line. Even before all these calamities struck, the UN (2019) had estimated the population of poor in India to be 364 million, or 29 percent of the total population. A silver lining to the dark clouds of COVID-19 has been the medical coverage of all sections of the population, an unparalleled feat in India's public health history.

Conclusion

India is in the throes of an economic and social challenge and needs development without leaving anyone behind. Poorly understood and distorted versions of sustainable development do more harm than good to this cause. Sustainable development is a broad concept, not a narrow one. In the words of the UNCSD "Living within our environmental limits is one of the central principles of sustainable development" but "the focus of sustainable development is far broader than just the environment. It is also about ensuring a strong, healthy and just society. This means meeting the diverse needs of all people in existing and future communities, promoting personal wellbeing, social cohesion and inclusion, and creating equal opportunity…. "Sustainable development is about finding better ways of doing things, both for the future and for the present. We might need to change the way we work and live now, but this doesn't mean our quality of life will be reduced."

Select References

"Why People Protest: An Analysis of Ecological Movements" Subhash Sharma, Publications Division, Ministry of Information & Broadcasting, Government of India, 2009.

"Social Movement: Narmada Bachao Andolan" Manjula Yadav, Tata Institute of Social Science, Hyderabad; Research gate, Decr.2015.

"Are Resettled Oustees from the Sardar Sarovar Dam Project 'Better off' Today", Swaminathan S. Anklesaria Aiyar and Neeraj Kaushal, Economic &Political Weekly. March 23 2019, Vol. LIV No.12.

"Narmada Dams Controversy –Case Summary", M.J. Petersen, Osman Kirati and Ercan", Version 1, September 2010 in "International Dimensions of Ethics Education in Sciences and Engineering – Case Study Series.

"Learning from Narmada", World Bank OED Precis, May 1995.

"Environmental Movements In India: A case study of Chipko Movement" Ramesh Kumar Department of Sociology, BBAU, Lucknow, International Journal of Innovative Social Science& Humanities Research.

"The Saving of the Silent Valley: a case study of Environmental Education in Action", D.S. Variava, The Environmental Science and Technical Education, edited by Baez, Knamiller, Smyth, Pergamon Press.

"Nuclear Power in a Clean Energy System", International Energy Agency (iea), May 2019; PRIS/IAEA : 2021.

"Report of the Western Ghats Ecology Expert Panel", MOEF, GOI, April 2011 (Madhav Gadgil Report).

"Report of The High Level Working Group on Western Ghats" April 2013 (Kasturirangan Report).